ETHICS
AND
ORGANIZATIONAL
DECISION MAKING

ETHICS AND ORGANIZATIONAL DECISION MAKING

A Call for Renewal

Ronald R. Sims

Q

QUORUM BOOKS
Westport, Connecticut • London

Library of Congress Cataloging-in-Publication Data

Sims, Ronald R.
    Ethics and organizational decision making : a call for renewal /
Ronald R. Sims
        p.   cm.
    Includes bibliographical references and index.
    ISBN 0-89930–860–0 (alk. paper)
    1. Business ethics. 2. Decision-making (Ethics).
3. Organizational behavior. I. Title.
HF5387.S57 1994
174'.4—dc20   93–50071

British Library Cataloguing in Publication Data is available.

Library of Congress Catalog Card Number: 93–50071
ISBN: 0–89930–860–0

First published in 1994

Quorum Books, 88 Post Road West, Westport, CT 06881
An imprint of Greenwood Publishing Group, Inc.

Printed in the United States of America

The paper used in this book complies with the
Permanent Paper Standard issued by the National
Information Standards Organization (Z39.48-1984).

10 9 8 7 6 5 4 3 2

Contents

Preface

Ethics underlies much of what happens in modern organizations, and ethical problems exist for all types of organizations — educational, government, religious, business, and so on. The interest in business ethics (or lack thereof) by some organizations has increased dramatically in the 1970s and 1980s. One need only look at the number of news reports, books, and other writings that focus on the topic of business ethics and what appears to be an accompanying flow of continuous unethical acts by corporations and their employees to document the increased concern and emphasis on business ethics.

A basic assumption underlying this book is that organizations that work to institutionalize ethics establish an organizational culture based on ethical values and consistently display them in all their activities. As a result of such behavior, these organizations will derive a number of positive benefits: improved top-management control, increased productivity, avoidance of litigation, and an enhanced organizational image that earns the public's good will and attracts talent. Another underlying assumption is that organizations committed to institutionalizing ethics see business ethics as focusing on business practices in light of some concept of human value, and for these organizations, the highest moral good is what ethics is all about.

A major aim of this book is to provide a better integration and understanding of a number of variables that are important to institutionalizing ethics within an organization. The book discusses the importance of ethics by paying particular attention to decision making, groupthink, organizational culture, and other related concepts, such as the role of top and middle management as key vehicles for increasing our understanding of the ethics equation in organizations. More specifically, the major points of this book are that organizations committed to developing ethically oriented cultures must understand: decision making (individual and group) in general and its relationship to ethics in particular, the concept of groupthink in linking decision making and ethical or unethical behavior in organizations, the relationship between leadership and organizational culture in the ethical equation, the potential implications of the changing employee-employer contract for ethical behavior in organizations, and the key components to institutionalizing ethics in organizations. In the end, if readers of this book gain a better appreciation and understanding of the causes of both ethical and unethical behavior and how to better establish, institutionalize, and maintain ethically oriented cultures, then this book will have accomplished its objective.

Acknowledgments

A book such as this grows through experience and, in particular, the delightful experience of interacting with a number of exceptional and fine individuals. Thus, although a single name is given as author of this publication, it was not a solitary effort. The School of Business Administration at the College of William and Mary deserves considerable recognition for its cooperative and wholehearted support of this undertaking. My continued appreciation and thanks go out to mentors, colleagues, and friends Herrington Bryce, the Life Insurance of Virginia Professor at the School of Business Administration, College of William and Mary, and Dave Kolb of Case Western Reserve University who continue to be instrumental in encouraging my professional growth and development.

Thanks must also go to the support staff (Julie Heck, Nancy Smith, and Phyllis Viandis) of the School of Business Administration who worked with me in the production process. Finally, my wife, Serbrenia, and daughters, Vellice, Nandi, Dangaia, and Sieya, always provide the much needed support and energy boosts that are necessary to undertake and complete such a book.

ETHICS
AND
ORGANIZATIONAL
DECISION MAKING

1

Ethics in Organizations

Public awareness of ethics in general and unethical behavior in organizations has increased in recent years. Part of this increased emphasis on business ethics can be attributed to the continued tension between the business world and the public at large. Such tension over the past century has often resulted in calls, by the public at large, for increased deterrence and stricter regulation of the business world.

Matthews (1988) has noted that there have been three distinct periods in the last 100 years in the United States when the public's distrust of big business reached extremely high levels. The first period extended from the late 1800s up to World War I, when the U.S. public became increasingly irate over abuses by the business world. As a result, the Interstate Commerce Commission was established in 1887, and the Sherman Antitrust Act was passed in 1890. In the first part of the new century, Upton Sinclair's treatise (1906) helped to create federal regulation of food and drugs, and other reforms followed, including the establishment of the Federal Reserve system, the passage of the Clayton Antitrust Act (1914), and the creation of the Federal Trade Commission (1914) to police business.

Public displeasure subsided until the Depression of the 1930s when, once again, distrust of big business became rampant. In this, the second period, the end result was New Deal legislation, including the establishment of new regulatory agencies such as the Federal Deposit Insurance Corporation (1933), the Securities and Exchange Commission (1934), the National Labor Relations Board (1935), and similar agencies.

Discontent with the business world did not emerge again until the 1960s — the years of the Vietnam War and the period when Ralph Nader became a nationally known consumer activist. This incipient stage was followed in the early 1970s by the overseas payments and scandals and the Watergate fiasco. Respect for the business world plummeted. This third period reached its peak from 1973 to 1980 — the era of social responsibility. It was during this time that business organizations and their leaders began to be seriously concerned with consumer calls for social responsibility. In the hope of staving off further external regulation, many corporate leaders attempted to demonstrate their social responsibility and social responsiveness through written codes of ethics, community involvement, philanthropic endeavors, and so forth.

The third period, like the earlier ones, brought about the establishment of a host of new federal regulatory agencies, for example, the Consumer Product Safety Commission (1972), Environmental Protection Agency (1970), National Highway Traffic Safety Administration (1970), and new legislation regulating corporations. The new laws and regulatory agencies were an outgrowth of the increased knowledge and concern about unsafe products and the deterioration of the environment. Matthews (1988) notes that:

It may be argued that this is an indication that the third period is over — the establishment of the regulatory agencies and legislation enacted during the seventies was the total outcome of the public's distrust of big business. On the other hand, it is possible that the early eighties may merely have been a dormant period. (p. 125)

Consumers and the general public are once again exhibiting signs of increasing distrust of the business world (Kellens, 1987). Defense contractors' overcharges, insider trading, false advertising on the part of diet centers. Union Carbide and the Bhopal accident, and the savings and loan (S & L) scandals are just a few examples that have been the subject of much media attention.

In a sense, one could say that a fourth period of public distrust and calls for increased policing of business has started in recent years, that is, as the legal and social environment of business has continued to change, public discontent with the corporate world is clearly on the rise once again. With this rise in public discontent, organizations and their leaders must work to improve their ethical image (deter the increase in unethical acts) in the eye of the public or face a new round of external regulation.

As with previous periods of reform, organizations must recognize the seriousness of the intensity a new round of external pressure may take if organizations do not get their ethical "act" together. If unethical actions continue in organizations to the level of 1992 and 1993, a new era of public concern, consciousness, and legislation is likely to occur in the very near future. Like Matthews (1988), it is our belief that the fourth period will, in effect, be a backlash against businesses' inability (or unwillingness) to police themselves and protect consumers (and the public at large) and that the resulting legal and social ramifications may be more than corporations are able to deal with.

ROOTS OF ETHICAL BEHAVIOR

Ethical behavior of today's employees has its roots in several aspects of contemporary society: the general culture of our society, values of the organization they work for and, often, the professions they are a part of, and their own personal values.

The General Culture

U.S. society, the culture itself, has established norms and values that undergird our behavior as a people. They are encompassed in our basic values and community standards and formalized into law.

The foundation consists of the basic U.S. values established by the Constitution and Bill of Rights, Declaration of Independence, and other traditions; democracy, freedom of speech and assembly, free enterprise, free public education for all, nondiscrimination, respect for work, and the like.

To this broad foundation we have added community standards, values established by custom and accepted by the majority of a region or individual community as right and proper behavior. Examples are respect for the aged and infirm, concern for wildlife and neighbors, and support for youth activities. Community standards reflect the values held by individual community members, value systems developed over a lifetime of experiences dominated by three basic social institutions — family, church, and schools.

Finally, as a nation, we have created a body of legal standards that codify our ethical values into law: the federal constitution, state constitutions, and the statutes. Examples are Title VII of the Civil Rights Act of 1964, the Occupational Safety and Health Act of 1970, the Equal

Employment Opportunity Act of 1972, and the Ethics in Government Act of 1978.

The Organization

The values of an organization — as reflected in management philosophy, its culture, and the products or services it offers — echo the values of the individuals who make it up: employees, supervisors, managers, and most significantly, the chief executive officer (CEO) and top leaders. Some commonly held organizational values are the importance of resources, return on investment, the welfare and well-being of employees, service to customers and clients, and loyalty to the organization.

Although the goals and values of an organization may be implicit or explicit, to a growing extent they are being placed in writing. Many companies have adopted codes of ethics or include sections in their policy statements that relate explicitly to the ethical realm. They address such issues as leadership, integrity, equity, employee rights, employee development, participation in policy formulation, nondiscrimination, quality of work life, and the like.

The Employee

People's own values are a reflection of their home life and rearing, education and training, and religious beliefs. They bring these values to the performance of their jobs. Examples are competence, honesty, a sense of personal responsibility, completing a task on time, and pride in workmanship.

ETHICS AND ADDRESSING ETHICAL ISSUES IN ORGANIZATIONS

Although no one will doubt that public awareness of ethics has increased in recent years, it is also an accepted fact that ethical issues are a daily component of business, and they are more important today than ever. Ethics are involved in many facets of a business: decision making, arbitration, marketing and sales, financial reporting, personnel, appraisal, and leadership. Managers and other employees must be able to see the ethical issues in the choices they face, make decisions within an ethical framework, and build and maintain an ethical work environment.

There are a lot of stakeholders in the game of ethics: corporate boards of control, the company itself, executives, managers, supervisors, employees, customers and clients, suppliers, competitors, the industry at large, the community, and the nation. At one time or another, ethical decisions involve all these constituents and have a profound impact on market share, competitive position, profitability, image, job satisfaction, and morale.

The crux of the matter is that ethical behavior often collides with the bottom line — at least in the short term. But things are changing. The word is getting out: ethical behavior is good business; it contributes to success in the marketplace. A reputation for honesty and integrity attracts and holds customers and will ultimately show up in the bottom line.

Organizations that have strong ethical values and consistently display them in all their activities derive other benefits, too: improved top-management control, increased productivity, avoidance of litigation, and an enhanced company image that attracts talent and earns the public's goodwill.

The question of business ethics focuses on business practices in light of some concept of human value. Thus, traditional business goals — profit, growth, or technological progress — are evaluated not for their own sake but for their contribution to some basic human good, such as investor satisfaction, improved services, or better working conditions. The ethical, the *right* thing to do in business is that which best serves the ideals of morality and good management practice. The highest moral good is what ethics is all about. The best solution to any problem almost always involves a cost of some kind.

Members of organizations often confront dilemmas. A few examples to illustrate this point: Is it unethical to "pad" an expense account? How about using the company telephone for personal long-distance calls or using company postage on personal mail? Is it wrong to use insider information for personal financial gain? Should someone follow orders that he or she does not personally agree with? Is it wrong for a manager to show favoritism in selection decisions or disciplinary practices? Is it ethical to "play politics" in an organization?

Ethics refers to the "rules or principles that define right and wrong conduct." Ethical questions like those stated in the previous paragraph have no "right" answers. These questions fall into a gray area where individuals must make judgments based on some ethical standards. There are three different ethical positions that can provide guidance to help employees deal with these issues and in evaluating their own ethical standards.

The first is the utilitarian view of ethics, in which decisions are made solely on the basis of their outcomes or consequences. The goal of utilitarianism is to provide the greatest good for the greatest number. This view tends to dominate business decision making. It is consistent with goals like efficiency, productivity, and high profits. By maximizing profits, for instance, a business executive can argue that he or she is securing the greatest good for the greatest number.

Another ethical perspective is the rights view of ethics. This calls upon individuals to make decisions consistent with fundamental liberties and privileges as set forth in documents like the Bill of Rights. The rights view of ethics is concerned with respecting and protecting the basic rights of individuals, such as the right to privacy, to free speech, and to due process. For instance, this position would protect employees who report unethical or illegal practices by their organization to the press or government agencies on the grounds of their right to free speech.

A third perspective is the justice view of ethics. This requires individuals to impose and enforce rules fairly and impartially so there is an equitable distribution of benefits and costs. Union members typically favor this view. It justifies paying people the same wage for a given job, regardless of performance differences, and it uses seniority as the criterion in making layoff decisions.

Each of these perspectives has advantages and liabilities. The utilitarian view promotes efficiency and productivity, but it can result in ignoring the rights of some individuals, particularly those with minority representation in the organization. The rights perspective protects individuals from injury and is consistent with freedom and privacy, but it can create an overly legalistic work environment that hinders productivity and efficiency. The justice perspective protects the interests of the underrepresented and less powerful, but it can encourage a sense of entitlement that reduces risk-taking, innovation, and productivity. The three ethical views presented here — utilitarian, rights, and justice — provide a frame of reference for analyzing these issues.

THE BUSINESS ORGANIZATION
AND ETHICAL DIMENSIONS

Sheppard (1988) stresses that, although it is difficult to pinpoint any one essential quality of business leadership, it is at least possible to quantify its market effects in statistical terms. This is not always the case when we encounter the term "business ethics." Indeed, to many, the term is contradictory, that is, an oxymoron. How, it may be asked, is it possible to do well in business and remain ethical? Others may claim that ethics belongs among the arcane mysteries of philosophic inquiry. What relevance does it have to organization effectiveness? Because business produces what consumers demand, that should suffice to justify its place in society. After all, is not the business coordinated with the economic system? Charles Wilson said that, "What is good for General Motors is good for the economy," while earlier, President Coolidge said that "the business of America is business."

Ethics is at the heart of any corporation. Corporations earn reputations for excellence by acting in accord with ethical commitments to provide high quality products and services, on-time delivery, dependability, reliability, guaranteed service, and more. People are proud of their employment, and the company has low turnover and high morale. Others stand at the gates, hoping to join the ranks as new hires. This is the company with a golden reputation, both for the product and service it offers and for the fair and equitable manner in which it treats its members at all levels of the organization.

This ideal description offered by Blake and McCanse (1991) is a goal toward which many companies strive; the actual realization of it is much less common. Almost every day we hear continuing revelations concerning the ethical wrongdoing of corporate America, and what we hear may only be the tip of the iceberg. In the face of growing media awareness of unethical practices, public distrust of business in general is widespread. Obviously, ethical problems in business organizations require effective leadership for their satisfactory resolution. Yet, it must be emphasized that only an individual is capable of ethical or unethical conduct, not a corporation or any other artificial entity. Clearly, ethical responsibilities are vested in all levels of executive, management, and employee conduct. Unquestionably, the cutting edge of moral awareness must be sharpened by effective business leadership if the leaders are to influence their followers. It is only on this basis that profit making can be combined with moral sensitivity; it is possible to do both.

Over the years we have been constantly reminded that the moral tone and example set by top management — the CEO and the board of directors — is probably the most important variable in building an ethical corporate atmosphere (Jones, 1982; Harrington, 1991; Srivastva, 1988). The personal values of the CEO and the other top executives, powered by their authority, set the ethical tone of an organization. And for that reason, standards of ethical conduct must be formulated systematically at the top level of management. Although top management's support and genuine commitment to an ethical climate is crucial, other champions for such a climate are needed — people who will take strong personal stands on the need for ethical behavior, role model the behaviors required to reinforce such behaviors, and assist with continually working to move the organization forward ethically.

Today's organizations must understand that the bedrock of moral action is a system of personal values such as honesty, truthfulness, courage, loyalty, moral integrity, affection, self-respect, and consideration of other human beings. That is, these values determine norms of individual conduct, which constitute the basic axioms under which an organization promotes ethical behavior.

To be ethically effective, organizations must understand that there is no one formula for decision making in their organizations. That is, conflicting motives require evaluation of duties, values, and consequences, and that exercise involves rational, reflective judgment. Should individuals in a corporation falsify reports for the prospect of future profitable defense contracts? Organizational members must have a conscience and ought to weigh duties to ensure that public safety prevails over duties to stockholders. In addition, they should possess values of honesty, fairness, noninjury, and respect for others; prevail over deceptive competitive practices; and, finally, ensure that the long-term consequences of an inferior and unsafe product prevail over short-term market opportunism.

Henderson (1992) has noted that the scale and scope of business ethics are shifting beneath our feet as well. It is a societal issue that embraces the entire world for the foreseeable future. Business ethics are here to stay. Gilbreath (1987) gives several reasons why ethics will be of increasing significance in the future:

The easy decisions, such as cost cutting, layoffs, and reorganizations have already been made.

All business is now public business; nothing is private.

Management prudence is the new standard because of new audits, reviews, and second-guessing of corporate action.

The list of stakeholders is growing.

The hero is vulnerable under the public spotlight.

Scapegoats are needed, and individuals will be found who can be blamed.

Traditional values are coming back, blending intellectual and economic soundness with definitions of the "good." (p. 25)

There is no doubt that business ethics will continue to be an important part of organizations. Polls indicate that the public does not regard the ethics of managers too highly. It is not easy to say whether businesses' ethics have declined or just seem to have done so because of the increased media coverage and the rising public standards against which ethics is being compared. Today's and tomorrow's organizations and their members will not have easy judgments to make. It is our belief that the ideas included in this book will help create organizational climates that will make such judgments easier than they are now.

OVERVIEW OF THE BOOK

As the twentieth century comes to an end, companies face a variety of changes and challenges that will have a profound impact on organizational dynamics and performance. In many ways, these changes will decide who will survive and prosper into the next century and who will not. Several of these challenges are in the areas of international competition, new technologies, an increased emphasis on quality, changing demographics and accompanying human resource management costs, and changing employee expectations. Although these challenges must all be met by organizations and managers concerned about survival and competitiveness in the future, Chapter 2 will focus on the challenge of ethical behavior and will provide a more detailed discussion and definition of ethics, briefly discuss the challenge of ethical behavior in organizations, present an in-depth discussion on some of the major reasons that unethical behavior occurs in organizations, and, finally, highlight the importance of organizational culture in establishing an ethical climate within organizations.

Decision making at best is a challenge for employees in general and managers in particular. For example, many decisions that management faces turn out to be ethical decisions or have ethical implications or consequences. Once we leave the realm of relatively ethical-free decisions (such as which production method to use for a particular product), decisions quickly become complex, and many carry with them an ethical dimension. Decision making in itself is not a simple process and is even more complicated when one thinks about the character and nature of decision making that includes ethical dimensions. It would be nice if decision making was indeed a simple process and that a set of ethical principles was readily available for employees to "plug in" and walk away from, with a decision to be forthcoming. However, in reality that is not, nor will it ever be, the case when it comes to ethics and decision making.

It is the contention of this book that the importance of increasing our understanding of organizational decision making (individual and group) in general and ethical decision making in particular is a key to improved decision making in organizations. Chapter 3 provides a detailed discussion of decision making as a backdrop for the remaining chapters and will discuss individual and group decision making and obstacles to quality decisions in general; it will also highlight the importance of decision making to ethical behavior in organizations.

Over the past several years, many news stories have portrayed social or ethical issues in the relationship between business (and public) organizations and segments of society. In many instances the situation was one in which an organization was being criticized for its behavior, actions, or decisions. Major examples of this include the accusation against General Dynamics of fraud in its dealings with the Pentagon; the E. F. Hutton scandal in which the brokerage firm was accused of fraud and illegal cash management practices; the action taken against A. H. Robbins and its ill-fated Dalkon Shield; the tragic accident at Union Carbide's plant in Bhopal, India; Morton Thiokol and the NASA Challenger disaster; the greed and mismanagement at Drexel Burnham Lambert, which partially resulted in the firm's bankruptcy; the massive S & L scandal, which resulted in the conviction of hundreds of executives for criminal fraud; the Salomon Brothers bond scandal; and false advertising by diet centers such as Nutri-System and Jenny Craig.

As a result of incidents like the ones above, people throughout the world are becoming increasingly quick to cry out "That's unethical!" And in many instances, efforts are made to tie the unethical or questionable behavior to ineffective decision making. In those instances where more than one individual is involved in the decision-making process, the behavior in question is traced to poor decision making by the group. To date, those who write about ethics and decision making have ignored what we believe is a significant contributor to unethical behavior and decision making, the concept of groupthink (a mode of thinking that people engage in when they are deeply involved in a cohesive in-group, when the members' striving for unanimity overrides their motivation to realistically appraise alternative courses of action (Janis, 1972).

Chapter 4 is concerned with groupthink and individuals who behave "unethically" and takes the perspective that the connection between groupthink and unethical behavior could be especially helpful in understanding the role of groupthink when individuals behave unethically as well as providing a basis for altering behavior in a more ethical direction. It will provide an elaboration of the groupthink effect and then discuss how groupthink contributed to unethical behavior in several organizations (for example, Beech-Nut, E. F. Hutton, and Salomon Brothers).

Many business analysts argue that top management routinely should be held responsible for their subordinates' actions (as cultural norms already dictate in Japan). The idea is that until top officials are made responsible for the unethical practices of their subordinates, organizational cultures will continue endorsing — if only tacitly — unethical actions that yield short-term profit. In other words, the top leaders may be the most effective way of inculcating a culture that discourages unethical behavior. This position assumes that leadership can make a difference in creating an ethical organizational culture.

Chapter 5 is concerned with the role of leadership in the creation of an organizational culture that results in unethical behavior. Chapter 5 discusses literature that highlights the importance of leadership in the ethics equation and provides a more detailed discussion of the Salomon Brothers fiasco while under the leadership of John Gutfreund to demonstrate how a leader can create a culture that is less than ethical.

Change is an organizational fact of life. If an organization has any chance of transforming itself from an unethical culture and experience (like Salomon Brothers), it must be able to handle change positively — to alter policies, structure, behavior, and beliefs — and do it with a minimum of resistance and disruption. It is far better to deal with the need for change — to modify it, redirect it, or disarm it — than to ignore or fight it. However, for companies like Salomon Brothers, a successful ethical turnaround does not just happen spontaneously; proper change management is the key to achieving this goal. But, in reality, can an organization like Salomon Brothers turn itself ethically? If so, what needs to happen for an organization like Salomon Brothers to make a successful ethical turnaround? Finding an answer to that question is the focus of Chapter 6, which focuses on models for managing organizational culture toward better ethical ends, reinforcing the importance of the relationship between culture and ethical or unethical behavior (as first suggested in Chapter 2). The discussion will then turn to a successful ethical turnaround in an organization. Finally, the chapter will revisit the Salomon Brothers situation by discussing Warren Buffet's efforts to change (or turn around) the ethical culture of Salomon Brothers.

The increased emphasis on ethics in the workplace organizations has found organizations themselves needing to develop and implement processes to counter unethical behavior. Countering unethical behavior is the focus of Chapter 7. Thus, the theme of Chapter 7 is that it is important that organizations be proactive in countering unethical behavior. A major point of this chapter is that organizations must work to improve their employees' decision-making skills when confronted with ethical dilemmas as individuals and working in groups. Chapter 7 will suggest that organizations must ensure that their employees learn to cope with the inevitable conflicts that arise among the members, improve the quality of employees' decisions by taking active steps to counter groupthink and unethical behavior, and foster disagreement and contrast into the decision-making process.

For a number of years there has been debate and controversy about whether ethics can and should be taught (or learned). One school of thought argues that ethics is personal, already embedded within the individual and, hence, not alterable or teachable. On the other hand, the other school of thought assumes that instruction in business ethics should be made a part of an organization's employee training efforts. Whether one agrees with one or the other school, ethics training has been identified as an important component in countering unethical behavior in organizations, and more and more organizations are now conducting their own ethics training for employees, sending them to public seminars, or contracting with ethics training specialists for tailored courses.

Chapter 8 highlights the importance of ethics training to the promotion of ethical behavior and suggests that voids in ethical standards can be filled. That is, ethics can be learned, and effective ethics training can occur when there is agreement about the organization's goals or objectives of ethics training, ethics training is perceived as relevant by employees, a debriefing (processing) phase is included as part of ethics training, and the design of ethics training is renewed by a well-designed and implemented outcomes assessment process.

Changing demographics, along with the shrinking labor pool and an expected increase in the number of minorities entering the workplace, are revolutionizing the work force. Employees of every race, sex, and age are insisting on corporate policies that respond to their changing expectations and still satisfy their professional ambitions. Expectations must also be balanced with ever-changing organizations. It is the premise of Chapter 9 that the extent to which today's and tomorrow's changing employee-employer relationships are understood and managed determines the likelihood that unethical behavior will occur in the organization.

Chapter 9 offers an overview of the origins of the changing employee-employer relationship and revisits the concept of the employee-employer contracts by introducing a model important to creating and maintaining an ethical climate in organizations in the midst of changing employees and organizations. Chapter 9 will also present a framework that organizations can use to develop ethical employee-employer contracts.

The importance of the institutionalization of ethics within an organization cannot be underestimated. No one can tell when employees will be confronted with ethical dilemmas. Any decision they make that involves ethics is likely to be based on values they have already learned and experiences they had prior to joining an organization. However, organizations must take proactive responsibility for ensuring that employees do not encounter organizational policies and practices that may be inappropriate. In addition, an organization must create an environment that encourages its employees to blow the whistle on those policies and practices. In reality, an organization that supports the institutionalization of ethics seeks employees who are willing to take a personal stand and perhaps put their own careers at risk if necessary to expose and eliminate unethical behavior.

Chapter 10 takes the stance that institutionalizing ethics is an important task for today's organizations if they are to effectively counteract the increasingly frequent occurrences of blatantly unethical and often illegal behavior within large and often highly respected organizations. It discusses a number of organizational variables (for example, psychological contract, organizational commitment, the commitment of top and middle management, organizational culture and the company's value system, and codes of ethics) that are, in our view, important to institutionalizing organizational ethics.

REFERENCES

Blake, R. R., & McCanse, A. A. 1991, Summer. Sound ethical reasoning in business. *Academy of Management ODC Newsletter*, pp. 7–8.

Gilbreath, R. D. 1987. The hollow executive. *New Management* 4(4): 25.

Harrington, S. J. 1991. What corporate America is teaching about ethics? *Academy of Management Executive* 5(1): 21–30.

Henderson, V. 1992. *What's ethical in business?* New York: McGraw-Hill.

Janis, I. 1972. *Victims of groupthink.* Boston, MA: Houghton Mifflin.

Jones, D. G. 1982. *Doing ethics in business.* Cambridge, MA: Ogleschlager, Ginn & Hain.

Kellens, G. 1987. Economic cycles and the attitudes of public prosecutors and businessmen toward the use of sanctions. Paper presented at the annual meeting of the American Society of Criminology in Montreal, Canada.

Matthews, M. C. 1988. *Strategic intervention in organizations: Resolving ethical dilemmas.* Newbury, CA: Sage Publications.

Sheppard, C. S. 1988, Spring. The ethical maze: Perspectives on business leadership and ethics. *William and Mary Business*, pp. 26–31.

Sinclair, U. 1906. *The jungle.* New York: Doubleday, Page & Co.

Srivastva, S. (ed.). 1988. *Executive integrity: The search for high human values in organizational life.* San Francisco, CA: Jossey-Bass.

2

Ethics and the Challenge of Ethical Behavior in Organizations

It has often been said that the only constant in life is change, and nowhere is this more true than in the workplace. As one survey concluded, "Over the past decade, the U.S. corporation has been battered by foreign competition, its own out-of-date technology and out-of-touch management and, more recently, a flood of mergers and acquisitions. The result has been widespread streamlining of the white-collar ranks and recognition that the old way of doing business is no longer possible or desirable" (*U.S. News & World Report*, 1989, p. 42). This trend has become even more pronounced as companies like IBM, AT&T, and others have laid off or eliminated tens of thousands of jobs.

As the twentieth century comes to an end, companies face a variety of changes and challenges that will have a profound impact on organizational dynamics and performance. In many ways, these changes will decide who will survive and prosper into the next century and who will not. Among these challenges are international competition, new technologies, increased quality, employee motivation and commitment, managing a diverse work force, increased human resource management costs (that is, health care), new employee-employer relationships (that is, the new psychological contract), and ethical behavior. Although these challenges must all be met by organizations and managers concerned with survival and competitiveness in the future, this chapter will focus on the challenge of ethical behavior. More specifically, this chapter will offer a definition of ethics; briefly discuss the challenge of ethical behavior in organizations; present an in-depth discussion of some of the major reasons unethical behavior occurs in organizations; and, finally, discuss the concept of organizational culture and, specifically, its relationship to establishing an ethical climate within an organization.

ETHICS AND THE CHALLENGE OF ETHICAL BEHAVIOR

The imperatives of day-to-day organizational performance are so compelling that there is little time or inclination to divert attention to the moral content of organizational decision making. Morality appears to be so esoteric and qualitative in nature that it lacks substantive relation to objective and quantitative performance. Besides, understanding the meaning of ethics and morality requires the distasteful reworking of long-forgotten classroom studies. What could Socrates, Plato, and Aristotle teach us about the world that confronts organizations approaching the twenty-first century? Possibly a gap in philosophical knowledge exists between organizational executives and administrators of different generations. Yet, like it or not, there has been and will continue to be a surge of interest in ethics.

The word "ethics" is often in the news these day. Ethics is a philosophical term derived form the Greek word "ethos," meaning character or custom. This definition is germane to effective leadership in organizations in that it connotes an organization code conveying moral integrity and consistent values in service to the public. Certain organizations will commit themselves to a philosophy in a formal pronouncement of a Code of Ethics or Standards of Conduct. Having done so, the recorded idealism is distributed or shelved, and all to often that is that. Other organizations, however, will be concerned with aspects of ethics of greater specificity, usefulness, and consistency.

Formally defined, "ethical behavior" is that which is morally accepted as good and right as opposed to bad or wrong in a particular setting. Is it ethical, for example, to pay a bribe to obtain a business contract in a foreign country? Is it ethical to allow your company to withhold information that might discourage a job candidate from joining your organization? Is it ethical to ask someone to take a job you know will not be good for their career progress? Is it ethical to do personal business on company time?

The list of examples could go on and on. Despite one's initial inclinations in response to these questions, the major point of it all is to remind organizations that the public-at-large is demanding that government officials, managers, workers in general, and the organizations they represent all act according to high ethical and moral standards. The future will bring a renewed concern with maintaining high standards of ethical behavior in organizational transactions and in the workplace.

Many executives, administrators, and social scientists see unethical behavior as a cancer working on the fabric of society in too many of today's organizations and beyond. Many are concerned that we face a crisis of ethics in the West that is undermining our competitive strength. This crisis involves business people, government officials, customers, and employees. Especially worrisome is unethical behavior among employees at all levels of the organization. For example, a study found that employees accounted for a higher percentage of retail thefts than did customers (Silverstein, 1989). The study estimated that 1 in every 15 employees steals from his or her employer.

In addition, we hear about illegal and unethical behavior on Wall Street, pension scandals in which disreputable executives gamble on risky business ventures with employees' retirement funds, companies that expose their workers to hazardous working conditions, and blatant favoritism in hiring and promotion practices. Although such practices occur throughout the world, their presence serves to remind us of the challenge facing organizations.

This challenge is especially difficult because standards for what constitutes ethical behavior lie in a "grey zone" where clear-cut right-versus-wrong answers may not always exist. As a result, sometimes unethical behaviors are forced on organizations by the environments in which they exist and laws such as the Foreign Corrupt Practices Act. For example, if you were a sales representative for a U.S. company abroad and your foreign competitors used bribes to get business, what would you do? In the United States, such behavior is illegal, but it is perfectly acceptable in other countries. What is ethical here? Similarly, in many countries, women are systematically discriminated against in the workplace; it is felt that their place is in the home. In the United States, again, this practice is illegal. If you ran a U.S. company in one of these countries, would you hire women in important positions? If you did, your company might be isolated in the larger business community, and you might lose business. If you did not, you might be violating what most Americans believe to be fair business practices.

As the previous paragraph notes, the matter of ethics is even more complicated when there are intercultural differences. Globalization is accompanied by inevitable misunderstandings and misinterpretations stemming from fundamental differences in beliefs, values, ethical considerations, and overall ways of doing business. In reality, globalization multiplies the ethical problems facing organizations and their employees. That is, although U.S. companies may have a set of general guidelines for appropriate behavior based on a particular value structure rooted in the country's Judeo-Christian heritage and federal law, such guidelines are not consistently applicable in other countries (Laczniak & Noar, 1985; Deresky, 1994).

"International ethics" refers to the business conduct or morals of multinational corporations (MNCs) in their relationships with individuals and entities (Asheghian & Ebrahimi, 1990). Such behavior is based largely on the cultural value system and the generally accepted ways of doing business in each country or society. Those norms, in turn, are based on broadly accepted guidelines from religion, philosophy, the professions, and the legal system. When employees go to another country with very different cultural traditions, the ethical framework they have come to rely on may no longer be appropriate. Cultural relativism recognizes that people's notions of right and wrong derive from their country's societal values (McWhirter, 1989).

Deeply rooted cultural traditions have tended to create country-specific ethical standards. When national borders were real barriers to trade and communication, cultural relativism created few ethical problems, because interactions were essentially intranational. The biggest single problem for MNCs in their attempt to define a corporatewide ethical posture is the great variation of ethical standards around the world. Many practices that are considered unethical or even illegal in some countries are accepted ways of doing business in others. U.S. companies are often caught between being placed at a disadvantage by refusing to go along with a country's accepted practices, such as bribery, and being subject to criticism at home for using "unethical" tactics to get the job done.

Deresky (1994) notes that whereas the upper limits of ethical standards for international activities are set by the individual standards of certain leading companies — or, more realistically, by the moral values of their top managers — it is more difficult to set the lower limits of those standards. Laczniak and Noar (1985) explain:

The laws of economically developed countries generally define the lowest common denominator of acceptable behavior for operations in those domestic markets. In an underdeveloped country or a developing country, it would be the actual degree of enforcement of the law that would, in practice, determine the lower limit of permissible behavior. (p. 152)

When companies operate in dozens of different countries with a multi-cultural work force, the lack of universal ethical standards creates major dilemmas for its employees. In such countries, organizations must find ways to help their employees decide on what standard of behavior to follow and the need to recognize the difference between ethical and unethical behavior.

WHY DOES UNETHICAL BEHAVIOR OCCUR IN ORGANIZATIONS?

Brumback (1991) identifies two kinds of unethical behavior, the illegal and the legal. The former gets more publicity but is vastly outnumbered by the latter. In addition, in many instances, the legal kind of unethical behavior has become so very ordinary, as we can see from these generic examples: embellishing claims, scapegoating personal failures, shirking distasteful responsibilities, knowingly making unreasonable demands, stonewalling questions, acting disingenuously, reneging on promises, making consequential decisions unilaterally, using chicanery in budgeting, and loafing and loitering.

None of these is scandalous, but each violates a sense of what is the morally correct behavior (for example, the behaviors of personal responsibility, honesty, fairness), abets cynicism and distrust, undermines integrity, and can be a stepping stone to egregious behavior.

The fact that unethical behavior has various origins, each is a mix of personal and situational conditions, makes it important that organizations understand that the effective management of ethical issues requires that organizations ensure that their members know how to deal with ethical issues in their everyday work lives. A basic premise of this book is that a key to knowing how to deal with ethical issues in everyday organizational life is that organizational members understand some of the underlying reasons for the occurrence of unethical practices.

What are the causes of unethical behavior or decisions? The answer to this question is important to understanding how to anticipate the circumstances in which special vigilance is necessary. Knowing the causes of unethical behavior can aid in its prevention, as will be highlighted in different parts of this book. Because the topic is sensitive, one should appreciate that this is not the easiest area to research or find agreement on. Over the years, the major evidence comes from surveys of executive or management opinions, case studies of prominent ethical failures, business game simulations, and responses to written scenarios involving ethical dilemmas.

The potential for individuals and organizations to behave unethically is limitless. Unfortunately, this potential is too frequently realized. Consider, for example, how greed overtook concerns about human welfare when the Manville Corporation suppressed evidence that asbestos inhalation was killing its employees or when Ford failed to correct a known defect that made its Pinto vulnerable to gas tank explosions following low-speed rear-end collisions (Bucholz, 1989). Companies that dump dangerous medical waste materials into our rivers and oceans also appear to favor their own interests over public safety and welfare. Although these examples are better known than many others, they do not appear to be unusual. In fact, the story they tell may be far more typical than we would like, as one expert estimates that about two-thirds of the 500 largest U.S. corporations have been involved in one form of illegal behavior or another (Gellerman, 1986).

Unfortunately, unethical organizational practices are embarrassingly commonplace. It is easy to define such practices as dumping polluted chemical wastes into rivers, insider trading on Wall Street, overcharging the government for Medicaid services, and institutions like Stanford University inappropriately using taxpayer money to buy a yacht or to enlarge their president's bed in his home as morally wrong. Yet, these and many other unethical practices go on almost routinely in many organizations. Why is this so? In other words, what accounts for the unethical actions of people in organizations; more specifically, why do people commit those unethical actions when individuals knew or should have known that the organization was committing an unethical act? An example provided by Baucus and Near (1991) helps to illustrate this distinction.

A federal court judge found Allegheny Bottling, a Pepsi-Cola bottling franchise, guilty of price fixing. The firm had ended years of cola wars by setting prices with its major competitor, Mid-Atlantic Coca-Cola Bottling (*New York Times*, 1988). Because evidence showed most executives in the firm knew of the illegal price-fixing scheme, the court not only fined Allegheny $1 million but also sentenced it to three years in prison — a sentence that was suspended because a firm cannot be imprisoned. However, the unusual penalty allowed the judge to place the firm on probation and significantly restrict its operations.

In another case, Harris Corporation pleaded no contest to charges that it participated in a kickback scheme involving a defense department loan to the Philippines (*Wall Street Journal*, 1989). Although this plea cost the firm $500,000 in fines and civil claims, Harris' chief executive said the firm and its employees were not guilty of criminal conduct; he maintained that top managers pleaded no contest because the costs associated with litigation would have been greater than the fines and litigation would have diverted management attention from firm operations.

Although both cases appear to be instances of illegal corporate behavior, there is an important distinction between them. In the first case, Allegheny's executives knew or should have known that the firm's activities were illegal; price fixing is a clear violation of antitrust law. Further, the courts ruled that evidence indicated that the firm had engaged in the illegal act. In contrast, it is not clear that Harris Corporation's managers committed an illegal act. Some areas of the law are very ambiguous, including the area relevant to this case, the Foreign Corrupt Practices Act, and managers may not at times know what is legal or illegal; thus, a firm may inadvertently engage in behavior that is later defined as illegal or unethical (Baucus & Near, 1991).

In *Moral Mazes: The World of the Corporate Manager*, Robert Jackall (1988) argues that the unethical actions of managers do not result from individual moral deficiencies. Rather, he argues that the bureaucratic structure of modern corporations encourages managers to behave unethically. Corporate success for managers is not a function of high ethical standards; rather, a willingness to compromise one's ethical standards in the interests of both the organization and oneself is positively related to managerial success (Wahn, 1993).

Numerous other authors also suggest that organizational life frequently pushes individuals to behave unethically. Barach (1985, p. 132) argues that different ethical standards hold in business than in other aspects of life: "Business has its own brand of hardball and the price of success involves ethical pressures — playing to win may involve hurting someone. Some say that business ethics is a contradiction in terms. It is true that sometimes businessmen are pressured to compromise their standards."

Grossman (1988) argues that much unethical behavior within the corporation occurs because individual employees are subject to pressures to conform to actions that might deviate from their personal moral code:

Young managers today, with few exceptions, will not exert the kind of moral fortitude that is necessary to disagree with corporate approaches, whether they relate to quality of products, the reliability of goods produced or concerns about the health and safety of consumers and the protection of the environment. Few feel secure enough in their positions to step out of line for fear of being fired. (p. 35)

Wahn (1993) notes that significant empirical work supports this basic argument. In a study by Posner and Schmidt (1987), nearly 40 percent of questionnaire respondents report that their superiors have asked them to do something they consider to be unethical. In an earlier study, respondents rated the behavior of superiors as the most important influence on unethical behavior (Posner & Schmidt, 1984). In another survey, 30 percent of respondents reported having been asked by their superior to behave in an unethical manner, and about two-thirds of this group felt that their jobs were at stake if they failed to comply (Modic, 1987).

Pressure to compromise one's own ethical standards need not be in the form of a direct supervisor request. In another questionnaire, almost 65 percent of respondents agreed with the following statement: "Managers today feel under pressure to compromise personal standards to achieve company goals" (Carroll, 1975, p. 77). Further examination of the data also revealed that this feeling was more widely felt at the middle and lower management levels. Senger (1971) reported that employee performance evaluation is affected by the evaluator's perceptions of his or her acceptance of organizational values. Furthermore, Pennings (1970) found that promotion rates were affected by employee values. Clearly, conformity has its rewards in organization life (Kanter, 1977, Chap. 3).

One clear answer to the question of why individuals knowingly commit unethical actions is based on the idea that organizations often reward behaviors that violate ethical standards. If organizations reward unethical behavior, then who will display "moral fortitude" and be willing to risk their jobs by whistleblowing or, less dramatically, risk inhibited career progression by failing to comply with ethically relevant conformity pressures? Although individual variables undoubtedly play a part, Wahn (1993) has noted that those employees who are less dependent on their employers will be less willing to comply. In other words, employees with more choices will display greater moral fortitude than employees with fewer alternatives.

Wahn's findings (1993) provide additional support for the notion that certain unethical behaviors other than conforming to organizational demands may also be rewarded within organizations. Kanter (1977) and Jackall (1988) both discuss the importance of image in career advancement. Actions that enhance one's own image or harm that of others may be regarded as unethical but be useful in preserving and/or enhancing one's own career.

Wahn's study (1993) also reminds us that organizations are elaborate structures of authority. This may be useful for the coordination of a complex system but can put pressure on individuals that may be difficult for them to ignore. The findings suggest that high organizational dependence will reduce the likelihood that an individual will ignore pressure to compromise ethical values. Consider, for example, how many business executives are expected to deal in bribes and payoffs, despite the negative publicity and ambiguity of some laws, and how good corporate citizens who blow the whistle on organizational wrongdoing may fear being punished for their actions.

Jansen and Von Glinow (1985) explain that organizations tend to develop counternorms, accepted organizational practices that are contrary to prevailing societal or ethical standards. Being open and honest is one of the prevailing norms identified by Jansen and Von Glinow (1985). Indeed, governmental regulations requiring full disclosure and freedom of information reinforce society's values toward openness and honesty. Within organizations, however, it is often considered not only acceptable but also desirable to be much more secretive and deceitful. The practice of stonewalling, willingly hiding relevant information, is quite common. One reason for this is that organizations may actually punish those who are too open and honest. Look at the negative treatment experienced by many employees who are willing to blow the whistle on unethical behavior in their organizations. Also, consider, for example, the disclosure that B. F. Goodrich rewarded employees who falsified data on the quality of aircraft brakes in order to win certification (Vandevier, 1978). Similarly, it has been reported that executives at Metropolitan Edison encouraged employees to withhold information from the press about the Three Mile Island nuclear accident (Gray & Rosen, 1982). Both incidents represent cases in which the counternorms of secrecy and deceitfulness were accepted and supported by the organization.

Other prevailing norms identified by Jansen and Von Glinow (1985) are follow the rules at all costs, be cost-effective, take responsibility, and be a team player. Other organizational counternorms that promote morally and ethically questionable practices are do whatever it takes to get the job done, use it or lose it, pass the buck, and take credit for your own actions — grandstand. Because these practices are commonly rewarded and accepted suggests that organizations may be operating within a world that dictates its own set of accepted rules. This reasoning suggests a second answer to the question of why organizations knowingly act unethically — namely, because managerial values exist that undermine integrity. In an analysis of executive integrity, Wolfe (1988) explains that managers have developed some ways of thinking (of which they may be quite unaware) that foster unethical behavior.

One culprit is referred to as the bottom-line mentality. This line of thinking supports the company goal of financial success as the only value to be considered. It promotes short-term solutions that are immediately financially sound, despite the fact that they cause problems for others within the organization or the organization as a whole. It promotes an unrealistic belief that everything boils down to a monetary game. As such, rules of morality are merely obstacles, impediments along the way to bottom-line financial success.

A similar bottom-line mentality, the political bottom line, is also quite evident in the public sector. For example, when it comes to spending money, the U.S. Congress has no equal. Although much of this expenditure is for purposes of national concern, a sizable portion is devoted to pork-barreling. "Pork-barreling" refers to the practice whereby a senator or representative forces Congress to allocate monies to special projects that take place in his or her home district. In many cases, the projects have little value and represent a drain on the taxpayers. They do, however, create jobs — and political support — in the home district. This practice is common because many members of Congress believe it will help them get votes in the next election.

In some more extreme — and definitely ethically questionable — situations, such actions are designed to reward some large-scale campaign contributors in the home district. A case in point is the Maxi Cube cargo handling system. Funds for testing the Maxi Cube cargo handling system were written into the fiscal 1989 defense budget during the final Senate-House appropriations conference at the request of Representative John Murtha of Pennsylvania. The $10 million item was specifically targeted for a Philadelphia businessman (and contributor to Murtha's campaign) who was to manufacture the truck in Murtha's home district. The only problem was that the U.S. Army had clearly said that it had "no known requirement" for the handler. In response, Murtha was reported to be "mad as hell" at the "nitpicking" by the army. He pushed ahead anyway and used his position on the House Appropriations Committee to freeze a series of military budgeting requests until he got his pet project approved.

And Murtha is not alone. Representative Les Aspin of Wisconsin got the Defense Appropriations Committee to include $239 million to continue making a certain ten-ton truck (in Wisconsin, naturally) that the army was trying to phase out. It, too, was unneeded, but Aspin wanted the project for his home district. Is this legal? Yes. Is it ethical? That depends upon your point of view (Morgan, 1989). Clearly, Murtha and

Aspin thought it was appropriate, given the realities of today's private and public organizations.

Wolfe (1988) also notes that managers tend to rely on an exploitative mentality — a view that encourages "using" people in a way that promotes stereotypes and undermines empathy and compassion. This is a highly selfish perspective, one that sacrifices concerns for others in favor of benefits to one's own immediate interests. In addition, there is a Madison Avenue mentality — a perspective suggesting that anything is right if the public can be convinced that it is right. The idea is that executives may be more concerned about their actions appearing ethical than about their legitimate morality — a public relations-guided morality. It is this kind of thinking that leads some companies to hide their unethical actions (by dumping their toxic wastes under cover of night, for instance) or otherwise justify them by attempting to explain them as completely acceptable.

It is not too difficult to recognize how individuals can knowingly engage in unethical practices with such mentalities. The overemphasis on short-term monetary gain and getting votes in the next election may lead to decisions and rationalizations that not only hurt individuals in the long run but also threaten the very existence of organizations themselves.

Within the literature on corporate illegality, the predominant view is that pressure and need force organizational members to behave unethically and develop corresponding rationalizations; however, according to research, this explanation accounts for illegal acts only in some cases (Baucus & Near, 1991). In their data, poor performance and low organizational slack (the excess that remains once a firm has paid its various internal and external constituencies to maintain cooperation) were not associated with illegal behavior, and wrongdoing frequently occurred in munificent environments.

According to the model developed by Baucus and Near (1991), illegal behavior occurs under certain conditions. For example, results from their research showed that large firms are more likely to commit illegal acts than small firms; although the probability of such wrongdoing increases when resources are scarce, it is greatest when resources are plentiful; illegal behavior is prevalent in fairly stable environments but is more probable in dynamic environments; membership in certain industries and a history of repeated wrongdoing are also associated with illegal acts; and the type of illegal activity chosen may vary according to the particular combination of environmental and internal conditions under which a firm is operating.

Baucus and Near (1991) also suggest that conditions of opportunity and predisposition are antecedents of illegal behavior. That is, rather than tightening conditions creating pressure for illegal acts, it may be that loosening, ambiguous conditions create opportunities to behave illegally. In terms of the model presented by Baucus and Near (1991), large firm size provided more opportunities to engage in illegal activities than small size; the former condition may make it easy to hide illegal activities. Rules, procedures, and other control mechanisms often lag behind growth of a firm, providing organizational members with an opportunity to behave illegally because no internal rules proscribe such behavior.

Predisposition indicates a tendency or inclination to select certain activities — illegal ones — over other activities because of socialization or other organizational processes. Baucus and Near (1991) avoid the assumption that a firm's managers or agents subscribe to a different set of ethical standards than the rest of society. Instead, they recognize that organizations, and industries, can exert a powerful influence on their members, even those who initially have fairly strong ethical standards.

As noted above, organizations operating in certain industries tend to behave unethically. Certain industry cultures may predispose organizations to develop cultures that encourage their members to select unethical acts. If an organization's major competitors in an industry are performing well, in part as a result of unethical activities, it becomes difficult for organizational members to choose only ethical actions, and they may regard unethical actions as a standard of industry practice. Such a scenario results in an organizational culture that serves as a strong precipitant to unethical actions. The next section looks at organizational culture and its relationship to ethical behavior.

ORGANIZATIONAL CULTURE AND ETHICAL CLIMATES

Organizational Culture

Watching an organization in action reveals many things in addition to routine-task-related activities. Close observation reveals a pattern of ceremonies, conventions about how to dress, use of jargon, way of acknowledging status, mutually agreed-upon standards for doing various jobs, and frequently recited stories about how the organization came into being and how it has dealt with various crises. Further observation, and a little thinking, would convince one that all of these features of the organization actually are only surface manifestations — artifacts, if you will — of an underlying core of fundamental beliefs that are shared by the organization's members. These shared beliefs are about what is true, right, appropriate, proper, necessary, desirable, and unthinkable for the organization and about how one ought to act in the context of that organization. The core beliefs and their artifacts are called the organization's culture.

Organizational culture has become an important, if contentious, focus in the study of organizational life. Managers of organizations have turned to organizational culture to explain what happens in ways that are consistent with organizational goals — to use culture to orchestrate organizational change. Organizational culture has been portrayed as a particularly promising tool in the managerial kitbag (Schwartz & Davis, 1981; Deal & Kennedy, 1982; Kilmann, Saxon, & Serpa, 1985).

Because it is shared and because it lies at the heart of what they do and think, the organization's culture provides its members with a common viewpoint that binds them together as a group (Sathe, 1983). It helps them understand the activities of others in the organization, and it guides their own activities within and on behalf of the organization. Because the shared beliefs include values about what is desirable and undesirable — how things should and should not be — they dictate the kinds of activities that are legitimate and the kinds that are illegitimate (Beyer, 1981). Thus, the culture not only places constraints upon activities of the organization and its members (cultural prohibitions), it also prescribes what the organization and its members *must* do (cultural imperatives). In short, the culture guides the activities of the organization and its members.

Harrison (1972) notes that an organization's culture serves at least seven important functions. It:

specifies what is of primary importance to the organization, the standards against which its successes and failures should be measured;

dictates how the organization's resources are to be used, and to what ends;

establishes what the organization and its members can expect from each other;

makes some methods of controlling behavior within the organization legitimate and makes others illegitimate, that is, it defines where power lies within the organization and how it is to be used;

selects the behaviors in which members should or should not engage and prescribes how these are to be rewarded and punished;

sets the tone for how members should treat each other and how they should treat nonmembers: competitively, collaboratively, honestly, distantly, or hostilely; and

instructs members about how to deal with the external environment: aggressively, exploitatively, responsibly, or proactively.

In short, the culture is the essence of what is important to the organization. As such, it prescribes and proscribes activities, and it defines the "dos and don'ts" that govern the behavior of its members.

Although popularized in recent years, organizational culture is not a new understanding. A well-established tradition of administrative research has demonstrated that organizations produce a mindset among individual members (that, in turn, is determined by, for example, structure or external pressures) that encourages people to behave in ways that are not necessarily consistent with individual or preexisting norms but are apparently induced by organizational membership (Merton, 1940; Whyte, 1956; Crozier, 1964; Hummerl, 1982; Baum, 1987; Jackall, 1988).

Administrative theory has not been alone in its attention to culture as a determinant of the moral content of what goes on in organizations. Scholars of corporate crime (Stone, 1975; Coleman, 1985) have concluded that the "climate" (Clinard, 1983) and culture of organizations exercise a powerful influence on unethical behavior in organizations. Clinard (1983) concluded from his study of retired middle managers in Fortune 500 companies that corporate crime was determined by top managers who pushed their subordinates so hard that illegal practices were tacitly necessary to survive. Clinard (1988) concludes that corporate lawbreaking is a product of the cultural norms operating in a corporation and that corporations "socialize" their members into patterns of law obedience or lawbreaking. Analysis of wrongdoing at Salomon Brothers and disasters such as the Challenger incident similarly concluded that corporate cultures were an important piece of the puzzle of precipitating events (Sims, 1992; Werhane, 1991).

The impact of organizational culture on the ethical standards and moral practices of people in organizations has also been increasingly documented (Fisse & Braithwaite, 1983). Several other studies and articles have also focused on the importance of the organization's culture in determining the morality of corporate activities (Robin & Reidenbach, 1987; Trevino, 1986; Hoffman, 1984). Of particular relevance is the work of Victor and Cullen (1988) that measures work climate. Work climates are defined as "perceptions that are psychologically meaningful molar descriptions that people can agree characterized a system's practice and procedures" (Schneider & Rentsch, 1991). The ethical climate questionnaire is designed to measure the ethical dimensions of organizational culture. These items, developed within the limited research context of four firms, measure five ethical climate dimensions characterized as caring, law and order, rules, instrumental, and independence.

The recognition that culture is an important determinant in ethical decision making has acceptance outside academic management circles. When asked about Drexel Burnham Lambert's guilty plea and the reasons behind it, Edward Markey, U.S. representative, replied that there was a solid foundation of criminal activity behind their success, and when asked if this criminality was pervasive in the financial industry during this time, Markey responded, "there was definitely a culture that tolerated it" (*Wall Street Journal*, 1988, p. B1). Organizational leaders also exhort the importance of managing organizational culture to promote a high standard of ethical conduct among organizational members (see, for example, Akers, 1989).

Ethical Climates

Do organizations vary in the "ethical climates" they establish for their members? The answer to the question is "Yes," and it is increasingly clear that the ethical tone or climate of organizations is set at the top. What top managers do, and the culture they establish and reinforce, makes a big difference in the way lower-level employees act and in the way the organization as a whole acts when ethical dilemmas are faced. For example, there was no doubt in anyone's mind at Johnson & Johnson what to do when the infamous Tylenol poisoning took place. Company executives immediately pulled their product from the marketplace — they knew that "the J & J way" was to do the right thing regardless of its cost. What they were implicitly saying was that the ethical framework of the company required that they act in good faith in this fashion.

The ethical climate of an organization is the shared set of understandings about what is correct behavior and how ethical issues will be handled. This climate sets the tone for decision making at all levels and in all circumstances. Some of the factors that may be emphasized in different ethical climates of organizations are personal self-interest, company profit, operating efficiency, individual friendships, team interests, social responsibility, personal morality, rules and standard procedures, and laws and professional codes (Hunt, 1991; Schneider & Rentsch, 1991).

As suggested by this list, the ethical climate of different organizations can emphasize different things. In the Johnson & Johnson example just cited, the ethical climate supported doing the right thing due to social responsibility, regardless of the cost. In other organizations — perhaps too many — concerns for operating efficiency may outweigh social considerations when similarly difficult decisions are faced.

When the ethical climate is not clear and positive, ethical dilemmas will often result in unethical behavior. In such instances, an organization's culture also can predispose its members to behave unethically. For example, research has found a relationship between organizations with a history of violating the law and continued illegal behavior (Baucus & Near, 1991). Thus, some organizations have a culture that reinforces illegal activity. In addition, some firms are known to selectively recruit and promote employees who have personal values consistent with illegal behavior; firms also may socialize employees to engage in illegal acts as a part of their normal job duties (Conklin, 1977; Geis, 1977). For instance, in his account of cases concerning price fixing for heavy electrical equipment, Geis (1977) noted that General Electric removed a manager who refused to discuss prices with a competitor from his job and offered his successor the position with the understanding that management believed he would behave as expected and engage in price-fixing activities (Geis, 1977; Baucus & Near, 1991).

One ethical climate mix guaranteed to produce wrongdoing is given in this "prescription" (Brumback, 1991, p. 355):

> Put a moral rationalizer
> Hurrying to succeed
> In a seductive position
> Give him/her ignoble expectations
> And upside-down incentive
> And walk away.

Although there may be additional conditions, such as personal insecurity and the best and worst of times, the six identified above are cornerstones of an unethical organizational climate. A brief explanation of each is provided below.

Rationalizations

When there are corrupting situations like the ones characterized above, people in them may behave unethically and rationalize their behavior as ethical. This "mind-over-matter" tendency is a big reason why people sometimes behave badly. Several examples of mind-over-matter rationalizations noted by Gellerman (1986) are denying or trivializing its significance — "Show me a victim," "It's not illegal," "You can't legislate morality," and "It's just a technicality"; invoking the double standard — "Morality is a personal matter," "I don't mix business with my personal feelings"; arguing necessity — "It's cutthroat out there," "If I don't do it, someone else will," "It's my job," and "It will save some jobs"; arguing relativity — "It's not illegal elsewhere," "In the United States, ideals are turned into laws," "No act is inherently illegal," and "We are no worse or better than society at large"; and professing ignorance — "I wasn't told," "Ethics is a gray area," and "The rules are inscrutable."

Impatient Ambition

Short-term success is valued in our society. As a federal budget director put it, "We seem on the verge of a collective now-now scream. I want my Maypo; I want it NOWWWWW!" (Dentzer, 1989). And wanting it now can drive people to cut ethical corners.

Seductive Positions

Any position that gives its holder power, considerable discretion, and/or access to funds is seductive. Such a position tests moral character.

Ignoble Expectations

Behind every great performance is usually a great expectation. Unfortunately, ignoble expectations also have a considerable influence on behavior. An ignoble expectation accentuates achievement of results and is silent on the manner of pursuing them (typically the case when management by objectives is used), gives implicit approval to unethical means (for example, "wink-and-nod" management), or gives explicit approval or even an order.

Upside-Down Incentives

As influential as expectations are, incentives are often tacked on for added emphasis. Sometimes they are tacked on upside down. A common example is giving bonuses based on inflated performance ratings. The bonuses further reinforce the dishonesty behind the ratings.

Unguarded Trust

Ethics clearly cannot be taken for granted when any of the other conditions exist. Unguarded trust, or a laissez-faire posture, in these circumstances will be counterethic.

Like the above six conditions, to understand unethical organizational climates rests on examining the following internal danger signs or common pitfalls that put any organization at ethical risk (Cooke, 1991; Stern, 1992):

If an organization normally emphasizes short-term revenues above long-term considerations, it is creating a climate for unethical behavior.

Organizational members become so fixated on a goal that they are blind to the fact that the plan they are embracing is resulting in unethical behavior.

An organization that routinely ignores or violates internal or professional codes of ethics increases the likelihood of unethical behavior.

Employees look for simple solutions to business and other ethical problems and are satisfied with "cutting corners" or "quick fixes."

Managers persist in a course of action and become victims of the escalation, or entrapment, mentality.

Management is unwilling to take an ethical stand when there is a financial cost to the decision.

An organization creates an internal environment that either discourages ethical behavior or encourages unethical behavior.

The organization communicates to its employees that they must "keep pace" with the competition, no matter what.

An organization sees ethics as simply a matter of compliance with existing laws and regulations.

The organization puts ethical form above substance to enhance its image by focusing on the mileage to be gained by good media coverage.

Employees are not treated equitably by the organization.

An organization is unfair or arbitrary in its performance-appraisal standards.

The organization has no clear-cut procedures or policies that employees can use as guides in handling ethical problems.

The organization provides no way in which potential problems can be brought to the attention (internal whistleblowing mechanisms) of upper management and other interested parties.

An organization lacks clear lines of communication, especially in cases of potential impropriety.

The organization ignores the interests of everyone but the shareholder.

Employees are encouraged to leave their personal ethical values at the office door.

The organization manages by commitment and produces an atmosphere that punishes or inhibits differences of opinion (for example, crises of agreement or groupthink).

These are but a few of the common pitfalls or danger signs that emerge in an analysis of an unethical organizational climate.

Important Causes of Unethical Behavior

As noted earlier in this chapter, pressure, opportunity, and predisposition can all lead to unethical activities. In understanding and summarizing some of the important causes of unethical behavior, one can focus on personal gain, competition, personality, and culture.

Personal Gain

Although the point might seem mundane, it is critical to recognize the role of temptation in unethical behavior or decision making. The anticipation of healthy reinforcement for following an unethical course of action, especially if no punishment is expected, should promote unethical decisions (Trevino, Sutton, & Woodman, 1985; Hegarty & Sims, 1978). Consider, for example, Dennis Levine, the Drexel Burnham Lambert investment banker who was convicted of insider trading in Wall Street's biggest scandal:

It was just so easy. In seven years I built $39,750 into $11.5 million, and all it took was a 20-second phone call to my offshore bank a couple of times a month — maybe 200 calls total. My account was growing at 125% a year, compounded. Believe me, I felt a rush when I would check the price of one of my stocks on the office Quotron and learn I'd just made several hundred thousand dollars. I was confident that the elaborate veils of secrecy I had created — plus overseas bank-privacy laws — would protect me. (Levine, 1990)

Competition

It has long been recognized that stiff competition for scarce resources can stimulate unethical behavior or decisions. This has been observed in both business game simulations and industry studies of illegal acts, in which trade offenses such as price fixing and monopoly violations have been shown to increase with industry decline (Staw & Szwajkowski, 1975). For example, observers cite a crowded and mature market as one factor prompting price-fixing violations in the folding-carton packaging industry (Sonnenfeld & Lawrence, 1989). One exception to the "competition stresses ethics" thesis should be noted. In cases in which essentially *no* competition exists, there is also a strong temptation to make unethical decisions. This is because the opportunity to make large gains is not offset by market checks and balances. Prominent examples have occurred in the defense industry, in which monopoly contracts to produce military hardware have been accompanied by some remarkable examples of overcharging taxpayers.

Personality

Are there certain types of personalities that are prone to unethical behavior? Perhaps. Business game simulations have shown that people with strong economic value orientations are more likely to behave unethically than those with weaker economic values (Hegarty & Sims, 1978; Hegarty & Sims, 1979). Also, there are marked individual differences in the degree of sophistication that people use in thinking about moral issues (Colby & Kohlberg, 1987). Other things being equal, it is sensible to expect that people who are more self-conscious about moral matters will be more likely to avoid unethical behavior or decisions. Finally, people with a high need for power might be prone to make unethical decisions when this power is used to further self-interests rather than for the good of the organization as a whole. In concluding, it is important to note that we have a tendency to exaggerate the role of dispositional factors, such as personality, in explaining the behavior of others. Thus, when we see unethical behavior, we must also look at situational factors, such as competition and the organization's culture, as well as the personality of the actor.

Culture

A study found that there were considerable differences in ethical values across the organizations studied (Victor & Cullen, 1988). These differences involved factors such as consideration for employees, respect for the law, respect for organizational rules, and so on. In addition, there were differences across groups within these organizations. This suggests that aspects of an organization's culture (and its subcultures) can influence the ethics of decision making. This corresponds to the repeated finding in executive surveys that peer and superior conduct are viewed as strongly influencing ethical behavior, for good or bad. The presence of role models helps to shape the culture. If these models are actually rewarded for unethical behavior, rather than punished, the development of an unethical culture is likely.

Observers of the folding-carton price-fixing scandal mentioned above note how top managers frequently seemed out of touch with the difficulty of selling boxes in a mature, crowded market. They put in place goal-setting and reward systems (for example, commission forming 60 percent of income) that almost guaranteed unethical decisions, systems that are much more appropriate for products on a growth cycle (Sonnenfeld & Lawrence, 1989; Hosmer, 1987).

Finally, a consideration of culture suggests the conditions under which corporate codes of ethics (see Chapter 10 for a more detailed discussion of corporate codes of ethics) might actually have an impact on behavior or decision making. If such codes are specific, are tied to actual business being done, and correspond to the reward system, they should bolster an ethical climate. If vague codes that do not correspond to other cultural elements exist, the negative symbolism might actually damage the ethical climate.

In this chapter we have suggested that organizations continue to face ethical challenges and that they must concern themselves with why unethical behavior occurs in organizations and gain an appreciation of the importance of organizational culture in the creation of an ethical or unethical organizational climate.

The challenge of ethical behavior must be met by organizations if they are truly concerned about survival and competitiveness. When the ethical climate is unclear and negative, employees do not know what is expected of them when confronted with ethical dilemmas. Organizations have to ensure that their employees know how to deal with ethical issues while at the same time making effective decisions in their everyday work lives. This can give employees the confidence to be on the lookout for unethical behavior and act with the understanding that what they are doing is considered correct and will be supported by top management and the entire organization.

REFERENCES

Akers, J. 1989. Ethics and competitiveness — Putting first things first. *Sloan Management Review 30*(2): 69–71.

Asheghian, P., & Ebrahimi, B. 1990. *International business*. New York: Harper & Row.

Barach, J. 1985. The ethics of hardball. *California Management Review 27*(2): 132–39.

Baucus, M. S., & Near, J. P. 1991. Can illegal corporate behavior be predicted? An event history analysis. *Academy of Management Journal 34*(1): 9–36.

Baum, H. 1987. *The invisible bureaucracy: The unconscious in organizational problem solving*. New York: Oxford University Press.

Beyer, J. M. 1981. Ideologies, values, and decision making in organizations. In *Handbook of organizational design*, ed. P. C. Nystrom & W. H. Starbuck. New York: Oxford.

Brumback, G. B. 1991. Institutionalizing ethics in government. *Public Personnel Management 20* (Fall): 353–64.

_____. 1989. Institutionalizing ethics: How to make ethics real. Paper presented at the ASPA national conference on ethics in government, Washington, DC, November.

Bucholz, R. A. 1989. *Fundamental concepts and problems in business ethics*. Englewood Cliffs, NJ: Prentice-Hall.

Carroll, A. B. 1978. Linking business ethics to behavior in organizations. *Advanced Management Journal 43*(3): 4–11.

_____. 1975. Managerial ethics: Post-Watergate view. *Business Horizons 28*: 75–80.

Clinard, M. 1988. Foreword of Cash Matthews, M., *Strategic interventions in organizations: Resolving ethical dilemmas*. Beverly Hills, CA: Sage.

_____. 1983. *Corporate ethics and crime*. Beverly Hills, CA: Sage.

Colby, A., & Kohlberg, L. 1987. *The measurement of moral judgment: Volume 1: Theoretical foundations and research validation*. Cambridge: Cambridge University Press.

Coleman, J. 1985. *The criminal elite*. New York: St. Martin's Press.

Conklin, J. 1977. *Illegal but not criminal*. Englewood Cliffs, NJ: Prentice-Hall.

Cooke, R. A. 1991. Danger signs of unethical behavior: How to determine if your firm is at ethical risk. *Journal of Business Ethics 10*: 249–53.

Crozier, M. 1964. *The bureaucratic phenomenon*. London: Tavistock.

Deal, T., & Kennedy, A. 1982. *Corporate cultures*. Reading, MA: Addison Wesley.

Dentzer, S. 1989. The Maypo culture. *Business Month 13*(4): 26–34.

Deresky, H. 1994. *International management: Managing across borders and cultures*. New York: Harper Collins.

Fisse, B., & Braithwaite, J. 1983. *The impact of publicity on corporate offenders*. Albany, NY: State University of New York Press.

Geis, G. 1977. The heavy electrical equipment antitrust case of 1961. In *White-collar crime: Offenses in business, politics, and the professions*, eds. G. Geis & R. Meier. New York: Free Press, pp. 117–32.

Gellerman, S. W. 1986, July-August. Why "good" managers make bad ethical choices. *Harvard Business Review*, pp. 85–90.

Gray, M., & Rosen, I. 1982. *The warning*. New York: Norton.

Grossman, B. 1988. *Corporate loyalty: A trust betrayed*. Markham, Ontario: Penguin.

Harrison, R. 1972, May-June. Understanding your organization's character. *Harvard Business Review*, pp. 119–28.

Hegarty, W. H., & Sims, H. P., Jr. 1979. Organizational philosophy, policies, and objectives: A laboratory experiment. *Journal of Applied Psychology 64*, 331–38.

_____. 1978. Some determinants of unethical decision behavior: An experiment. *Journal of Applied Psychology 63*(4): 451–57.

Hoffman, W. M. 1984. The Ford Pinto. In *Business Ethics*, eds. W. M. Hoffman & J. Mills Moore. New York: McGraw-Hill, p. 419.

Hosmer, L. T. 1987. The institutionalization of unethical behavior. *Journal of Business Ethics 6*, 439–47.

Hummerl, R. 1982. *The bureaucratic experience*, 2nd ed. New York: St. Martin's Press.

Hunt, J. G. 1991. *Toward a leadership paradigm change*. Newbury Park, CA: Sage.

Jackall, R. 1988. *Moral mazes: The world of the corporate manager*. New York: Oxford University Press.

Jansen, E., & Von Glinow, M. A. 1985. Ethical ambivalence and organizational reward systems. *Academy of Management Review 10*(4): 814–22.

Kanter, R. 1977. *Men and women of the corporation*. New York: Basic Books.

Kilmann, R., Saxon, M., & Serpa, R. 1985. *Gaining control of the corporate culture*. San Francisco, CA: Jossey-Bass.

Laczniak, G. R., & Noar, J. 1985, July-August-September. Global ethics: Wrestling with the corporate conscience. *Business*, pp. 3–10.

Levine, D. B. 1990, May 21. The inside story of an inside trader. *Fortune*, pp. 80–85, 88–89.

McWhirter, W. 1989, October 9. I came, I saw, I blundered. *Time*, p. 72.

Merton, R. 1940. Bureaucratic structure and personality. *Social Forces 18*, pp. 560–68.

Modic, S. 1987. Forget ethics — and succeed? *Industry Week 235*(2): 17–18.

Morgan, D. 1989, August 12. Truck Army does not want to be tied up in house turf battle. *Washington Post*, p. A2.

New York Times. 1988, September 1. Corporate prison term for Allegheny bottling, p. D2.

Pennings, J. M. 1970. Work-value systems of white collar workers. *Administrative Science Quarterly 15*(1): 69–79.

Posner, G., & Schmidt, W. 1987. Ethics in American companies, a managerial perspective. *Journal of Business Ethics 6*, 383–91.

_____. 1984. Values and the American manager: An update. *California Management Review 24*(3): 206–16.

Robin, D. P., & Reidenbach, R. E. 1987. Social responsibility, ethics, and marketing strategy: Closing the gap between concept and application. *Journal of Marketing 51*(1): 44–58.

Sathe, V. 1983, Autumn. Implications of corporate culture: A manager's guide to action. *Organizational Dynamics*, pp. 5–23.

Schneider, B., & Rentsch, J. 1991. Managing climates and cultures: A futures perspective. In *Future of organizations*, ed. J. Hage. Lexington, MA: Lexington Books.

Schwartz, H., & Davis, S. 1981, Summer. Matching corporate culture and business strategy. *Organizational Dynamics*, pp. 31–48.

Senger, J. 1971. Managers' perceptions of subordinates' competence as a function of personal value orientation. *Academy of Management Journal 14*, 415–23.

Silverstein, S. 1989, December. One in 15 employees in study caught stealing. *Los Angeles Times*, p. D1.

Sims, R. R. 1992. Linking groupthink to unethical behavior in organizations. *Journal of Business Ethics 11*, 651–62.

Sonnenfeld, J., & Lawrence, P. R. 1989. Why do companies succumb to price fixing? In *Ethics in practice: Managing the moral corporation*, ed. K. R. Andrews. Boston, MA: Harvard Business School Press.

Staw, B. M., & Szwajkowski, E. E. 1975. The scarcity-munificence component of organizational environments and the commission of illegal acts. *Administrative Science Quarterly 20*, 345–54.

Stern, A. L. 1992, May. Why good managers approve bad ideas. *Working Women*, pp. 75, 104.

Stone, C. 1975. *Where the law ends: The social control of corporate behavior*. New York: Harper & Row.

Trevino, L. K. 1986. Ethical decision making in organizations: A person-situation interactionist model. *Academy of Management Review 11*(3): 601–17.

Trevino, L. K., Sutton, C. D., & Woodman, R. W. 1985, August. Effects of reinforcement contingencies and cognitive moral development on ethical decision-making behavior. Paper presented at the annual meeting of the Academy of Management, San Diego.

U.S. News & World Report. 1989, January 16. The new organization man. p. 42.

Vandevier, K. 1978. The aircraft brake scandal: A cautionary tale in which the moral is unpleasant. In *Interpersonal behavior: Communication and understanding relationships*, eds. A. G. Athos & J. J. Babarro. Englewood Cliffs, NJ: Prentice-Hall, pp. 529–40.

Victor, B., & Cullen, J. B. 1988, March. The organizational bases of ethical work climates. *Administrative Science Quarterly 33*, 101–25.

Wahn, J. 1993. Organizational dependence and the likelihood of complying with organizational pressures to behave unethically. *Journal of Business Ethics 12*, 245–51.

Wall Street Journal. 1989, June 5. Harris Corp. is convicted in kickback plan. p. A7
____. 1988, December. Mixed feelings about Drexel's decision. p. B1.

Werhane, P. 1991. Engineers and management: The challenge of the Challenger incident. *Journal of Business Ethics 10*(8): 605–18.

Whyte, W. 1956. *The organization man*. New York: Simon & Schuster.

Wolfe, D. 1988. Is there integrity in the bottom line: Managing obstacles to executive integrity. In *Executive integrity: The search for high human values in organization life*, ed. S. Srivastva. San Francisco, CA: Jossey-Bass, pp. 140–71.

3

The Nature of Decision Making in Organizations

Remember the film adaptation of *The Bonfire of the Vanities*? Remember New Coke? Both were multimillion-dollar disasters — the result of good managers making the decision to allow bad ideas to snowball. More recently, you remember hearing about how far Chambers Development Company would go for profits. We have all seen the phenomenon and may have even taken part in it. An opinionated senior manager ignores the red flags, employees fearful of political reprisals do not speak out, or a team becomes so caught up in fulfilling its objective that it fails to consider the downside of a plan with major flaws. The end is always the same — a lousy product, wasted time and money, and a sullied reputation. In each situation, poor decision making was a major factor in the final results.

Decision making at best is a challenge for employees in general and managers in particular. For example, many decisions management faces turn out to be ethical decisions or have ethical implications or consequences. Once we leave the realm of relatively ethical-free decisions (such as which production method to use for a particular product), decisions quickly become complex, and many carry with them an ethical dimension. Decision making in itself is not a simple process and is even more complicated when one thinks about the character and nature of decision making that includes ethical dimensions. It would be nice if decision making was indeed a simple process and that a set of ethical principles was readily available for employees to "plug in" and walk away from, with a decision to be forthcoming. However, in reality that is not, nor will it ever be, the case when it comes to ethics and decision making.

This chapter will provide a detailed discussion of decision making as a backdrop for the remaining chapters of this book. More specifically, this chapter will discuss individual and group decision making and obstacles to quality decisions in general. The chapter will also highlight the importance of decision making to ethical behavior in organizations.

THE NATURE OF DECISION MAKING

It is safe to say that decision making is one of the most important — if not *the* most important — of all individual and group efforts within an organization. Given the central importance of decision making in organizational life, we will begin our discussion by highlighting some of the accepted knowledge on individual and, then, group decision making.

Traditionally, theorists have looked at decision making as the multistep process by which a problem is identified, solution objectives are defined, a predecision is made (that is, a decision about how to make a decision), alternatives are generated and evaluated, and an alternative is chosen, implemented, and then followed up. This type of rational model of decision making assumes that the decision maker is aware of the problem, is aware that the decision must be made, has a set of alternatives, and possesses a criterion for making the decision, but these are significant assumptions. Such an ideal model of decision making also assumes that the decision maker is aware of all possible alternatives and that he or she decides after examining them all. A contemporary approach recognizes that decisions are made in an automatic, intuitive fashion. Specifically, image theory claims that people will adopt a course of action that best fits their individual principles, current goals, and plans for the future.

The decisions made in organizations can be characterized as programmed — routine decisions made according to preexisting guidelines — or nonprogrammed — decisions requiring novel and creative solutions. Decisions also differ with respect to the amount of risk involved, ranging from those in which the decision outcomes are relatively certain to those in which outcomes are highly uncertain. Uncertain situations are expressed as statements of probability based on either objective or subjective information.

Two major approaches to individual decision making have been identified (Greenberg & Baron, 1993). The rational-economic model characterizes decision makers as thoroughly searching through perfect information to make an optimal decision. In contrast, the administrative model recognizes the inherent imperfections of decision makers and the social and organizational systems within which they operate. Limitations imposed by people's ability to process the information needed to make complex decisions (bounded rationality) restrict decision makers to making satisficing decisions — solutions that are not optimal but are good enough.

INDIVIDUAL DECISION MAKING

The picture of an imperfect decision maker operating in a complex world is supported by studies that point to the seemingly confused and irrational decisions people make. The imperfections of decision makers take many forms, several of which we will review here.

Cognitive Biases in Decision Making: Framing and Heuristics

Probably the most obvious limitation on people's ability to make the best possible decisions is imposed by their restricted capacity to process information accurately and thoroughly (like a computer). For example, people often focus on irrelevant information in making decisions. They also fail to use all of the information made available to them. Obviously, limitations in people's abilities to process complex information adversely influence their decisions. Beyond this general limitation in information-processing capacity, we may note the existence of several systematic biases in decision making: framing and heuristics.

Framing

Because not all elements of each image or aspect are relevant to any one decision, the events leading up to the discussion as well as the particular context in which the decision arises define some elements as relevant and the rest as irrelevant. The decision maker's interpretation of the history and present context and the consequent definition of relevant image elements are called framing the decision. This well-established decision-making bias has to do with the tendency for people to make different decisions based on how the problem is presented to them, that is, the framing of a problem.

Decision framing is one of the least understood aspects of decision making. It is abundantly clear that it is — even crucial, but it is not clear how the standards that are applied to decision-maker ideas are selected.

Certainly, mental set has something to do with it. The way in which the decision is presented to the decision maker can determine the way in which it is framed. For example, in some situations, exactly opposite decisions may be reached depending upon whether the possible outcomes are presented in terms of losses or of gains. Specifically, problems framed in a manner that emphasizes the positive gains to be received tend to encourage conservative decisions (that is, decision makers are said to be risk aversive), whereas problems framed in a manner that emphasizes the potential losses to be suffered lead to risk-seeking decisions.

Analogy also affects framing. For example, if a problem is analogous to a problem the decision maker has seen before, he or she may assume that they are identical and require the same solution. Similarly, a decision maker may tend to view all decisions that involve people as "people problems," even though many such decisions actually are "systems problems" in which the system of which the people are a part is not designed so they can perform well within it. Framing the difficulty as a people problem means that the standards that are deemed relevant to deciding on a solution may be quite different from those that would be used for a systems problem. Clearly, if a decision maker frames a problem incorrectly, he or she may make the wrong decision.

Heuristics

Framing effects are not the only cognitive biases to which decision makers are subjected. For example, people often attempt to simplify the complex decisions they face by using heuristics — simple rules of thumb that guide them through a complex array of decision alternatives. Although heuristics are potentially useful to decision makers, they represent potential impediments to decision making. Two very common types of heuristics may be identified: availability and representativeness.

"Availability heuristic" refers to the tendency for people to base their judgments on information that is readily available to them, even though it might not be accurate. Suppose, for example, that an executive needs to know the percentage of entering college freshmen who go on to graduate. There is not enough time to gather the appropriate statistics, so she bases her judgments on her own recollections of when she was a college student. If the percentage she recalls graduating, based on her own experiences, is higher or lower than the usual number, her estimate will be off accordingly. In other words, basing judgments solely on information that is conveniently available increases the possibility of making inaccurate decisions. Yet, the availability heuristic is often used when making decisions.

The representativeness heuristic refers to the tendency to perceive others in stereotypical ways if they appear to be typical representatives of the category to which they belong. For example, suppose you believe that accountants are bright, mild-mannered individuals, whereas salespeople are less intelligent but much more extroverted. Further, imagine that there are twice as many salespeople as accountants at a party. You meet someone at the party who is bright and mild-mannered. Although mathematically the odds are two-to-one that this person is a salesperson rather than an accountant, chances are you will guess that the individual is an accountant because he possesses the traits you associate with accountants. In other words, you believe this person to be representative of accountants in general — so much so that you would knowingly go against the mathematical odds in making your judgment.

Heuristics do not always deteriorate the quality of decisions made. In fact, they can be quite helpful. People often use the rules of thumb to help simplify the complex decisions they face. For example, heuristics are useful aids in decisions regarding such matters as where to locate warehouses or how to compose an investment portfolio. We also use heuristics in our everyday lives, such as when we play chess ("control the center of the board") or blackjack ("hit on 16, stick on 17"). However, the representatives heuristic and the availability heuristic may be recognized as impediments to superior decisions because they discourage people from collecting and processing as much information as they should. Making judgments on the basis of only readily available information or on stereotypical beliefs, although making things simple for the decision maker, does so at a potentially high cost — poor decisions. Thus, these systematic biases represent potentially serious impediments to individual decision making.

Escalation of Commitment

Because decisions are made all the time in organizations, some of these will inevitably be unsuccessful. What would you say is the rational thing to do when a poor decision has been made? Obviously, the ineffective action should be stopped or reversed. In other words, it would make sense to "cut your losses and run." This is what Fisher-Price and Coca-Cola did in response to some of their own ineffective actions. However, it has been established that people do not always respond in this manner. Indeed, it is not unusual to find that ineffective decisions are sometimes followed up with still further ineffective decisions. Imagine, for example, that you have invested money in a company, but the company appears to be failing. Rather than lose your initial investment, you may invest still more money in the hope of salvaging your first investment. The more you invest, the more you may be tempted to save those earlier investments by making later investments. That is to say, people sometimes may be found "throwing good money after bad." This is known as the escalation of commitment phenomenon — the tendency for people to continue to support previously unsuccessful courses of action.

Although this might not seem like a rational thing to do, this strategy is frequently followed. Consider, for example, how large banks and governments may invest money in foreign governments in the hope of turning them around even though such a result becomes increasingly unlikely. Similarly, the organizers of Expo 86 in British Columbia continued pouring money into the fair long after it became apparent that it would be a big money-losing proposition (Ross & Staw, 1986). Another interesting example of escalation of commitment involved the epic film *Heaven's Gate*. Writer-director Michael Cimino initially proposed to United Artists that the film would cost $7.5 million. By the time production began, this figure had increased to $10 million. Production was behind schedule from the very first week, and Cimino was spending $200,000 a day. At this rate, the projected cost of the film would be close to $50 million, and the film would have to had to do better than almost any movie ever made to break even! United Artists finally capped production costs at over three times the initial estimate and ordered Cimino to construct a commercial product from the thousands of feet of film he had shot. *Heaven's Gate* turned out to be one of the biggest box office flops in the movie industry. Why do people do this? If you think about it, you may realize that the failure to back your own previous courses of action in an organization would be taken as an admission of failure — a politically difficult act to face in an organization. In other words, people may be very concerned about "saving face," looking good in the eyes of others. Staw and his associates have recognized that this tendency for self-justification is primarily responsible for people's inclination to protect their beliefs and others that they made the right decision all along and are willing to back it up (Staw, 1981). To conclude, the escalation of commitment phenomenon represents a type of irrational decision making that may occur, but only under certain circumstances.

Organizational Impediments to Decision Making

Thus far, the discussion in this chapter has emphasized the human cognitive shortcomings and biases that limit effective decision making. However, the discussion would be remiss if we were to ignore several important organizational factors that also interfere with rational decisions. Indeed, the situations faced by many organizational decision makers cannot help but interfere with their capacity to make decisions.

One obvious factor is time constraints. Many important organizational decisions are made under severe time pressure. Under such circumstances, it is often impossible for more exhaustive decision-making processes to occur. This is particularly the case when organizations face crisis situations requiring immediate decisions. In crisis situations, decision makers have been found to limit their search for information that may help them make optimal decisions (Tjosvold, 1984). Time constraints can contribute to a higher number of decisions that result in unethical or illegal behavior, as will be discussed later in this book.

The quality of many organizational decisions also may be limited by political "face saving" pressure. In other words, decision makers may make decisions that help them save face at work, although the resulting decisions might not be in the best interest of their organizations. Imagine, for example, how an employee might distort the available information needed to make a decision if the correct decision would jeopardize his or her job. Unfortunately, such misuses of information to support desired decisions are common. One study on this topic reported that a group of businessmen working on a group decision-making problem opted for an adequate — although less than optimal — decision rather than risk generating serous conflicts with their fellow group members (Johnson, 1984). In an actual case, a proponent of medical inoculation for the flu was reported as having decided to go ahead with the inoculation program on the basis of only a 2 percent chance of an epidemic (Neustadt & Feinberg, 1978). Apparently, people may make the decisions they *want* to make even though these may not be the optimal ones for the organizations involved.

Besides the time constraints and political pressures that limit quality of organizational decisions, note also the limitations imposed by moral and ethical constraints — what is known as bounded discretion. According to this idea, decision makers limit their actions to those that fall within the bounds of current moral and ethical standards. So, although engaging in illegal activities such as stealing may optimize an organization's profits (at least in the short run), ethical considerations may discourage such actions. Obviously, decision makers do not always act in an ethical manner. Sometimes, unethical decisions are made because of the inherent tendency of some individuals to be unethical, and other times, unethical decisions result from the tendency of the organization to encourage, or fail to discourage, unethical behavior.

GROUP DECISION MAKING

Decision-making groups are a well-established fact of modern organizational life. More than ever in today's organizations, groups and teams such as committees, study teams, task forces, or review panels are often charged with the responsibility for making important organizational decisions. They are so common, in fact, that it has been said that some administrators spend as much as 80 percent of their time in committee meetings (Delbecq, Van den Ven, & Gustafson, 1975; Greenberg & Baron, 1993). Given this, it is important to consider the strengths and weaknesses of using groups to make organizational decisions. The advantages of group decision making are pooling of resources, specialization of labor, and decision acceptance. Disadvantages of group decision making are wasted time, group conflict, and intimidation by group leaders.

There is little doubt that much can be gained by using decision-making groups. Several potential advantages of this approach may be identified. First, bringing people together may increase the amount of knowledge and information available for making good decisions; in other words, there may be a pooling of resources. A related benefit is that in decision-making groups, there can be a specialization of labor. With enough people around to share the work load, individuals can perform only those tasks at which they are best, potentially improving the quality of the group's efforts. Another benefit is that group decisions are likely to enjoy greater acceptance than individual decisions. People involved in making decisions may be expected to understand those decisions better and be more committed to carrying them out than decisions made by someone else (Murningham, 1981).

Of course, there are also some problems associated with using decision-making groups. One obvious drawback is that groups are likely to waste time. The time spent socializing before getting down to business may be a drain on the group and be very costly to organizations. Another possible problem is that potential disagreement over important matters may breed ill will and group conflict. Although constructive disagreement can actually lead to better group outcomes, highly disruptive conflict may interfere with group decisions. Indeed, with corporate power and personal pride at stake, it is not surprising to find that lack of agreement can cause bad feelings to develop among group members. Finally, we may expect groups to be ineffective sometimes because of members' intimidation by group leaders. A group composed of several "yes" men or women trying to please a dominant leader tends to discourage open and honest discussion of solutions. In view of these problems, it is no wonder we often hear the adage "A camel is a horse put together by a committee."

Given the several pros and cons of using groups to make decisions, we must conclude that neither groups nor individuals are always superior. Obviously, there are important trade-offs involved in using either one to make decisions.

COMPARING INDIVIDUAL AND GROUP DECISIONS

Because there are advantages associated with both individual and group decision makers, a question arises as to when each should be used, that is, under what conditions might individuals or groups make superior decisions?

When Are Groups Superior to Individuals?

Imagine a situation in which an important decision has to be made about a complex problem — such as whether one company should acquire another. This is not the kind of problem about which any one individual working alone would be able to make a good decision. Its highly complex nature may overwhelm even an expert, thereby setting the stage for a group to do a better job.

Whether or not it actually will do better depends on several important considerations. For one, we must consider who is in the group. Successful groups tend to be composed of heterogeneous group members with complementary skills. For example, a group composed of lawyers, accountants, real estate agents, and other experts may make much better decisions on complex problems than one composed of specialists in only one field. The diversity of opinions offered by group members is one of the major advantages of using groups to make decisions.

As you imagine, it is not enough to have skills. For a group to be successful, its members must also be able to freely communicate their ideas to each other in an open, nonhostile manner. Conditions under which one individual (or group) intimidates another from contributing his or her expertise can easily negate any potential gain associated with composing groups of heterogeneous experts. After all, having expertise and being about to make a contribution by using that expertise are two different things. Thus, for groups to be superior to individuals, they must be composed of a heterogeneous collection of experts with complementary skills who can freely and openly contribute to their group's product.

In contrast to complex decision tasks, imagine a situation in which judgment is required on a simple problem with a readily verifiable answer. For example, imagine that you are asked to translate a relatively obscure language into English. Groups might do better than individuals on such a task, probably because the odds are increased that someone in the group knows the language and can perform the translation for the group. However, there is no reason to expect that even a large group will be able to perform such a task better than a single individual who has the required expertise. In fact, an expert working alone may do even better than a group, because an expert individual performing a simple task may be distracted by others and suffer from having to convince them of the correctness of his or her solution. For this reason, exceptional individuals tend to outperform entire committees on simple tasks (Hill, 1982). In such cases, for groups to benefit from a pooling of resources, there must be some resources to pool. The pooling of ignorance does not help. In other words, the question: Are two heads better than one? can be answered this way: on simple tasks, two heads may be better than one if at least one of those heads has enough of what it takes to succeed. In summary, groups *may* perform better than individuals, depending on the nature of the task performed and the expertise of the people involved.

When Are Individuals Superior to Groups?

As has been described thus far, groups may be expected to perform better than the average or even the exceptional individual under certain conditions. However, there are also conditions under which individuals are superior to groups.

Most problems faced by organizations require a great deal of creative thinking. A company deciding how to use a newly developed adhesive in its consumer products is facing decisions on a poorly structured task.

Although you would expect that the complexity of such creative problems would give groups a natural advantage, this is not the case. On poorly structured, creative tasks, individuals perform better than groups.

A great part of the problem — and it is a problem, given the prevalence of decision-making groups in organizations — is that some individuals feel inhibited by the presence of others (this is even the case in brainstorming sessions, where one rule is that even far-out ideas may be shared). To the extent that people wish to avoid feeling foolish as a result of saying silly things, their creativity may be inhibited when in groups. Similarly, groups may inhibit creativity by slowing down the process of bringing ideas to fruition. Thus, although groups may be expected to help stimulate the creative process, any such benefits of groups are clearly more than offset when it comes to creative problems.

Thus far, this chapter has noted several problems underlying the relatively poor performance of groups compared with individuals. Now we will highlight important contributing factors to quality group decisions that in turn may lead to unethical group decision making.

OBSTACLES TO QUALITY GROUP DECISIONS

Many behaviors that are documented in behavioral science research affect the probability of success when groups participate in the decision-making process. For example, group function may be impaired when powerful leaders are present, commitment is required, goals must be set, or the members of the group perceive that risks are shared. This section identifies a few types of group dysfunctional behaviors that can serve as obstacles to quality group decisions and concludes with a comparison of the two most famous variants — groupthink and the Abilene paradox.

As they evolve, groups exhibit different patterns of behavior. First, there is socialization leading to focused work. Then, specific dysfunctional behavior may occur. In addition, groups evolve in four stages: forming, storming, norming, and performing. Forming includes introductions, the identification of participants' experience and skills, and preliminary task definition. Before actual work begins, groups experience a storming period characterized by conflicts over individual roles or the allocation of tasks and resources. Groups develop norms for behavior (norming) that guide interaction, facilitate task assignments, and influence discretionary rewards. Norms also help resolve conflict and route communications; they are helpful in identifying what types of problems are handled by specific participants or how conflict should be resolved. Finally, groups enter the performing stage, working toward their objective. The group follows procedures, evaluates alternatives, makes choices, and sets specific goals. As these processes occur, nonproductive activities (for example, ineffective decisions) may also occur.

Although groups are generally recommended as a means to improve decision making, build commitment, and facilitate implementation, organizational members must be cautioned that unusual outcomes have been recorded when groups work on problems. These outcomes are the result of certain behaviors that have unexpected results and that are attributed to group perceptions that may not reflect reality. For our purposes, there are five specific types of behavior that are obstacles to quality group decisions: groupthink, risky-shift behavior, commitment errors, goal-setting challenges, and the Abilene paradox.

Groupthink

In successful groups, individuals learn to work together. They become a cohesive group as they work on specific tasks or projects. However, cohesive groups may develop and implement strategies that are inappropriate. This behavior is attributed to changes in the group's reaction to new or conflicting information. Cohesive groups tend to close themselves off to unsettling information, whether from inside or outside the group. This behavior was labeled groupthink by Janis (1972, 1982).

The concept of groupthink was proposed initially as an attempt to explain ineffective decisions made by U.S. government officials that led to fiascoes such as the Bay of Pigs invasion in Cuba and the Vietnam War. Groupthink does not occur only in governmental decision making, of course, but also in the private sector (although the failures may be less well-publicized). For example, analyses of the business policies of large corporations such as Lockheed and Chrysler have suggested that it was the failure of top management teams to respond to changing market conditions that at one time led them to the brink of disaster (Janis, 1988). The problem is that members of very cohesive groups may have considerable confidence in their group's decisions, making them unlikely to raise doubts about these actions (that is, "the group seems to know what it's doing"). As a result, they may suspend their own critical thinking in favor of conforming to the group. When group members become fiercely loyal to each other, they may ignore potentially useful information from other sources that challenges the group's decisions. The result of this process is that the group's decisions may be completely uninformed, irrational, or even immoral (Moorehead & Montanari, 1986) (see Chapter 4 for a more detailed discussion of the concept of group-think and its relationship to unethical behavior).

Risky-Shift Behavior

Conventional wisdom suggests that groups act conservatively as a result of demands for conformity. However, researchers have found that many groups made more risky decisions than individuals (Walker & Main, 1973). So, for example, if four individuals recommended that the riskier course of action be taken if the odds of success were 40 percent, a group composed of these same individuals might recommend that the riskier course of action be taken if the odds of success were lower, say 20 percent. Because of this shift in the direction of riskiness by groups compared with individuals, the phenomenon became known as the risky shift. Apparently, the risky shift is part of a more general tendency for group members to shift their individual views in a more extreme direction, a phenomenon known as group polarization (Lamm & Myers, 1978). The group polarization effect refers to the tendency for group members to shift their views about a given issue to ones that are more extreme in the same direction as the views they held initially. Someone who is initially in favor of a certain decision will be more favorable toward it following group discussion, and someone who is initially opposed to a certain decision will be more opposed to it following group discussion.

Groups make riskier decisions because individual members do not fear personal retribution as a result of a group decision. If this behavior is not recognized, it increases the probability of failure. For example, failure can be defined as making a decision that has group support but that cannot be successfully implemented within current resource or time constraints.

Commitment Errors

Individuals may also make risky commitments. When individuals make public commitments, they are likely to attempt to live up to them despite evidence suggesting that they cannot be met. In laboratory and field experiments examining a portfolio manager's stock selections, managers who publicly selected certain stocks held those stocks longer than managers who made their selections privately, even when the stocks incurred substantial losses. Employees often commit to completion of tasks by a particular date. In one case, when a scheduled date was missed, the employees were persistent in stating they would be finished soon but did not provide accurate forecasts of completion dates.

Goal-Setting Challenges

Groups are not especially effective at setting goals. For example, the lower a group's achieved level of results relative to its goal, the more likely is the group to increase its goal for the subsequent year. Explanations for this odd behavior range from a shared group perception that there is no shame in failing at a more difficult task (that is, higher goal) to group compensation for previous failure. Either way, groups frequently do not adjust their goals to be more realistic after failure.

Erratic goal-setting behavior occurs when groups set goals to accomplish projects in less time or at lower cost than they have historically accomplished with similar projects. As new projects begin, previous experiences may be used as a reference. The group's composition frequently changes, particularly if poor performers have been removed. The group may believe that it will exceed its performance in previous tasks. Individuals may also believe they have learned more from their previous experiences than is actually the case. These perceptions, coupled with changes in requirements from situation to situation, increase probabilities of error when groups set goals.

The Abilene Paradox

The last problem behavior has to do with implied group agreement and has been dubbed the Abilene paradox by Jerry Harvey (1974). It has implications similar to those described previously, but its effects are more subtle.

In groups where there is strong pressure to avoid conflict, an alternative may be selected without any serious evaluation. There may be no discussion at all; the group may simply accept the first offered solution. Individuals seeking to avoid conflict may respond with neutral comments or look for some positive aspect of an idea or alternative considered. The general tone of a group meeting may leave participants feeling that they have reached consensus even though many participants may have severe personal reservations about the outcome selected (the behavior gets its name from an incident in which a group, feuding over where to eat, accepted the idea of driving 50 miles to a restaurant in Abilene, despite everyone's better judgment).

Harvey suggests that the Abilene paradox occurs because group members do not raise serious objections (if they raise any at all) because they fear separation from the group. Agreement is assumed simply because there is no disagreement. Groups often adopt courses of action in direct opposition of the desires of many or all of their members. The Abilene paradox can be especially troublesome because the appearance of consensus can lead to the allocation of resources. If there are real problems that are not discussed, then substantial effort may be wasted before problems surface and are resolved.

Although these obstacles to quality group decisions are all important, the remainder of this chapter will provide a more detailed discussion and comparison of the two most famous obstacles (Abilene paradox and groupthink). More specifically, the next section will attempt to gain a greater understanding of what makes individuals reluctant to voice dissent when they are aware of the negative ramifications of their silence in groups and will serve as the foundation for the discussion in the next chapter on the relationship between groupthink and unethical behavior in organizations.

The Abilene Paradox and Groupthink: A Brief Comparison

Like Harvey's Abilene paradox, other authors (for example, Janis, 1972, 1982; Tuchman, 1984) have written about obstacles to quality decisions (for example, group pursuit of disadvantageous policies after the risks of doing so have become apparent). Janis and Tuchman have each focused on a variety of historically noteworthy decision fiascoes that moved them to speculate about why people in authority frequently act contrary to enlightened self-interest by making decisions that are likely to be counterproductive. Examples of such decisions include, among others, the U.S. failure in Vietnam, the Kennedy administration's decision to invade Cuba at the Bay of Pigs, and the Watergate cover-up. Other (Janis, 1998; Sims, 1992) have also documented ineffective group decision making in the private sector (Beech-Nut, Chambers Development Company, Chrysler, E. F. Hutton, Heinz, Hertz, Lockheed, and Salomon Brothers). In addition, the literature is filled with discussions on the group decision fiasco that led to the Challenger disaster (Esser & Lindoerfer, 1989; Moorehead, Ferrence, & Neck, 1991).

A key point emphasized by these authors is that when many or all individuals within a group privately express doubts about the group's decisions or processes while publicly supporting them and are aware that their reservations are shared by many or all other group members, the group's decisions will often result in a fiasco. For example, the Abilene paradox is based on the commonplace, even trivial, experience suffered by Harvey (1974, 1988), his wife, and in-laws. They each agreed to leave the relative comfort of a shaded porch where they had been playing dominoes and drinking lemonade in order to take a miserably long car ride in the scorching Texas sun for a substandard meal at a cafeteria in Abilene. Later, each disgruntled family member revealed that his or her true preference had been to stay at home.

The Abilene paradox can be extrapolated to serious organizational crises. Harvey (1977) defines the paradox as "Organizations frequently taking actions in contradiction to the desires of any of their members and therefore defeating the very purposes the organizations are designed to achieve." Taras (1991) notes that the conditions necessary to diagnose Abilene are clear. In general, group members as individuals are fully aware of the problems facing the organization and of its poor responses. They admit, to themselves, to serious reservations. They often even agree, unknown to one another, about the solution required to solve the problem. Nonetheless, in collective situations, such as group meetings, they withhold their private feelings and allow other group members to believe that decisions are unanimously supported. The group makes defective decisions, producing the paradox. Individuals suffer frustration, irritation, anger, and feelings of impotence. They assign blame, choosing as targets themselves, the group, the task, or the organization as a whole. The organization begins to experience what Harvey calls "phoney conflict." More than likely, it also could plummet into a low-energy, low-motivation state best described as generalized malaise (Golembiewski, 1989).

The more famous of the two obstacles, groupthink, bears some superficial similarities to the Abilene paradox (Taras, 1991). As noted earlier, Janis and others have offered mesmerizing accounts of defective group decision making leading to fiascoes such as the failure to foresee the Japanese attack on Pearl Harbor. The groupthink decision-making procedure is defective, with premature convergence on a single option and the closing-off of sources of alternative information and courses of action. Although the decisions are poorly conceived, they are endorsed in both settings. It is also exceedingly difficult for a group or individual to admit fault (Silver & Mitchell, 1990; Gouran, 1982; Nisbett & Ross, 1980). It seems that one of the outcomes of defective decision-making modes is that the window of opportunity in which dissent may be voiced is very brief and slams precipitously and completely shut. Groups exhibit a tendency to push ahead even in the face of evidence that the decision may have been faulty (Taras, 1991).

Both groupthink and the Abilene paradox begin with an individual's attraction to a group, so much so that he or she will express concurrence with a decision perceived to the group's rather than voice dissent and suffer the real or imagined consequences. The expected negative consequences need to be based on reality. Indeed, catastrophic fantasies are as inhibitive to the individual as real threats.

Harvey goes no further than this stage of explanation. Janis, however, created a rich conceptual model, providing descriptions that exacerbate the tendency toward defective decision making (Janis & Mann, 1977; Janis, 1982; Hirokawa, 1980, 1987; Hirokawa, Gouran, & Martz, 1988).

Groupthink's antecedent conditions are easily specified: the group is cohesive, insulated, and homogeneous and has neither a tradition of impartial leadership nor norms requiring a systematic information search. Defective decisions are triggered by provocative situational contexts, composed of high stress from external threats, low self-esteem of group members, and decisions that involve questions of morality. Faced with an intolerably elevated degree of uncertainty, individuals seek greater affiliation with the group as a protective device. This banding together produces overestimations of the group — that it is invulnerable, inherently moral, and superior.

Recall the label "best and brightest" as it was applied to President Kennedy's inner circle. The group becomes close-minded and develops defenses against both internal and external dissent. Personal identities are, to some extent, dependent on group affiliation (Raven, 1974). At this point, group members are prepared to make, and support, decisions they might not have made as individuals had they not been seduced by group membership.

Groupthink can be distinguished from the Abilene paradox on four different levels (Taras, 1991). First, the consciousness of participants must be examined. Abilene riders each knowingly lives a lie that he or she perceives as the communal truth whose absurdity is enormously and psychically oppressive. Groupthink situations lack this paradoxical element where individuals want to do one thing but willingly, although in despair, do the opposite. In groupthink, the situation is not absurd until after the fog lifts. Not surprisingly, the strongest support of Janis' model is culled from the reflections and recriminations of group participants, in which hindsight is crystal clear. At the time they made defective decisions, however, they were often described as "euphoric," enjoying high morale and heightened sense of efficacy. To put it in simple, although somewhat extreme, terms, groupthink makes people feel good about bad public decisions, while the Abilene paradox makes people feel bad about good private decisions withheld from the group.

Second, at the group or organizational level, the Abilene paradox engenders conflict and/or malaise, while groupthink creates esprit de corps, optimistic portrayals of the future, and loyalty to the organization. What differentiates descriptions of groupthink from the Abilene paradox is the lack of conflict after faulty decisions are made.

Third, the relevant unit of analysis differs in the two conditions. In groupthink, individual entities become submerged and the group as a whole becomes analogous to a single organism; it responds to stimuli in patterned ways, is self-correcting, and expends energy to maintain homeostasis. In groupthink, the group is "more than" the sum of its parts; in contrast, Abilene paradox groups are "less than" the sum of their real parts. Individuals and their expectations dominate in the Abilene paradox.

The third distinction raises a troubling issue of morality and responsibility. Post mortems of Abilene paradoxes illuminate the individual's inability to speak out, and his or her awareness of the paradox mitigates the capacity to deflect culpability. The Abilene paradox offers no recourse to absolution of guilt by seeking refuge in group dynamics. In groupthink, however, the *group* is guilty of poor decision making, and because group members have surrendered their separate identities, they are exonerated from individual responsibility. Janis (1982) suggests that

Every executive who participates in group decisions is potentially susceptible to groupthink. Irrespective of the personality characteristics and other predispositions of the members who make up the policy-making group, the groupthink syndrome is expected to emerge whenever the situational conditions that are conducive to it are present. (p. 243)

In case after case, Janis mounts a brilliant line of defense for individuals who are accused of contributing to defective decisions. Pressure toward conformity, he argues, is the main factor that leads individuals to make and own defective decisions.

Fourth, intervention strategies differ. As the logical outcome of the preoccupation with group-level forces, groupthink interventions have focused on group structures and processes (Janis, 1982; Sauser, 1988). The Abilene paradox, with its focus on the individual, suggests interventions at the impersonal level — stressing disclosure, feedback, openness, and owning of privately held views (Harvey, 1988, 1977; Harvey & Albertson, 1971; Golembiewski, 1989).

Although there are similarities between these two obstacles to quality group decisions, the two are distinguishable because they invoke different individual member cognition, they have dramatically dissimilar consequences on group cohesion, they involve different levels of analysis, and, from a practical standpoint, each condition requires custom-tailored diagnostic strategies. Because groupthink more frequently pops up quickly and wreaks havoc before anyone realizes what is going on, it is the premise of this book that it causes more problems for organizations and, thus, can be more easily tied to unethical behavior in organizations, as highlighted in the next chapter.

Studies comparing the decisions made by groups and by individuals reveal a complex pattern. Groups have proven superior to individual members when they are composed of a heterogeneous mix of experts who possess complementary skills. However, groups may not be any better than the best member of the group when performing a task that has a simple, verifiable answer. Compared with individuals, groups tend to make inferior decisions on creative problems. However, no matter whether one focuses on individual or group decision making, having an understanding of both is important to the success of an organization.

There is no doubt that organizations make a variety of decisions that impact their culture, values, leaders, managers, employees, and both strategic and operational initiatives. It is the contention of this book that all of these decisions are important to understanding ethics and to institutionalizing ethics in organizations. Based on the overview of individual and group decision making provided in this chapter, the next chapter presents a discussion of the relationship between groupthink and unethical behavior.

REFERENCES

Delbecq, A. L., Van de Ven, A. H., & Gustafson, D. H. 1975. *Group techniques for program planning*. Glenview, IL: Scott, Foresman.

Esser, J. K., & Lindoerfer, J. S. 1989. Groupthink and the space shuttle accident: Toward a quantitative case analysis. *Journal of Behavioral Decision Making 2*, 167–77.

Golembiewski, R. T. 1989. *Ironies in organization development*. New Brunswick, NJ: Transaction.

Gouran, D. S. 1992. *Making decisions in groups: Choices and consequences*. Glenview, IL: Scott, Foresman.

Greenberg, J., & Baron, R. A. 1993. *Behavior in organizations*. Needham Heights, MA: Allyn and Bacon.

Harvey, J. B. 1988, Summer. The Abilene paradox: The management of agreement. *Organizational Dynamics 17*, 16–43.

_____. 1977. Consulting during crises of agreement. In *Current issues and strategies in organization development*, ed. W. Warner Burke. New York: Human Science Press.

_____. 1974, Summer. The Abilene paradox: The management of agreement. *Organizational Dynamics 17*, 16–43.

Harvey, J. B., & Albertson, R. 1971. Neurotic organizations: Symptoms, causes, and treatment. Parts I and II. *Personnel Journal*, p. 50.

Hill, G. W. 1982. Group versus individual performance: Are N + 1 heads better than one? *Psychological Bulletin 91*, 517–39.

Hirokawa, R. Y. 1987, February. Why informed groups make faulty decisions: An investigation of possible interaction-based explanations. *Small Group Behavior 18*, 3–29.

_____. 1980. A comparative analysis of communication patterns within effective and ineffective decision-making groups. *Communication Monographs 47*, 312–21.

Hirokawa, R. Y., Gouran, D. S., & Martz, A. E. 1988, November. Understanding the sources of faulty group decision making: A lesson from the Challenger disaster. *Small Group Behavior 19*, 411–33.

Janis, I. L. 1988. *Crucial decisions: Leadership in policy making and crisis management*. New York: Free Press.

_____. 1982. *Groupthink* 2nd ed. revised. Boston, MA: Houghton Mifflin.

_____. 1972. *Groupthink*. Boston, MA: Houghton Mifflin.

Janis, I. L., & Mann, L. 1977. *Decision making: A psychological analysis of conflict, choice, and commitment*. New York: Free Press.

Johnson, R. J. 1984. Conflict avoidance through acceptable decisions. *Human Relations 27*, 71–82.

Lamm, H., & Myers, E. C. 1978. Group-induced polarization of attitudes and behavior. In *Advances in experimental social psychology*, ed. L. Berkowitz. New York: Academic Press, Vol. 11, pp. 145–95.

Moorehead, G., & Montanari, J. R. 1986. An empirical investigation of the groupthink phenomenon. *Human Relations 39*, 399–410.

Murningham, J. K. 1981. Group decision making: What strategies should you use? *Management Review 25*, 56–62.

Myers, D. G., & Lamm, H. 1976. The group polarization phenomenon. *Psychological Bulletin 83*, 602–27.

Neustadt, R. E., & Fineberg, H. 1978. The swine flu affair: Decision making on a slippery disease. Washington, DC: U.S. Department of Health, Education and Welfare.

Nisbett, R. E., & Ross, L. 1980. *Human inference: Strategies and shortcomings of social judgment*. Englewood Cliffs, NJ: Prentice-Hall.

Raven, B. 1974. The Nixon group. *Journal of Social Issues 30*, 304–20.

Ross, J., and Staw, B. M. 1986. Expo 86: An escalation prototype. *Administrative Science Quarterly 31*, 274–97.

Sauser, W. I., Jr. 1988. Injecting contrast: A Key to quality decisions. *Advanced Management Journal 53*(4): 20–23.

Silver, W. S., & Mitchell, T. R. 1990. The status quo tendency in decision making. *Organizational Dynamics 18*(4): 34–46.

Sims, R. R. 1992. Linking groupthink to unethical behavior in organizations. *Journal of Business Ethics 11*, 651–62.

Staw, B. M. 1981. The escalation of commitment to a course of action. *Academy of Management Review 6*, 577–87.

____. 1976. Knee-deep in the big muddy: A study of escalating commitment to a chosen course of action. *Organizational Behavior and Human Performance 16*, 27–44.

Taras, D. G. 1991, Winter. Breaking the silence: Differentiating crises of agreement. *Public Administration Quarterly*, pp. 401–18.

Tjosvold, D. 1984. Effects of crisis orientation on managers' approach to controversy in decision making. *Academy of Management Journal 27*, 130–38.

Tuchman, B. 1984. *The march of folly.* New York: Knopf.

Walker, T. G., & Main, E. C. 1973. Choice-shifts in political decision making: Federal judges and civil liberties cases. *Journal of Applied Social Psychology 2*, 93–98.

4

The Relationship between Groupthink and Unethical Behavior in Organizations

Issues of corporate morality and business ethics are of concern to both management and their organizations (Jansen & Von Glinow, 1985; Schermerhorn, Hunt, & Osborn, 1991). These issues include social responsibility, conflict of interest, payoffs, product safety, liability, and whistleblowing (Jansen & Von Glinow, 1985). On the popular front, many national newspapers and business magazines offer continuing glimpses of corporate and managerial misbehavior. Despite all the attention, such inquiries rarely and explicitly examine the link between organizational culture (and, more specifically, groupthink) and individuals who behave unethically. It is far more common and dramatic to focus on individual culpability, a practice organizations may support out of sheer self-interest. However, greater knowledge of the role of groupthink in unethical actions may change attributions of individual culpability.

The connection between groupthink and unethical behavior could be especially helpful in understanding the role of groupthink when individuals behave unethically as well as providing a basis for altering behavior in a more ethical direction. The purpose of this chapter is to discuss the importance of groupthink in contributing to unethical behavior in organizations. The chapter will provide a further elaboration of the groupthink effect and then discuss how groupthink contributed to unethical behavior in several organizations (Beech-Nut, E. F. Hutton, and Salomon Brothers).

GROUPTHINK: AN ELABORATION

As noted in Chapter 3, Janis (1972, 1982, 1989) laid the basis for a theory of causes and effects of groupthink and has offered several definitions of the concept. The shortest and most explicit definition is concurrence seeking (see Janis, 1982, Figure 10-1). In text, the definition is amplified to mean "a mode of thinking that people engage in when they are deeply involved in a cohesive group, when the members' strivings for unanimity override their motivation to realistically appraise alternative courses of action" (Janis, 1982, p. 9). It is important to be clear that groupthink is not simply a group making a bad decision, that is, a decision that turns out badly. Groupthink is concurrence seeking that interferes with adequate consideration of decision alternatives, which in turn leads to poor decisions (Janis, 1982, Figure 10-1). But the linkage from groupthink to defective decision-making procedures to bad decisions is probabilistic rather than deterministic. Groupthink can sometimes produce a good decision, and high-quality decision-making procedures will occasionally produce a bad (unsuccessful) decision.

Groupthink is most likely to occur when a group experiences antecedent conditions such as high cohesion, insulation from experts, limited methodological search and appraisal procedures, directive leadership, and high stress, combined with low self-esteem and little hope of finding a better solution than that favored by the leader or influential group members. Such conditions lead to symptoms of groupthink such as illusions of invulnerability, collective rationalization, belief in the inherent morality of the group, stereotypes of outgroups, pressure on dissenters, self-censorship, illusions of unanimity, and self-appointed mindguards. Groupthink is hypothesized to result in poor quality decisions and defective decision-making symptoms such as incomplete survey of alternatives and objectives, failure to examine risks of preferred solution, failure to reappraise initially rejected alternatives, poor information search, selective bias in processing information at hand, and failure to develop contingency plans. Janis described several shared characteristics of cohesive decision-making groups that have been responsible for some policy debacles. The following quotation from Janis and Mann (1977, p. 130) is a good example.

Many historic fiascoes can be traced to defective policy making on the part of government leaders who receive social support from their ingroup advisors. A series of historic examples by Janis (1972) suggests that the following four groups of policy advisors, like Kimmel's ingroup of naval commanders, were dominated by concurrence seeking or groupthink and displayed characteristic symptoms of defensive avoidance: Neville Chamberlain's inner circle, whose members supported the policy of appeasement of Hitler during 1937 and 1938, despite repeated warnings and events that it would have adverse consequences; President Truman's advisory group, whose members supported the decision to escalate the war in North Korea despite firm warnings by the Chinese Communist government that U.S. entry into North Korea would be met with armed resistance from the Chinese; President Kennedy's inner circle, whose members supported the decision to launch the Bay of Pigs invasion of Cuba despite the availability of information indicating that it would be an unsuccessful venture and would damage U.S. relations with other countries; and President Johnson's close advisors, who supported the decision to escalate the war in Vietnam despite intelligence reports and other information indicating that this course of action would not defeat the Vietcong or the North Vietnamese and would entail unfavorable political consequences within the United States. All these groupthink-dominated groups were characterized by strong pressures toward uniformity, which inclined their members to avoid raising controversial issues, questioning weak arguments, or calling a halt to soft-headed thinking.

There also is evidence that groupthink was at work in the Nixon entourage, which was responsible for the Watergate cover-up, although there is some question of the cohesiveness of this group (Janis, 1982).

As noted in the previous chapter, Janis' concept of groupthink has been an influential one. The appeal of the concept is evidenced by the ease with which it can be applied to numerous group decisions such as Nazi Germany's decision to invade the Soviet Union in 1941, Israel's lack of preparedness for the October 1973 war, Gruenthal Chemie's decision to market the drug thalidomide (Raven & Rubin, 1976), governmental decisions regarding earthquake retrofitting before the Loma Pietra earthquake (Turner & Pratkanis, 1991), the National Aeronautics and Space Administration's and Morton Thiokol's decision to launch the Challenger space shuttle (Aronson, 1988), the decision by top executives of the Buffalo Mining Company to continue to dump slag into the Buffalo River (Wheeler & Janis, 1980), the Carter administration's decision to use military measures to rescue Iranian hostages (Ridgeway, 1983; Smith, 1984), the check-kiting scheme at E. F. Hutton (Moorehead & Griffin; 1989, Sims, 1992), and the potential for groupthink to occur in various work situations (Manz & Sims, 1982; Moorehead & Montanari, 1986).

The tragedy of the space shuttle Challenger provides a more contemporary example of groupthink and the decision-making process. This decision was the product of a flawed group decision as much as it was a failure of technology. The presidential committee that investigated the accident pointed to a flawed decision-making process as a primary contributory cause. Strong pressures for uniformity also characterized the process surrounding the flawed decisions of the Reagan administration to exchange arms for hostages with Iran and to continue commitment to the Nicaraguan Contras in the face of several congressional amendments limiting or banning aid.

Initial investigations of the groupthink phenomenon focused on policy decision making in government and military settings. However, evidence suggests that it frequently occurs in the business world. The design and marketing of the ill-fated Edsel automobile have been attributed to groupthink (Huseman & Driver, 1979). A more recent example is the film *The Bonfire of the Vanities*. In the *Devil's Candy: The Bonfire of the Vanities Goes to Hollywood*, the book chronicling the making of the $50 million box-office bomb, author Julie Salamon details how many of the people involved in the making of the movie privately doubted casting decisions and changes in the story line, but no one voiced these doubts to the director, Brian De Palma. De Palma had reservations as well, but because everyone seemed to be in agreement, he convinced himself that he had made the right decisions (Stern, 1992). Similarly, the following example shows how another organization form the world of business succumbed to its pressures (Harvey, 1974; Sims, 1992).

The Ozyx Corporation is a relatively small industrial company. The president of Ozyx has hired a consultant to help discover the reasons for the poor profit picture of the company in general and the low morale and productivity of the R&D division in particular. During the process of investigation, the consultant becomes interested in a research project in which the company has invested a sizable proportion of its R&D budget.

When asked about the project by the consultant in the privacy of their offices, the president, the vice president for research, and the research manager each describe it as an idea that looks great on paper but will ultimately fail because of the unavailability of the technology required to make it work. Each of them also acknowledges that continued support of the project will create cash flow problems that will jeopardize the very existence of the total organization.

Furthermore, each individual indicates he or she has not told the others about these reservations. When asked why, the president says he cannot reveal his "true" feelings because abandoning the project, which has been widely publicized, would make the company look bad in the press. In addition, it would probably cause his vice president's ulcer to kick up or perhaps even cause her to quit, "Because she has staked her professional reputation on the project's success."

Similarly, the vice president for research says she cannot let the president or the research manager know her reservations because the president is so committed to it that "I would probably get fired for insubordination if I questioned the project."

Finally, the research manager says he cannot let the president or vice president know of his doubts about the project because of their extreme commitment to the project's success.

All indicate that, in meetings with one another, they try to maintain an optimistic facade so the others will not worry unduly, writing ambiguous progress reports so the president and the vice president can "interpret them to suit themselves." In fact, the research manager says that he tends to slant them to the "positive" side, "given how committed the brass are."

In a paneled conference room, the research budget is being considered for the following fiscal year. In the meeting itself, praises are heaped on the questionable project, and a unanimous decision is made to continue it for yet another year.

Why do skilled, experienced, and ethical executives and employees occasionally make decisions like these, in which vital interests of their organization are likely to be hurt? By facilitating the development of shared illusions and related norms, groups make such decisions. That is, groupthink is likely to occur when members of a group or team begin to think alike. People are either quiet about their reservations or they convince themselves that everybody else agrees with the plan. It appears that in many instances, groupthink pops up and quickly wreaks havoc before anyone realizes what is going on.

Strong dynamics perpetuate groupthink. First and foremost, because retention of membership in the group is imperative, individuals remain silent because they dread separation from the group. In groupthink, when an individual's dissonance poses a danger to membership, a primal separation anxiety is activated and fear of abandonment, however irrational, takes hold (Janis, 1963). If a person feels depersonalized or alienated within a large organization, he or she may react by clinging excessively to a group, seeking friendship, support, and affirmation (Golembiewski, 1989).

One must appreciate that, despite all organizational assurances to the contrary, a person who contemplates breaking a silence and exposing a defective group decision faces actual danger. A whistleblower is usually pressured by the group to conform or, failing that, is punished if possible. Even in groups that allow members to express doubts about decisions, research suggests that, after an initial burst of activity to elicit conformity, the amount of communication directed to the deviant member precipitously declines. If necessary, group members eject the deviant member or redefine the boundaries of the group in some way as to exclude the deviant member (Cartwright & Zander, 1968).

A review of our current understanding on group dynamics yields a long list of conditions that likely contribute to the propensity for obstacles to quality group decisions like groupthink to occur. These distinct, though not mutually exclusive, conditions interact to produce groupthink.

It is the contention of this book that, given the heavy emphasis on teamwork within modern organizations and on groups in general, the dissemination of the groupthink concept is desperately needed and can assist us in acquiring a better understanding of why unethical behavior occurs in organizations. Therefore, based upon the groupthink explanation discussed to this point, the remainder of this chapter will demonstrate how the groupthink effect can be directly tied to unethical actions committed in organizations.

CAN GROUPTHINK BE A PRECURSOR TO UNETHICAL BEHAVIOR?

What guides the behavior of managers and employees as they cope with ethical dilemmas? Or, keeping in line with the main focus of this book, what results in the unethical behavior of some groups in organizations? Trevino (1986) has developed a model that suggests that individuals' (and groups') standards of right and wrong are not the sole determinant of their decisions. Instead, these beliefs interact with other individual characteristics (such as locus of control) and situational forces (such as an organization's rewards and punishments and its culture). All of these factors shape individual and group decisions and the behavior that results from them. Trevino's model shows how people can choose to engage in acts they consider unethical when the culture of an organization and its prevailing reward structure overwhelm personal belief systems.

As evidenced in Trevino's (1986) work, organizational culture is a key component when looking at ethical behavior. It is the contention of this chapter that the literature on "groupthink" (Janis, 1972) may help explain why some organizations develop cultures in which some individuals and groups knowingly commit unethical acts or ignore them even though they believe the activities to be wrong. The presence or absence of ethical behavior in organizational members' actions is both influenced by the prevailing culture (ethical climate) (as introduced in Chapter 2) and, in turn, partially determines the culture's view of ethical issues. The organizational culture may promote the assumption of responsibility for actions taken by individuals and groups, thereby increasing the probability that both will behave in an ethical manner. Alternatively, the culture may diffuse responsibility for the consequences of unethical behavior, thereby making such behavior more likely. In addition, there is the increased potential for groupthink, a precursor to organizational counternorms and unethical behavior.

As noted previously, according to Janis (1972), groupthink is "a mode of thinking that people engage in when they are deeply involved in a cohesive in-group, when the members' striving for unanimity overrides their motivation to realistically appraise alternative courses of action." During groupthink, small groups develop shared illusions and related norms that interfere with critical thinking and reality testing. Bales' (1950) studies of groups whose members did not previously know one another supports Janis' concept of groupthink. For the purposes of our discussion, groupthink occurs when a group places a higher priority on organizational counternorms that lead to organizational benefits, thus, encouraging and supporting unethical behavior. In addition, these counternorms are shaped and maintained by key organizational actors and the organization's reward system.

From his analysis of good and bad decisions made by such groups, Janis (1972) argues that antecedent conditions lead to a concurrence-seeking tendency (groupthink) in small decision-making groups. Antecedents to groupthink are high cohesiveness and the insularity of the decison-making group and a lack of methodological procedures for searching for and appraising information; the group may be led in a highly directive manner, and it may operate under conditions of high stress combined with low hope for finding a better solution than the one favored by the leader or other influential people. Particularly under stress, members of the group develop a number of cognitive defenses that result in a collective pattern of avoidance. These defenses include misjudging relevant warnings, inventing new arguments to support a chosen policy, failing to explore ominous implications of ambiguous events, forgetting information that would enable a challenging event to be interpreted correctly, and misperceiving signs of the onset of actual danger.

A revised model of groupthink (Moorehead, Ference, & Neck, 1991) has proposed two variables (time and leadership style) as moderators of the impact of the group characteristics on groupthink symptoms. In effect, the model proposes that the groupthink symptoms result from the group characteristics, as proposed by Janis (1972), but only in the presence of the moderator variables of time and certain leadership styles.

Time, as an important element in the model, is relatively straightforward. When a decision must be made within a very short time frame, pressure on members to agree, to avoid time-consuming arguments and reports from outside experts, and to self-censor themselves may increase. These pressures inevitably cause group members to seek agreement. In Janis' original model, time was included indirectly as a function of the antecedent condition, group cohesion. Janis (1963) argued that time pressures can adversely affect decision quality in two ways. First, it affects the decision makers' mental efficiency and judgment, interfering with their ability to concentrate on complicated discussions, to absorb new information, and to use imagination to anticipate the future consequences of alternative courses of action. Second, time pressure is a source of stress that will have the effect of inducing a policy-making group to become more cohesive and more likely to engage in groupthink.

Leadership is shown to be a moderator because of the importance it plays in either promoting or avoiding the development of the symptoms of groupthink. The leader, even though she or he may not promote a preferred solution, may allow or even assist the group seeking agreement by not forcing the group to critically appraise all alternative courses of action. The focus of this leadership variable is on the degree to which the leader allows or promotes discussion and evaluation of alternatives. It is not a matter of simply not making known a preferred solution; the issue is one of stimulation of critical thinking among the group.

The major symptoms of a group caught in groupthink (Janis, 1972, Hodgetts, 1990) and several potential hazards related to ethical behavior (Sims, 1992) are:

an illusion of invulnerability shared by most or all members of the group, which creates excessive optimism and encourages extreme risks;

collective efforts to rationalize the group's course of action in order to discern their belief in the inherent morality of the group and an unwillingness to reconsider their assumptions before they recommit themselves to their past policy decisions;

an unquestioned belief in the group's inherent morality, inclining the members to ignore the ethical or moral consequences of their decisions;

stereotyped views of those not in the group (rivals and enemies) as "colored by naivete and impractical ideals" (Janis, 1972, p. 73), too evil to warrant genuine attempts to negotiate, or too weak or stupid to counter whatever risky attempts are made to defeat their purposes (no attempt is made to understand others' ethical concerns, and group members may underestimate others' potential to contribute relevant information to goal accomplishment);

direct pressure on any member who expresses strong arguments against any of the group's stereotypes, illusions, or commitments, making clear that such dissent is contrary to what is expected of all loyal members;

self-censorship of deviations from the apparent group consensus, reflecting each member's inclination to minimize to himself/herself the importance of his/her doubts and counterarguments (group members falsely assume that silence means consent);

a shared illusion of unanimity, partly resulting from this self-censorship and augmented by the false assumption that silence implies consent; and

the emergence of self-appointed mindguards — members who protect the group from adverse information that might shatter their shared complacency about the effectiveness and morality of their decisions.

Evidence of most of these symptoms appears in the unedited transcripts of the deliberations of the people involved in the Watergate cover-up (Van Fleet, 1991) and records on discrimination violations, horizontal or vertical price-fixing, and intentional securities fraud.

The flaws in the groupthink decision-making process (Janis, 1972; Moorehead, 1982) often result in the kinds of ethical decision-making defects and outcome variables (Sims, 1992) listed below:

perception of few ethical alternatives,

no reexamination of preferred unethical alternative,

no reexamination of rejected ethical alternatives,

rejection of dissenting opinions,

selective bias of new information, and

win at all costs.

The result of the antecedent conditions and the symptoms of group-think is a defective decision-making process that can result in the kinds of ethical decision-making defects and outcome variables like unethical decisions and lower decision quality. Groupthink occurs in organizations that knowingly commit unethical acts when the group is cohesive, a leader promotes solutions or ideas even if they are unethical, and the group has no internal rules or control mechanisms to continually prescribe ethical behavior (Sims, 1992).

Just like entering an organization, employees entering a group are provided opportunities to become schooled in and committed to the group's goals, objectives, and ways of conducting business. Such commitment is the relative strength of an individual's identification with and involvement in a particular group. It usually includes the following factors that lead to the following group characteristics: group cohesiveness — a strong belief in the group's goals and values; a willingness to exert considerable effort on behalf of the group; a strong desire to continue as a group member; excessive and almost blind loyalty to the group; arrogance and overconfidence; a bottom-line mentality; insulation from ethical opinion and control; and leader promotion of unethical solutions, that is, any behaviors that ensure that the group wins (Moorehead, 1982; Sims, 1992). This kind of commitment to the group, then, is not simply loyalty to a group; rather, it is an ongoing process through which group members express their concern for the group and its continued success and well-being even to the extent of committing unethical actions.

Keeping in line with the discussion in the previous section, a major factor contributing to the group's defective decision making is that for each member of the cohesive group, one particular incentive looms large: the approval or disapproval of his or her fellow group members and their leader. The group is likely to perceive few ethical alternatives and to ignore potential problems with the preferred alternative. The group may reject any opinion that does not support the preferred alternative, and it is unlikely to reconsider an alternative previously dismissed by the group, even in light of new evidence. Decisions made through such a process are not always unethical, but there is a higher probability of the occurrence of unethical behavior.

As pointed out earlier, groupthink can occur in decision making within almost any organization, as may have been the case of Ford Motor Company's decision to market the Edsel and at Beech-Nut and E. F. Hutton. Both the Beech-Nut and E. F. Hutton experiences provide examples of how even the most reputable of companies can suffer from an ethical breakdown through groupthink and subsequent poor judgment.

The admission by Beech-Nut, the second largest baby-food producer in the United States, that it sold millions of jars of "phony" apple juice shocked many company employees as well as industry executives. Since 1891, purity, high quality, and natural ingredients had served as the foundation of its corporate culture and had been a consistent marketing theme. What had caused Beech-Nut to stray from its heritage and reputation?

Perhaps some portion of motive can be inferred from a report Hoyvald wrote to Nestle, the company that had acquired Beech-Nut in the midst of his cover-up. "It is our feeling that we can report safely now that the apple juice recall has been completed. If the recall had been effectuated in early June [when the FDA had first ordered it], over 700,000 cases in inventory would have been affected. . . . Due to our many delays, we were only faced with having to destroy 20,000 cases" (Kindel, 1989, p. 48).

Beginning in 1977, the company began buying a chemical concoction, made up mostly of sugar and water, and labeling it as apple juice. Sales of that product brought Beech-Nut an estimated $60 million between 1977 and 1982 while reducing material costs about $250,000 annually.

When various investigators tried to do something about it, the company stonewalled. Among other things, they shipped the bogus juice out of a plant in New York to Puerto Rico, to put it beyond the jurisdiction of federal investigators, and they even offered the juice as a giveaway to reduce their stocks after they were finally forced to discontinue selling it.

In the end, the company pleaded guilty to 215 counts of introducing adulterated food into commerce and violating the Federal Food, Drug and Cosmetic Act. The FDA fined Beech-Nut $2 million. In addition, Beech-Nut's president, Neils Hoyvald, and its vice president of operations, John Lavery, were found guilty of similar charges (Kindel, 1989). Again, why did they do it?

The answer to this question is complex. However, underlying the company's ethical failure were strong financial pressures. Beech-Nut was losing money, and the use of the cheap, adulterated concentrate saved millions of dollars. Beech-Nut employees seemed to use two arguments to justify their actions: they believed that many other companies were selling fake juice, and they were convinced that their adulterated juice was perfectly safe to consume. In addition, some employees took refuge in the fact that no conclusive test existed to determine natural from artificial ingredients. With regard to this latter point, Beech-Nut seems to have shifted the burden of proof around. Other juicemakers have been known to cut off suppliers if the supplier cannot demonstrate that their product is genuine. At Beech-Nut, senior management apparently told R&D that *they* would have to prove that an inexpensive supplier's product was adulterated before the company would switch to another supplier. Beech-Nut compounded their problems when government investigations began by stonewalling rather than cooperating, apparently in order to gain time to unload a $3.5 million inventory of tainted apple juice products. Thus, although at first Beech-Nut appears to have been the innocent victim of unscrupulous suppliers, the company by its later actions changed a civil matter into criminal charges (Welles, 1988).

Strong pressures also characterize the process surrounding the unethical decisions of E. F. Hutton's check kiting.

In 1985, the E. F. Hutton Group Inc., one of the nation's largest brokerage firms, pleaded guilty to 2,000 counts of wire and mail fraud, paid a fine of almost $3 million, and put over $9 million into funds to pay back defrauded banks and investors. The court case focused the nation's attention on banks' overdraft policies, but it also provided an example of how groupthink can cause trouble for even the mightiest institutions.

Hutton's crime involved a form of check kiting. A money manager at a Hutton branch office would write a check on an account in bank A for more money than Hutton had in that account. Because of the time lag in the check-collection system, these overdrafts sometimes went undetected, and Hutton could deposit funds to cover the overdraft in bank A's account on the following day. Even if the bank noticed the overdraft, it was unlikely to complain, because Hutton was such an important customer and because certain kinds of overdrafts are fairly routine.

In any case, the Hutton manager would deposit the check from bank A into an account in bank B, where the money would start earning interest immediately. In effect, the scheme allowed Hutton to earn a day's interest on bank A's account without having to pay anything for it. A day's interest may not sound like much, but Hutton was getting as much as $250 million in free loans every day, and a day's interest on such a sum is substantial (Goleman, 1988; *ASA Banking Journal*, 1987; Seneker, 1986).

Eventually, complaints from banks arrived at the desk of the vice president and money manager. It was not long before the media picked up the explanation. No contingency plan was in place. As the full tale unfolded, Hutton's senior executives debated whether the problem was internal or external. Defensive doubting gave way to aggressive anger. Had they actually done something drastically wrong or only pushed a common but dubious practice too far?

Hutton top management hired former Attorney General Griffin Bell, Jr., to investigate their overdraft practices. He discovered that branch managers received a percentage of any interest earned from the over-drafting. The accounting practice failed to distinguish between the interest earned from cash management and commissions earned from brokerage transactions. This minor discrepancy was enough to inspire a new and easy way to hit gross revenue targets. Because of the Hutton culture, officers and company personnel either failed to grasp the implications of their system or simply took liberties with what was becoming a clearly enunciated ethic.

Hutton concluded that their officers were not basically at fault and rationalized that they were just overzealous. They supported this view even though it was found that the Hutton culture evidently provided supervisory slippage at all three levels, from branch manager to executive money manager to the chief financial officer. They reasoned that their real ethical problem was external and not internal — that is, how they were perceived by clients. Thus, they decided against an in-house ethical "cleanup" program that could have created a tighter organization with articulated standards. They hired Bill Cosby, at a cost of more than $1 million, to recapture their reputation.

Comments from victims of the Hutton caper indicate that they were most offended at the arrogance of the executives who expected special favors. They were not just cheated. They treated their banking colleagues as slaves rather than equals. The Hutton money managers seemed unmindful or unaware of any possible cost or inconvenience to others. They were imperialistic. Little, if any, consideration was extended to clients. Hutton executives abused a fine reputation. They expected to be treated differently. The overdrafts were neither casual nor occasional. They were planned. Hutton was distinguished by these motives and methods that led to the groupthink effect and the decision to commit unethical acts.

Excuses for Hutton's behavior are easy to find if one wants to. The increased competition among brokerage firms and signals from Washington provided impetus for "ethical innovation," to put it politely. Increased pressure on the financial bottom line always puts pressure on the quality of group decision making and the ethical bottom line. In a sense, one might say that "something's got to give." The mounting deficits in Washington, along with its probusiness attitude, gave birth to an "anything goes" mentality. Couple that with the Hutton organizational culture in particular, and it is easy to understand the resulting groupthink effect and the check kiting.

E. F. Hutton misread public reaction and treated their check kiting as a public relations issue. They hired Bill Cosby to recapture their reputation. Although they understood the importance of public perception, they failed to see that their problems were internal and a result of an organizational culture that allowed check kiting (an unethical behavior) to occur.

More recently, wrongdoings by Salomon Brothers in the Treasury auction scandal provides another example of how groupthink can be linked to unethical behavior. A chronology of how the Salomon Brothers fiasco unfolded is as follows:

December 1990 — Salomon submits bids in the names of customers who had not authorized them at an $8.57 billion auction of four-year notes. The bids enable the firm to buy 46 percent of the securities, breaching Treasury rules that bar individual bidders from buying more than 35 percent at any single sale.

February 1991 — Through unauthorized customer bids, Salomon buys 57 percent of securities sold at an auction of $9.04 billion of five-year Treasury notes.

As a "practical joke" against a Salomon employee, a managing director persuades an unidentified customer to submit a bogus bid for $1 billion at the $11.01 billion auction of 30-year Treasury bonds. This plan goes awry, and the bid is actually submitted.

April — In a $9.06 billion auction of five-year notes, Salomon exceeds the bidding limit with a 35 percent bid for its own account, in addition to a $2.5 billion bid for a customer and the repurchase of $600 million of that bid at the auction price.

Late April — Paul Mozer, managing director in charge of government bond trading, informs Salomon Chairman John Gutfreund, President Thomas Strauss, and Vice Chairman John Meriwether about the illegal bidding in February. No immediate action is taken.

May 22 — In the Treasury's $12.26 billion auction of two-year notes, Salomon effectively buys at least 44 percent of the issue. The firm bids $2 billion for a customer and repurchases $500 million from the customer at the auction price, in addition to "inadvertently" failing to disclose its own position of $497 million. Government investigators allege that Salomon may have controlled as much as 85 percent of the issue. Dealers charge that Salomon forced up prices to squeeze its competitors.

June — The Securities and Exchange Commission and Justice Department issue subpoenas to Salomon and certain clients.

July — Salomon reviews its government bond operations and launches "full" investigation.

August 9 — Salomon first discloses that it violated bidding rules in December, February, and May and suspends Mozer, his top aide, Thomas Murphy, trader Christopher Fitzmaurice, and clerk Henry Epstein.

August 14 — Salomon discloses that Gutfreund, Strauss, and Meriwether knew of the violations in April and releases details of additional violations.

August 16 — Gutfreund and Strauss announce they will resign at August 18 board meeting. Warren E. Buffet is named interim chairman.

August 18 — The Treasury Department bars Salomon from participating in government securities auctions for customers' accounts but allows the firm to continue bidding for its own accounts. Deryck C. Maughan, former head of Salomon's Tokyo operations, is named chief operating officer in charge of day-to-day operations. Salomon board accepts resignations of Gutfreund, Strauss, and Meriwether and fires Mozer and Murphy (Siconolfi & Cohen, 1991, p. A4).

Gutfreund, a one-time bond trader, kept his tough-guy image to the end. After formally offering to resign, Gutfreund told top executives at a closed door meeting: "I'm not apologizing for anything to anybody. Apologies don't mean [expletive]. What happened, happened" (Siconolfi & Cohen, 1991, p. A4). The same arrogance that enabled Gutfreund to build Salomon into the dominant force in the $2.3 trillion Treasury securities market also led to his becoming ensnared in a government trap that became his and other key company executives' undoing.

Collusion and price fixing in the $2.3 trillion Treasury securities market have been routine for more than a decade, according to traders and top Wall Street executives (Siconolfi, Sesit, & Mitchell, 1991). The most prevalent and potentially damaging practice has been the sharing of confidential information among an elite group of bond dealers about their bids at auctions of Treasury securities. Current and former traders at several prominent Wall Street investment banks say they regularly have shared secrets about the size and price of their bids at these multibillion-dollar government auctions.

Buffett, the interim chairman, conceded that Salomon's freewheeling, aggressive style probably contributed to its current difficulties. He said that style would be toned down. "There were aspects of the culture that could have contributed to that," Buffett said. "[It is] what some might call macho, some might call cavalier" (Siconolfi & Cohen, 1991, p. A4).

Everyone knows that selling jars of "phony" apple juice is unethical. In addition, everyone who has a checking account knows that bouncing checks is wrong, and you do not have to be a financial wizard to know that writing bad checks is illegal. And, finally, everyone now knows that illegal bidding in Treasury auctions is wrong. So how could some of the country's most sophisticated executives and money managers become involved in such unethical behavior? The answer in all likelihood may well be groupthink, that is, groupthink that may be fostered by the "bottom-line mentality" (Wolfe, 1988). This line of thinking supports financial success as the only value to be considered. It promotes short-term solutions that are immediately financially sound, despite the fact that they cause problems for others within the organization or the organization as a whole. It promotes an unrealistic belief in some organizational groups that everything boils down to a monetary game. As a result, such rules on ethical conduct are merely barriers, impediments along the way to bottom-line financial success.

Beech-Nut's employees were under a lot of financial pressures, and instead of cooperating with government investigators, they compounded their problems by stonewalling rather than cooperating. Hutton's employees were under a lot of pressure to make money, and the company no doubt paid more attention to profit figures than to how those figures were achieved. The practice may even have started accidentally, but once it got going, the money managers apparently wrote unnecessary checks solely to profit from the check kiting scheme as the money passed from bank to bank.

Company employees evidently had the necessary company loyalty and commitment to enable groupthink to come into play. Most important, once it became clear that high-level executives were not going to stop the scheme, employees became very good at ignoring any information that might lead them to conclude that the practice was illegal. An internal Hutton memo recommended that "if an office is overdrafting their ledger balance consistently, it is probably best not to request an account analysis" (Goleman, 1988). Executives at Salomon showed group characteristics found in groupthink experiences — for example, they exhibited excessive or blind loyalty, a bottom-line mentality, arrogance and overconfidence, and a promotion of unethical solutions by its leaders. In addition, like Beech-Nut and E. F. Hutton, Salomon Brothers also showed clear symptoms of groupthink, decision-making defects, and outcome variables presented earlier in this chapter. In each organization, individuals were willing to take the approach of "Let's all close our eyes to this problem."

In a sense, individuals and groups in Beech-Nut, E. F. Hutton, and Salomon Brothers committed unethical acts because of an overabundance of characteristics that did not allow them to operate ethically in a large, free-wheeling organization. The values of organizational members in all three organizations were important, that is, groupthink and the ensuing unethical behavior may have been precipitated by arrogance. Arrogance is the illegitimate child of confidence and pride found in groups experiencing groupthink. Arrogance is the idea that not only can you never make a mistake but also no one else can ever be right.

In Beech-Nut, E. F. Hutton, and Salomon Brothers, this arrogance was an insurmountable roadblock to ethical behavior. The flip side of arrogance is the ability to shine, to star, while working within the limits of ethical policies and guidelines. Another reason why groupthink may have occurred in these organizations is that they lacked the value of ethical commitment, that is, a willingness to commit to a goal that is bigger than they are — to keep acting ethically, even when there is a threat of failure, until they finally come up with ethical business decisions.

A third reason for the unethical acts committed by Beech-Nut, E. F. Hutton, and Salomon Brothers has to do with another human value — loyalty. It is something valued in all organizations. No one wants to work with anyone who has no concern for anyone or anything else. Loyalty counts in organizations; however, it should not be an unwillingness to question the unethical behavior of a group or organization. Groupthink occurs when arrogance, overcommitment, and loyalty help a group to shine above the ethical interests of an organization.

When groupthink occurs, organizations like Beech-Nut, E. F. Hutton, and Salomon Brothers are more likely to strive for unanimity, ignore the voices of dissenters and conscience, and make less than quality decisions that result in unethical behavior. However, by ignoring voices of caution and conscience and working with a bottom-line mentality for short-term profit, all three companies' managers ended up severely damaging their company's reputation. By not doing a better job of promoting positive and ethical organizational cultures (climates), these organizations increased the likelihood of unethical behavior and the probability of groupthink.

Organizations that support financial success as the only value to be considered increase the likelihood of accompanying employee attitudes, a bottom-line mentality, and an unrealistic belief that everything boils down to a monetary game. By emphasizing short-term revenues above long-term consequences, organizations create a climate in which individuals and groups understand that unethical behavior is acceptable. In addition, these same organizations are unwilling to take a stand when there is a financial cost to any group's decision. This stand contributes to the groupthink effect and encourages ethical shortcuts by its members.

Organizations must create organizational cultures and climates that run counter to a "win at all cost" mentality. These same organizations must recognize how the organizations' strategy and culture can lay the foundation for groupthink and unethical behavior to flourish. Organizations must develop measures to counter the negative effects of groupthink and unethical behavior, as highlighted in the next few chapters.

REFERENCES

Aronson, E. 1988. *The social animal*. New York: Freeman.

ASA Banking Journal. 1987, July. A violation of business ethics or outright fraud? pp. 30–34.

Bales, R. 1950. *Interaction process analysis*. Reading, MA: Addison-Wesley.

Cartwright, D., & Zander, A. 1968. Pressures to uniformity in groups: Introduction. In *Group dynamics: Research and theory*, eds. D. Cartwright and A. Zander. New York: Harper & Row.

Goleman, D. 1988, October. Following the leader. *Science 85*, 18.

Golembiewski, R. T. 1989. *Ironies in organization development*. New Brunswick, NJ: Transaction.

Harvey, J. 1974, Summer. Managing agreement in organizations: The Abilene paradox. *Organizational Dynamics*, pp. 63–80.

Hodgetts, R. M. 1990. *Modern human relations at work* 4th ed. Hinsdale, IL: Dryden Press.

Huseman, R. C., & Driver, R. W. 1979. Groupthink: Implications for small-group decision making in business. In *Readings in organizational behavior: Dimensions of management actions*, eds. R. C. Huseman and A. B. Carroll. Boston, MA: Allyn & Bacon.

Janis, I. L. 1989. *Crucial decisions: Leadership in policy making and crisis management*. New York: Free Press.

_____. 1982. *Groupthink*. Boston, MA: Houghton Mifflin.

_____. 1972. *Victims of groupthink*. Boston, MA: Houghton Mifflin.

_____. 1963. Group identification under conditions of external danger. *British Journal of Medical Psychology 36*, 227–38.

Jansen, E., & Von Glinow, M. A. 1985. Ethical ambivalence and organizational reward systems. *Academy of Management Review 10*(4): 814–22.

Kindel, S. 1989, June 27. Bad apple for baby. *Financial World*, p. 48.

Manz, C. C. & Sims, H. P. 1982. The potential for "groupthink" in autonomous work groups. *Human Relations 35*, 773–84.

Moorehead, G. 1982, December. Groupthink: Hypothesis in need of testing. *Group and Organization Studies*, p. 434.

Moorehead, G., Ference, R., & Neck, C. P. 1991. Group decision fiascoes continue: Space shuttle Challenger and a revised groupthink framework. *Human Relations 44*(6): 539–50.

Moorehead, G., & Griffin, R. W. 1989. *Organizational behavior*, 2nd ed. Boston, MA: Houghton Mifflin.

Moorehead, G., & Montanari, J. R. 1986. An empirical investigation of the groupthink phenomenon. *Human Relations 39*, 399–410.

Raven, B. H., & Rubin, J. Z. 1976. *Social psychology: People in groups.* New York: Wiley.

Ridgeway, C. L. 1983. *The dynamics of small groups.* New York: St. Martin's Press.

Salamon, J. 1991. *Devil's candy: The bonfire of the vanities goes to Hollywood.* Boston, MA: Houghton Mifflin.

Schermerhorn, J. R., Jr., Hunt, J. G., & Osborn, R. N. 1991. *Managing organizational behavior.* New York: John Wiley & Sons.

Seneker, H. 1986, January 27. Nice timing. *Forbes*, p. 102.

Siconolfi, M., & Cohen, L. P. 1991, August 19. Sullied solly: How Salomon's hubris and a U.S. trap led to leaders' downfall. *Wall Street Journal*, pp. A1, A4.

Siconolfi, M., Sesit, M. R., & Mitchell, C. 1991, August 19. Collusion, price fixing have long been rife in treasury market. *Wall Street Journal*, p. A1.

Sims, R. R. 1992. Linking groupthink to unethical behavior in organizations. *Journal of Business Ethics 11*, 651–62.

Smith, S. 1984. Groupthink and the hostage rescue mission. *British Journal of Political Science 15*, 117–26.

Stern, A. L. 1992, May. Why good managers approve bad ideas. *Working Woman*, pp. 75, 104.

Trevino, L. K. 1986. Ethical decision making in organizations: A person-situation interactionist model. *Academy of Management Review 11*, 601–17.

Turner, M. E., & Pratkanis, A. R. 1991. Groupthink as social identity maintenance: Evidence from the field and the laboratory. Unpublished manuscript, San Jose State University.

Van Fleet, D. D. 1991. *Behavior in organizations.* Boston, MA: Houghton Mifflin.

Welles, C. 1988, February. What led Beech-Nut down the road to disgrace. *Business Week*, pp. 124–28.

Wheeler, D., & Janis, I. L. 1980. *A practical guide for making decisions.* New York: Free Press.

Wolfe, D. 1988. Is there integrity in the bottom line: Managing obstacles to executive integrity. In *Executive integrity: The search for high human values in organization life*, ed. S. Srivastva. San Francisco, CA: Jossey-Bass, pp. 140–71.

5

Leadership and Unethical Behavior in Action

Should an organization's leadership take the rap for groupthink and unethical behavior? History can provide valuable lessons. During the 1970s, U.S. President Richard Nixon was forced to resign from office in large part because the evidence was not convincing that he did not have any knowledge of — or actually authorized — illegal acts associated with the Watergate break-in. A decade later, when some officials of President Reagan's administration were accused of selling arms to political factions in Nicaragua, they conscientiously distanced the president from their actions, keeping the nation's chief executive in the dark so that he could not be blamed for their questionable actions. In the E. F. Hutton situation, Hutton concluded that their senior officers were not basically at fault. They were just overzealous. Interestingly, when similar questions of unethical behavior by subordinates or top leaders are raised about public and private institutions in Japan, the top leaders tend to resign in disgrace, shouldering the blame for the unethical conduct — whether or not they actually were directly responsible.

Given the complexities of most organizational designs — especially those for large bureaucratic organizations — it is usually difficult to identify who exactly is to blame for a particular unethical event. One individual may have committed the impropriety, but he or she may only be following the orders of an immediate supervisor, who is following the orders of a still-higher-ranking official, and so on. Who is *really* responsible? Philosophers would say that it is morally wrong to "pull the trigger," even if one is "only following orders" (a common plea made by people accused of committing the Nazi atrocities during World War II — a similar plea is presented in many groupthink and corporate fraud incidents); to kill is morally wrong, for whatever reason. However, psychologists recognize the intense social pressures a subordinate is likely to feel when ordered by a superior to act unethically, especially when a superior explicitly shoulders the blame for the actions.

As a case in point, consider what happened at Hertz Car Rental's Boston office in the 1980s. The company was accused of overcharging rental customers by some $13 million by sending them phoney and inflated bills for repair damage (Alsway, 1988). In response, the chairman of Hertz, Frank Olson, fired the head of the Boston office, Alan Blicker (who was five levels below Olson!), and 18 others. He also redesigned the organization by shifting control over repair matters from the regional offices to the corporate office itself (increased centralization). Such actions ostensibly suggest that the company does not approve of these practices. Regardless, Blicker contended that he was made the scapegoat and that management actually approved of these practices! By instituting a policy that lower-level employees have to follow, top-level employees may effectively make themselves immune from any questionable actions by lower-level employees that are taken in an attempt to implement the policy. Put differently, top officials may be able to camouflage themselves from unethical actions by hiding within the organizational chart.

Many business analysts argue that top management routinely should be held responsible for their subordinates' actions (as cultural norms already dictate in Japan). The idea is that until top officials are made responsible for the unethical practices of their subordinates, organizational cultures will continue endorsing — if only tacitly — unethical actions that yield short-term profit. In other words, the top leaders may be the most effective way of inculcating a culture that discourages unethical behavior. This position assumes that leadership can make a difference in creating an ethical organizational culture. This chapter is concerned with the role of leadership in the creation of an organizational culture that results in unethical behavior. More specifically, this chapter will first briefly discuss recent literature that highlights the importance of leadership in the ethics equation, that is, highlight the leaders' role in creating different followers and organizational cultures. Then, the chapter will discuss leadership and unethical and ethical behavior. Finally, the chapter will provide a more detailed discussion of the Salomon Brothers fiasco introduced in Chapter 4, while under the leadership of

John Gutfreund, to demonstrate how a leader can create a culture that is less than ethical.

THE ROLE OF LEADERSHIP IN
THE ETHICS EQUATION

A strong set of values, including concern for employees, customers, honesty, and fairness, must be a part of today's corporate leadership roles. Such values are necessary, in this view, to keep leaders and their companies free of the taint of ethical scandals in business, religion, and government. In addition, today's leaders must establish the direction and motivation in promoting ethical behavior within their organization and an ethically oriented culture. There should be little question that the ethical behavior of an organization, or any group or individual within an organization, depends largely on the ethical quality of its leadership. With this in mind, the leader is a key to the promotion of ethics within an organization.

By definition, a leader must have followers, and followers must have a leader. But the effective business leader ought not to outdistance the followers with visionary impracticality, and followers ought not to mistake unclear communication for the gospel. Inspirational motivation and instructional communication are necessarily conjoined under effective business leadership; therefore, business leaders themselves must realize that they are the ultimate sources of ethical decision making. Because they represent significant others in the organizational lives of employees, they often have their behavior modeled by employees. Thus, they must set the organization on its path to an ethical corporate culture. Their example and decisions affect not only the employees who report to them but also the stockholders, suppliers, customers, community, country, and even the world. Considerations of the ethical component in day-to-day decisions will set the tone for others who interact with the company. Thus, the image of the business leader will affect how others choose to deal with the company and will have long-term effects.

Upper management is critical in determining the ethical culture of an organization. In particular, the philosophies of top managers as well as immediate supervisors represent a critical organizational factor influencing the ethical behavior of employees. In addition, the development of sound ethical practices becomes a realistic possibility when those who hold positions of leadership at all levels acquire an understanding of how ethical reasoning changes as individuals mature, how organization culture supports or inhibits the practice of sound ethics, and how to strengthen and reinforce decision making that supports highest standards of ethical reasoning and conduct.

The work of Howell and Avolio (1992) on ethical and unethical charismatic leaders highlights the importance of the leader in the ethics equations. For example, Howell and Avolio note that charismatic leaders can be very effective leaders, yet they may vary in their ethical standards, and such difference create very different types of followers and organizational cultures. The ethical charismatic leader uses power to serve others, aligns vision with followers' needs and aspirations, considers and learns from criticism, stimulates followers to think independently and to question the leader's view, opens two-way communication, coaches, develops, and supports followers, shares recognition with others, and relies on internal moral standards to satisfy organizational and societal interests. The unethical charismatic leader uses power only for personal gain or impact, promotes own personal vision, censures critical or opposing views, demands own decisions be accepted without question, suppresses two-way communication, is insensitive to followers' needs, and relies on convenient external moral standards to satisfy self-interests. The difference between the ethical and unethical charismatic leader determines the extent to which an organization builds an ethically oriented culture, the types of values followers will be exposed to, and the role models with whom employees will have their most direct personal contact.

LEADERSHIP AND UNETHICAL BEHAVIOR

As suggested in the discussion on leadership to this point, leaders (or top management), because they are in influential positions, have the power to influence ethical issues and decisions affecting many people. There should be no doubt that the moral tone of an organization is set by the organization's top leadership. This is because all managers and employees look to the highest level for their cues as to what is acceptable. A former chairman of Bethlehem Steel Corporation stated it well: "Starting at the top, management has to set an example for all the others to follow" (Foy, 1975). Top management, through its capacity to set a personal example and to shape policy, is in the ideal position to provide a highly visible role model. The authority and ability to shape policy, both formal and implied, forms one of the vital characteristics of the leader's job in any organization. Fortunately, those leaders who are interested in establishing an ethical organization are provided ethical standards and guidelines by our culture, religion, and values. Many of these guidelines have been enacted into laws to ensure that ethical standards are adhered to by the citizenry.

Sometimes it takes laws a long time to have an effect. For instance, two of the most powerful and influential leaders in the first half of the 1980s were Ivan F. Boesky and Michael F. Milken. The top graduate schools of business in the United States sought them out to speak to their MBA students. They were role models for many of these students, and the most desired career field upon graduation was the financial world of Wall Street and investment banking. Milken was considered the most powerful financier since J. P. Morgan and led Drexel Burnham Lambert, through innovative junk bond financing, to become Wall Street's most profitable firm.

Both men ended up being criminals. In 1987, Boesky and others were given stiff jail sentences and fines for using confidential knowledge about companies to their advantage in stock market trading. Boesky was also barred from Wall Street for life. Actually, he may have gotten off relatively easy "because he promised to put in prison stripes an even bigger crook: Mike Milken" (Galen, Faust, & Schine, 1990). Then, in late 1988, Drexel Burnham Lambert pleaded guilty to six felony counts of mail, wire, and securities fraud and agreed to pay $650 million in fines and restitution.

In 1989, facing a 98-count federal indictment charging him with racketeering and other securities trading offenses, Milken admitted to six felonies involving dealings with Boesky and Salomon. Accusing Milken of not going further for fear of increasing the risk of being caught, Judge Kimba M. Wood stated that Milken had the habit of "stepping just over to the wrong side of the law." She ordered him to serve ten years in jail and three years in full-time community service. In addition, he will have to pay $200 million in fines and penalties to the federal government and $400 million to settle the Securities and Exchange Commission's (SEC) civil suit. This latter amount is to settle the claims of victims if they win pending lawsuits (Welles & Galen, 1990; Schwartz, 1989; *Wall Street Journal*, 1988). Notice that the judge accused Milken of going over the line from *unethical* to *illegal* behavior.

Carroll (1992) provides an example of bad ethical leadership he encountered in a small company where a long-time employee was identified as having embezzled about $20,000 over a 15-year period. When the employee was approached and questioned as to why she had done this, she explained that she thought it was all right because the president had led her to believe it was. She further explained that any time during the fall, when the leaves had fallen in his yard and he needed them raked, he would simply get company personnel to do it. When the president needed cash, he would take it out of the company's petty cash box or get the key to the soft drink machine and raid its coin box. When he needed stamps to mail his personal Christmas cards, he would take them out of the company stamp box. The woman's perception was that it was all right for her to take the money because the president did it frequently. Therefore, she thought it was an acceptable practice for her! The Salomon Brothers fiasco elaborated upon in the next section demonstrates a more detailed example of the extent to which leadership can make a difference in the type of organizational culture that develops and the ethical behavior exhibited by its employees.

THE CASE OF SALOMON BROTHERS: AN EXAMPLE OF LEADERSHIP AND UNETHICAL BEHAVIOR IN ACTION

We're not talking about the failure to cross a "t" or to dot an "i" in this kind of case. It is not an adequate ethical standard to aspire to get through the day without being indicted.

Richard Breeden, SEC Chairman on charges
against Salomon (Salwen, 1991, p. A18)

The scandal that rocked Salomon Brothers, the investment banking division of Salomon, Inc., can be traced to its culture, which was directed by the controversial chief executive officer (CEO), John Gutfreund. Gutfreund's leadership style helped to mold a corporate culture that eventually resulted in unethical and illegal behavior in its members. This section seeks to address how Gutfreund's leadership led to a culture that was tailor-made for greedy and power-hungry employees whose commitment to ethical behavior was suspect. Schein's (1985) five primary mechanisms by which a leader can both embed and reinforce aspects of an organization's culture will be used to describe the culture developed by John Gutfreund at Salomon Brothers.

John Gutfreund successfully molded Salomon's culture by employing each of these tools — attention, reactions to crises, role modeling, allocation of rewards, and criteria for selection and dismissal (Yukl, 1989). Attention refers to what the leader asks employees and what he or she measures, praises, and criticizes. Reactions to crises, Schein (1985) argues, are important because the "emotionality surrounding them increases potential for learning about values and assumptions." Using the leader as a role model can also communicate to the employees the expectations of their own actions. Allocation of rewards is who gets pay increases or promotions from the leader. Finally, a leader's criteria for selection and dismissal of employees signal what will be important to get ahead in the organization.

In the wake of the Salomon scandal and Gutfreund's voluntary resignation from the firm, Salomon's majority shareholder, Warren Buffett, stepped in as interim chairman in an attempt to restore the firm's position in the financial community — in part, by changing its culture. (Schein's primary mechanisms will also be used in Chapter 7 to highlight the actions of Buffett and show how a drastic culture change is being undertaken at Salomon in order to restore the firm's credibility.)

Gutfreund's Cultural Leadership

As noted in Chapter 2, the concept of organizational culture is important in understanding ethical behavior in organizations. Schein (1985) defines culture as the basic assumptions and beliefs shared by members of a group or organization. These assumptions and beliefs involve the group's view of the world and their place in it, the nature of time and space, human nature, and human relationships (Yukl, 1989). In addition, he asserts that culture impacts employees' or group members' behavior because one of its major functions is "to help us understand the environment and determine how to respond to it, thereby reducing anxiety, uncertainty, and confusion" (Schein, 1985, p. 86). Therefore, an organization's culture dictates to its members how situations are to be handled and what their expected behavior will be. It can be said that, in reality, a strong leader who has been in power for a substantial length of time can mold a corporation's culture. And, indeed, that was what John Gutfreund was able to do at Salomon Brothers.

Attention

Schein describes attention as what the leader focuses employees to concentrate on (what is criticized, praised, or asked about), which communicates his/her values to them. Gutfreund's tenure at Salomon was marked by an absolute attention to a short-term business focus and what was happening that day or that week. Through this short-term perspective, Gutfreund forced his employees to produce profits immediately. As Cooke (1991) has indicated, dedication to short-term revenues above long-term considerations creates a climate where unethical behavior thrives. The consequences of pushing ethical and legal boundaries are not immediately realized, and a short-term profit maximizer often ignores any possible long-term ramifications of his or her actions.

John Gutfreund focused his attention and his employees' attention on the day-to-day operations of the Salomon Brothers trading floor. His desk was at the front of The Room (with a capital "R") that housed the trading area. The Room was 100 feet long and two stories high, with double-height windows looking out over the New York Harbor. Gutfreund also had a ceremonial office that his second wife Susan, had redecorated, but the desk on the floor was where he was in control — "all-seeing and instantly accessible" (Taylor, 1989). Gutfreund thought that privacy in this business was too dangerous. The traders in The Room worked from a capital base of over \$3.5 billion, buying stocks and bonds as quickly as possible and reselling them at a profit. Gutfreund wanted to make sure he was always close to the pulse of the organization (Taylor, 1989).

Gutfreund often left his desk and walked around the floor. This style has been well-publicized as "management by walking around." One Salomon insider claimed, "Those walks mean a lot — to everybody. John finds out everything that's going on. People on the floor know that and are encouraged to do their best" (Leinster, 1984). "Encouraged" may be too soft a word to describe the way Gutfreund affected those around him. One senior executive stated that "There are a lot of people here, I mean senior people who measure their day by whether John smiles at them" (Sterngold, 1988). Young traders and bankers were challenged by Gutfreund with impromptu quizzes in the hall: "He'll ask you about something outside your area just to get you to think broadly. But if you can't give him an answer on something you should know, he'll take you apart on the spot" (Bianco, 1985). To impress John Gutfreund, you had to keep on your toes and know every detail of your business. This is a characteristic of many successful managers. Gutfreund's lack of hesitation in harshly chastising employees, even in front of clients, however, led to a desperate need for employees to please his whims.

As noted earlier, Gutfreund's attention was always focused on short-term results (short-term horizons are crucial to traders). There is no evidence that Gutfreund ever created a long-term strategy for Salomon's future. Decision making had been instantaneous for John Gutfreund as a trader, and he may have continued to agonize over long-term or complex management problems as CEO. He always had an executive committee to help make the crucial decisions of the firm. This should not, however, be confused with delegation of power. No one was allowed to forget who was in charge of the destiny of Salomon (McGoldrick, 1986). Most of the daily decisions were made quickly, "on the fly," by two or three members of the executive committee while they were on the floor (Bianco, 1985). When a more difficult decision needed to be made, Gutfreund's preferred style was "to virtually overwhelm a problem with ideas and suggestions until they [the committee] find a solution" (McGoldrick, 1986). One could surmise that Gutfreund was not ever comfortable making long-range or personnel-related decisions without group discussion and brainstorming.

This short-term aspect, which is a function of being in the trading business, may have been particularly dangerous during Gutfreund's tenure at Salomon. When an organization's entire focus is on next quarter's profits, its future is in jeopardy. In addition, dedication to short-term profits usually means those profits will be gained at any cost, including breaking ethical standards or the law.

Reactions to Crises

A crisis situation, Schein (1985) asserts, allows followers to see what is valued by the leader, because its emotionality brings these values to the surface. John Gutfreund reacted to crises by using arbitrary dismissal criteria, executing firing decisions ruthlessly, using "sneaky" tactics to secure his own job, and covering up and lying about ethical indiscretions. Gutfreund showed a commitment to saving his own position, not to any professional or personal code of ethics. When a legal violation by the firm was brought to his attention, he reacted by attempting a cover-up, not by disciplining the violators. Clear signals were sent that ethical and legal principles were not important to the management of Salomon.

After completing a lengthy strategic review in 1987, John Gutfreund decided that for Salomon Brothers to remain competitive in the investment banking industry, 12 percent of his staff needed to be fired (Taylor, 1989). Because he took so long in analyzing the situation, fine-tuning was not enough. A crisis situation was allowed to develop, because excess employees were hired freely in the good times, but the organization was too fat in lean times. Unfortunately, news of the firings was leaked to the press. These employees read in the newspaper on Friday that their jobs would not exist on Monday. They were then asked "en masse into a conference room and informed over a speakerphone that their department no longer existed" (Taylor, 1989). Interestingly, Gutfreund described himself as "too paternalistic" and "deliberate on people issues" (Sterngold, 1988). When the severity of the situation was realized by Gutfreund, he concentrated on short-term benefits at the expense of his employees. He said, [It was emotionally unsettling. But in the short term it was more attractive to gain those cost benefits. In an ideal world, I would have downgraded rather than excised" (Sterngold 1988, p. 20). Gutfreund's message was clear: there were no long-term guarantees of employment at Salomon (in a sense, this is true at most U.S. companies). People were expendable when times were tough.

Also, in 1987, Gutfreund faced an external crisis when Salomon's majority shareholder, Minorco, wanted to sell its stock. After Gutfreund failed to respond to their initial interest, Minorco's investment bank put the stock on the market and the company "in play." Gutfreund snapped to attention when the notorious hostile takeover specialist Ronald Perelman expressed interest in purchasing the company. Although Perelman asked for only two seats on Salomon's board, his history of ousting current management convinced Gutfreund that he wanted full control. "Believing Mr. Perelman has no hostile intention," he said, "is like believing the tooth fairy exists" (Taylor, 1989). The stakes for Gutfreund were high, and his lawyer, Martin Lipton, recalled, "I was embarrassed for John. John sees Salomon as occupying a special place in the financial system, and that could have been wrecked. From that moment on, it was crystal clear to John that the continuation of the firm was in jeopardy" (Sterngold, 1988). All weekend, Gutfreund secretly worked to solidify his own deal with an "old friend," the billionaire investor Warren Buffett. Gutfreund went to Salomon's board on Monday afternoon and said he would resign as chairman and CEO if his deal with Buffett was not chosen over Perelman's, even though Gutfreund's offer was substantially lower. He claimed, "I never stated it as a threat. I was stating a fact" (Sterngold, 1988, p. 27). The board acquiesced, and Gutfreund had temporarily secured his position as Salomon's leader (Sterngold, 1988). The master deal maker was dealing to ensure his own fate, at the expense of the shareholders. Secret maneuverings were his modus operandi, and his first priority was to save his own job. Employees could see that his crisis reaction began with his desire to stay at the helm of Salomon, and he would employ any methods to achieve this goal.

Finally, Gutfreund's crisis management strategy was seen in his reaction to the knowledge that someone at his firm had placed bids on Treasury bills in excess of the legal maximums. Salomon, Inc., released information in August 1991 that the firm had overextended themselves in several U.S. Treasury bill auctions (*The Economist*, 1991). Securities laws limit the percentage of any one auction to 35 for each dealer, so that no one can secure the market and influence the pivotal T-bill interest rate. This auction is at the cornerstone of the U.S. economy and the rest of the capital markets, as well as all other interest rates guided by it. Many scandals rocked Wall Street in the late 1980s and early 1990s, but none touched as close to the foundation of the U.S. financial system (*The Economist*, 1991). By the end of the disclosures, it had been revealed that Salomon owned up to 94 percent of one Treasury auction and was well over the allowed limit in several other instances (Galen, 1991).

When the first memo was released on August 9, 1991, it did not mention any prior knowledge of the legal infractions by Salomon's top management, including John Gutfreund. Internally, Gutfreund claimed to be as shocked as the rest of the company in discovering this illegal activity (Bianco, 1991a). Just five days later, however, at the urging of E. Gerald Corrigan, president of the Federal Reserve Bank of New York, another memo disclosed that Gutfreund and other top management executives had known in late April about the irregularities (Cohen, 1991). Although details remain to be sorted out, it is "clear already, though, that Gutfreund not only failed to inform federal authorities of the violations but deceived his colleagues in an attempt to save his own neck" (Bianco, 1991b). At the final meeting of his executive committee, Gutfreund said, "Apologies are bull. . . . This is just a lifestyle change" (Bianco, 1991b). Two days later, Gutfreund voluntarily gave his resignation to Warren Buffett, the majority shareholder who would become Salomon's "interim" chairman (Cohen, 1991).

It is clear that Gutfreund's reaction to unethical and illegal behavior in his organization was to try to cover it up. When the initial cover-up failed, he then lied and attempted to save his position as CEO. It is little wonder that employees of Salomon were motivated to commit unethical acts and break the law when they were shown the way by their leader. His management of crises indicated that ethical wrongdoing was to be hidden from the authorities at any cost. There is no evidence that Gutfreund took any actions against the transgressors. His action, or inaction, showed that Salomon was not committed to any sort of ethical or legal standard.

Role Modeling

A leader communicates strong messages to employees about his or her values through his or her own actions, and Schein (1985) labels this role modeling. Employees who wished to emulate Gutfreund's rise to power at Salomon saw that his hard work and aggression had paved the road to his success. Although aggressiveness is certainly desirable in the fast-paced investment banking community, Gutfreund's rise to power included the betrayal of his mentor, Salomon's owner, Billy Salomon, to further his career. He once again used "below-the-board" deals, which signaled that this type of maneuvering would be tolerated, and perhaps encouraged, at Salomon. To be like John Gutfreund, one could not hold to a strong sense of personal ethics.

Gutfreund was short and pudgy, with an unremarkable appearance, but he was a ruthless trader. His sense of humor and salesman's manner coupled with his drive and ambition allowed him to rise through the ranks of the firm quickly. Within ten years, he was made a partner in the firm (Taylor, 1989). Salomon Brothers was headed by Billy Salomon, son of the firm's founder, from 1963 to 1978, and many credit him for planting the seeds of the culture that would come to full fruition under Gutfreund (McGoldrick, 1986). Salomon had built his family's company from a small bond house to a major power in most trading activities. The firm's one-word reputation was "aggressive," and Gutfreund embodied this description. Many believe Billy Salomon deserved the treatment he eventually received from Gutfreund for starting the aggressive culture that nurtured Gutfreund and others: "It was Billy's fault. . . . He had put a group of tough, hard-nosed greedy people in charge. And, quite-simply, they were not going to do anything more for him, or for anyone, than they had to do" (Taylor, 1989). Greed is a quality that can push people to break ethical standards to further their cause and make more money. By placing people like Gutfreund in charge, Salomon was endangering the future of the firm. Salomon became Gutfreund's mentor and, in 1978, made him the chairman of the firm. When reflecting upon this time, Salomon said:

When I made John heir apparent, he was the most conservative person in the partnership, no question. Frugal is an understatement. If you turned in an expense account and you have taken a client to Caravelle for dinner or something, John would ask you if it was really necessary. I thought that was a good example for the boys. (Sterngold, 1988)

In an unbelievable act of betrayal, John Gutfreund sold Billy Salomon's company to Philip Brothers (Phibro) in 1982 without even discussing it with the man whose name still appeared on the door. Employees looking on were being told that anyone could be double-crossed at Salomon, even top managers. Gutfreund had decided, without consulting his mentor, that the changes in the investment banking industry necessitated that Salomon build up its capital base in order to remain competitive. Phibro was a giant commodities trading firm, and it bought the company for $554 million (which many considered to be well below what could have been obtained for the firm). Billy Salomon was understandably bitter and humiliated by the sale of his own company without his knowledge. Although he made just under $10 million on the sale (which pales in comparison to the $32 million made by Gutfreund), he did not even receive a premium for his shares (Taylor, 1989). A case could be made that Gutfreund's betrayal of Billy Salomon to further his own ambition indicated that similar behavior would be tolerated, even rewarded, at Salomon.

Whether the business community was impressed by Gutfreund's results at Salomon or not, in 1985, John Gutfreund was crowned "The King of Wall Street" by *Business Week* magazine (Bianco, 1985). Citing the fact that he had built the firm from being marginally profitable in 1978 to 1985 net earnings of close to $600 million, they felt that Gutfreund "personifies Wall Street in this era of performance. No longer can an investment bank get by on old-school ties and fancy china in the partners' dining room. To compete today, a firm must be able to put huge sums of its own money at risk in complex and volatile markets" (Bianco, 1985). "King" Gutfreund's financial performance could not be questioned, but his leadership style and the culture that he had created were doomed to turn on him one day. Those who wanted to model themselves after Gutfreund saw that any opportunity for power should be seized and capitalized upon for personal gain. Adherence to a code of ethics would be only a deterrent if you wanted to get ahead at Salomon. Those who were like Gutfreund did not hesitate to twist a situation to their advantage, regardless of the ethical consequences.

Allocation of Rewards

The behavior displayed by people the leader decides to reward with pay increases or promotions signals to others what is necessary to succeed in an organization — Schein's (1985) allocation of rewards mechanism. Further, research has indicated that the contingencies of reinforcement are critical in explaining the incidence of unethical decisions in the workplace (Worrell, Stead, Stead, & Spalding, 1985). Decisions about ethical or unethical behavior stemmed, during laboratory experiments from subjects' immediate superiors' expectations and evaluations. The reward system created by a leader indicates what is prized and expected in the organization.

Aggression

John Gutfreund continued in his mentor's tradition by rewarding aggressiveness. The people he promoted lived for Salomon. He said, [I'm addicted to this business" (McGoldrick, 1986), and he expected his employees to display a similar loyalty and commitment. A former employee said, "You have to learn to never say no, to always find a way to get the deal done, no matter what. Salomon people never give up" (McGoldrick, 1986). A source close to the firm claimed, "The ones who succeed at Salomon are not the nice ones. They're the ones who scream and rant and rave, who kick butt" (McGoldrick, 1986). Gutfreund told a class of trainees that they had "to be in shape, and I don't mean jogging and all that crap. You've got to be ready to bite the ass off a bear every morning" (Taylor, 1989).

Lewis Ranieri was the perfect example of the kind of extremely aggressive man that John Gutfreund promoted. In 1986, it appeared that Gutfreund was grooming Ranieri as his potential successor (Sterngold, 1988). Ranieri's quick rise through the company mirrored Gutfreund's own. He had joined the firm in 1966 as a mailroom clerk for $70 a week. Twenty years later, he was a vice chairman overseeing Salomon's mortgage-backed securities department, which would have qualified as the country's fourth-largest investment bank on its own (Taylor, 1989). Ranieri was a loud and aggressive man who kept a ceremonial sword over his desk. When overcome with emotion during a meeting, he raised the sword and slammed it on the desk (Taylor, 1989). He felt that "we [Salomon] got where we are today through sheer guts. You don't get where we are by being someone's equal, but by being better" (McGoldrick, 1986). Could it be that the amount of aggression at Salomon created an atmosphere where getting ahead was the number one priority and the firm's commitment to ethical behavior was suspect?

Greed

As early as 1984, more than 30 officials at the firm made more than $1 million; Gutfreund made $2.3 million in cash alone (McGoldrick, 1986). The competition among young MBAs was fierce to join Salomon, because of their reputation for rewarding young talent handsomely. Employees were expected to work long hours and dedicate themselves to the firm in exchange for these handsome salaries. Although some say that greed is a key aspect of the Wall Street environment, it appears that it was a definite part of the Salomon corporate culture from the time Billy Salomon ran the firm. Although there is nothing wrong with large salaries for deserving employees, rewarding those who will do anything for money creates a dangerous environment ripe for unethical behavior.

Short-term Performance

Unlike Wall Street firms of the past, promotion at Salomon Brothers was certainly not dependent upon your background (educational, family, or otherwise.) Promotion was based primarily on performance but, unfortunately, only on recent performance. A former corporate finance associate said of Salomon employees: "I worked with people who talked with their mouths full and spat tomatoes through their teeth, but I never met anyone who was incompetent" (McGoldrick, 1986). Like John Gutfreund, these people were not necessarily the smartest, but they were good and they could think quickly. Unfortunately, however, they either could not or did not think in terms of long-range consequences. As mentioned previously, the consequences of unethical or illegal actions are not usually realized until much later than when the act is committed. In addition, the unethical or illegal route is often the most lucrative and, therefore, would be the most attractive to Salomon's employees.

The Trader Mentality

Other firms considered traders "too brutal" to be in charge of the company, but traders reigned in Gutfreund's kingdom. Traders are not known for their tact and must yell to be heard on the floor:

Iron lungs and a thick hide are certainly prerequisites for trading. It also requires muscle and daring, quick reflexes rather than contemplative intellect. Traders profit by moving faster than anyone else, not by thinking more profoundly. That explains why traders, all trying to get in front of each other, often stampede herdlike through the market. (Taylor, 1989)

There is a reason that most firms do not promote traders to senior executive positions — their personalities are simply too harsh. In order to be successful as a trader you have to be brutal and fast, while a management position requires more tact, long-range planning, and thought. By promoting traders, Salomon may have opted to narrow its focus to short-term profits, with little regard for long-term organizational consequences.

According to Kelly (1987), "No action of management has more impact on its operational ethics than the people it promotes, dismisses, or allows to stagnate." Further, John Gutfreund seems to exemplify Kelly's destructive achiever (DA) who "has the charisma of a Leader [ethical manager] but lacks his operational values; this achiever's net effect on the long-term welfare of the organization is negative" (Kelly, 1987). In addition, the promotion of employees who were like himself led Gutfreund to contaminate the entire Salomon Brothers organization: "Every time a DA is promoted and the ethical difference between the DA and other candidates is apparent to the staff, the organization's value base is diminished and the way is opened to even faster deterioration" (Kelly, 1987). John Gutfreund selected those employees who shared his aggressive, win-at-all-costs mentality. His short-term view may have prevented him from seeing what the long-term costs of this kind of personality could be on the organization as a whole.

Criteria for Selection and Dismissal

Schein's (1985) last mechanism by which a leader shapes a corporate culture, criteria for selection and dismissal, describes how a leader's decisions about whom to recruit or dismiss signals his or her values to all the employees. Gutfreund's leadership style selected ambitious, aggressive young people and gave them the chance to create new departments and new products and enjoy success they could not achieve at other firms. Gutfreund said, "We listen to young people. We give them responsibility" (McGoldrick, 1986). Unfortunately, the criteria by which he dismissed employees were vague and led to ambiguous performance standards. When people are not sure what to do, unethical behavior may flourish as aggressive individuals pursue what they believe to be acceptable.

If Gutfreund decided that employees could not handle the responsibilities they were given, he would dismiss them. His potential successor, Ranieri, as previously discussed, was a great force within Salomon, and his mortgage-trading department "was the kind of fiefdom that challenged management's control" (Berry, 1988). Although Ranieri was thriving in Salomon's management system, he forgot the most important thing — Gutfreund insisted that he be "perceived as the brightest star in Salomon's galaxy. He will accept no competition" (McGoldrick, 1986). When interest rates dropped in early 1987, Gutfreund seized the opportunity to eliminate his "competition." On July 13, 1987, Gutfreund called Ranieri in to what seemed to be a normal meeting at their lawyers' offices. Much to Ranieri's surprise, his mentor demanded his resignation. When Gutfreund was interviewed about why he fired his former superstar, he compared the firing to a divorce. The causes, he claimed, were numerous — a series of things over the years, not one specific act. On his disappointment with Ranieri, he said, "When I promoted Lewis, I wanted him to help run the firm and remove himself from the day-to-day functioning of the mortgage-securities business. . . . Some people are happier when they are writing [order] tickets" (Bianco, 1987). No attempt was made to find a place where Ranieri may have been more capable of performing according to Gutfreund's expectations — he was simply fired. Perhaps Gutfreund feared that the man he had nurtured the way Billy Salomon had nurtured him may have one day turned against him. Specific performance guidelines were lacking at Salomon — criteria for dismissals were vague. Although Ranieri's dismissal stands out (because he was so close to the top), many others were fired by John Gutfreund. When the company was downsized by 12 percent of his staff in 1987, the group was fired together, without focus on individual acts or any behavior of specific people. As Drake and Drake (1988) have noted, there are both ethical and legal risks associated with Gutfreund's chosen leadership style: "Reliance solely on subjective measures (e.g., 'what my feelings tell me is right') can lead to vague and inconsistent management policies." These ambiguities can also lead to crossing ethical and legal boundaries, as Salomon's employees proceeded to do.

The Culture Created at Salomon by Gutfreund

One author speculated at the beginning of the Salomon T-bill auction crisis that "the biggest casualty may well be Salomon's corporate culture. Despite inroads made in the more genteel investment banking business, Solly is at bottom a bond house run by and for traders . . . greed might have pushed them outside the rules" (Weiss, 1991). Another author ridiculed Susan Gutfreund, John Gutfreund's wife, when she said, in explanation of much of her husband's behavior, "He's a trader" (Taylor, 1989). Hers is the best of all explanations. His short-term horizon, his ability to make split-second decisions but not long-term plans, his aggressiveness and lack of tact all were strengths that allowed him huge success as a trader. By instilling these kinds of attributes in all of his employees, however, he created a culture that pushed everything to the limit with little thought for the long-term implications to the firm. Gutfreund employed all of Schein's culture mechanisms to leave his impression on the firm:

Attention — He looked at the most recent bottom-line profits and disregarded long-term implications of employee actions.

Reactions to Crises — He lied, covered up ethical and legal transgressions, and tried to preserve his own position at any cost.

Role Modeling — He set an example for secret deals and for unethical behavior being tolerated and hidden.

Allocation of Rewards — He promoted those who were most like him, lacking any commitment to ethical principles.

Criteria for Selection and Dismissal — He had vague policies that confused employees and let them make their own decisions about how to "win" the internal Salomon competition.

In his book *Liar's Poker*, Michael Lewis (1989) provides a hilarious but partially confirming and troubling description of the corporate culture at Salomon Brothers under Gutfreund. Lewis served as a bond salesman and detailed his impressions as a trainee and salesman in London and New York.

The culture described by Lewis is characterized by the macho swaggering of the successful salesman and traders. The trading floor was the site of idiotic feats of gluttony (for example, guacamole was ordered in five-gallon drums), practical jokes and horseplay (such as throwing telephones at trainees), and childish (except for the scale) bravado. The book's title refers to a legendary game of liar's poker (a sort of card game played by using serial numbers on dollar bills) in which the stakes were $1 million.

The organization described in Lewis' book is not one in which examples from the top contributed to the ethical behavior of lower-level employees. Warren Buffett stepped in as interim chairman of Salomon in an attempt to restore Salomon to its previous position of respect within the financial community. The scandal has highlighted Gutfreund's win-at-all-costs culture and its unethical and illegal consequences. As will be noted in Chapter 7, Buffett's first steps all reflected a conscious effort to move away from the culture that developed under Gutfreund and toward one that is committed to ethical behavior and obeying the law.

The Salomon Brothers situation provides a vivid example of how a leader's actions and behavior communicate important messages for others in the organization. Thus, it is important to acknowledge that examples from the top have both a direct and an indirect effect on the ethical culture of an organization. The norms and values demonstrated by individuals at the top of the organization affect the culture of the organization, which in turn affects the behavior of other organizational members. The most important role of top-level managers, at least with regard to modeling ethical behavior in the workplace, may be to establish a climate in which organizational members lower in the hierarchy will be likely to provide positive role models for one another and for new members of the organization.

Business leaders must see part of their role as establishing a strong ethically oriented culture that views ethics as important for survival and profitability in a highly competitive environment. Although there have been and will always be leaders like Boesky, Milken, Keating, and Gutfreund, other business leaders have chosen to adopt an ethical attitude in their organization. For example, the CEO of Borg-Warner said, "values and profits are inseparable" (Harrington, 1991); IBM maintained that "people generally think of us as competent, successful, and ethical" and believes the three are directly related (Cook, 1988). Johnson & Johnson executives suggest that ethics is good business: ethics credo saved Johnson & Johnson during the Tylenol crisis, when employees were quickly making hundreds of unsupervised decisions (Miller, 1984; Modic, 1987). The senior vice president of human resources of Merck & Company, voted "America's most admired company" in three successive *Fortune* polls of CEOs, suggested that Merck employees are constantly asking, "What is the right thing to do?" in the absence of policy or precedent; employees use the statement "profit derived from work that is beneficial to society" to guide decisions. Overall, 63 percent of Fortune 500 CEOs maintain that strong ethics result in strategic advantage (Public Broadcasting Service and Ethics Resource Center, 1988).

Raelin (1987) cites some examples of companies that have benefitted from business leaders promoting organizational morality. For example, the 3M Company implemented its Pollution Prevention Pays policy in 1975 to generate savings from the prevention of environmental pollution. Professionals within 3M were encouraged to submit suggestions for reducing pollution by changing their company's manufacturing processes. Through 1987, company scientists generated over 1,700 proposals that not only helped minimize environmental pollution but also reportedly saved some $300 million. Similar success stories have been reported at companies such as Polaroid and Atlantic Richfield. Apparently, business leaders who have the foresight to promote ethical consciousness starting at the highest corporate levels may reap large benefits for doing so. Indeed, it has been estimated that whereas $30,000 invested in Dow-Jones stocks in 1952 would have grown to $134,000 by 1986, the same money would have grown to over $1 million if invested in 15 highly socially responsible companies (Burns, 1987). Clearly, when business leaders emphasize and reinforce ethical behavior in their organizations, it may pay off even more than the short-term benefits of unethical behavior.

Public concern about unethical behavior in organizations expressed by the pressures of various interest groups and government regulation, is greater than ever before, due to higher education levels in our society and the sophisticated media that keep the community well-informed. Gandossy (1988) has noted that ethics problems are not yet under control in some organizations for the following reasons: the responsibility of ethics is too widely distributed, there are strong financial incentives to overlook ethical issues, there is a lack of support for those who suspect wrongdoing, and management does not take a stand to encourage or discourage unethical practices.

This chapter supports the notion that a very important factor in improving the ethical behavior in organization is the actions taken by business leaders, especially in the impression they leave on the firm through a number of culture mechanisms: attention, reactions to crises, role modeling, allocation of rewards, and criteria for dismissal. In the end, business leaders must be sensitive to these culture mechanisms, take the responsibility for creating an ethically oriented organizational culture, and change the culture when it may not be oriented in such a manner.

REFERENCES

Alsway, W. 1988, February 15. Hertz is doing body work — on itself. *Business Week*, pp. 56–58.

Berry, J. F. 1988, June. Under siege. *Business Month*, pp. 65–68.

Bianco, A. 1991a, September 2. At Salomon, the king is dead — But few are crying. *Business Week*, p. 68.

_____. 1991b, September 9. "I'd be happy to have my name removed from the door." *Business Week*, p. 80.

_____. 1987, August 17. The decline of the superstar. *Business Week*, pp. 90–98.

_____. 1985, December 9. The king of Wall Street. *Business Week*, pp. 98–104.

Blake, R. R., & McCanse, A. A. 1991, Summer. Sound ethical reasoning in business. *Academy of Management ODC Newsletter*, pp. 7–8.

Bowie, N. 1982. *Business ethics*. Englewood Cliffs, NJ: Prentice-Hall.

Burns, S. 1987, April 15. Good corporate citizenship can pay dividends. *Dallas Morning News*, p. C1.

Carroll, A. B. 1992. *Business and society*, 2nd ed. Cincinnati, OH: South-Western.

Cohen, L. P. 1991, November 8. Buffett shows tough side to Salomon — and Gutfreund. *Wall Street Journal*, p. A6.

Cook, M. F. 1988, April. What's ahead in human resources. *Management Review*, pp. 41–44.

Cooke, R. A. 1991. Danger signs of unethical behavior: How to determine if your firm is at ethical risk. *Journal of Business Ethics 10*, 249–53.

Drake, B. H., & Drake, E. 1988, Winter. Ethical and legal aspects of managing corporate cultures. *California Management Review*, pp. 107–23.

Freeman, R. E. 1984. A typology of enterprise strategy. In *Strategic management: A stakeholder approach*. Marshfield, MA: Pitman Publishing, pp. 101–7.

Foy, L. W. 1975. Business ethics: A reappraisal. Distinguished Lecture Series, Columbia Graduate School of Business, January 30, 1972, p. 2.

Galen, M. 1991, September 9. The lawyer who'll ride herd on Salomon's cowboys. *Business Week*, p. 79.

Galen, M., Faust, D., & Schine, E. 1990, May 7. Guilty, your honor. *Business Week*, p. 33.

Gandossy, R. P. 1988, September. The tough job of shutting down corporate fraud. *Management Review*, pp. 39–43.

Harrington, S. J. 1991. What corporate America is teaching about ethics. *Academy of Management Executive 5*(1): 21–30.

Howell, J. M., & Avolio, B. J. 1992. The ethics of charismatic leadership: Submission or liberation? *Academy of Management Executive 6*(2): 43–54.

Kelly, C. M. 1987, Summer. The interrelationship of ethics and power in today's organization. *Organizational Dynamics*, pp. 5–18.

Leinster, C. 1984, December 24. The man who seized the throne at Phibro-Salomon. *Fortune*, pp. 108–20.

Lewis, M. 1989. *Liar's poker*. New York: Norton.

Main, J. 1987, September 28. Wanted, leaders who can make a difference. *Fortune*, p. 92.

McGoldrick, B. 1986, March. Salomon's power culture. *Institutional Investor*, pp. 67–76.

Miller, W. H. 1984, October 29. Business' new link: Ethics and the bottom line. *Industry Week*, pp. 49–53.

Mixed feelings about Drexel's decision. 1988, December 22. *Wall Street Journal*, p. B1.

Modic, S. J. 1987, December 14. Corporate ethics: From commandment to commitment. *Industry Week*, pp. 33–36.

Public Broadcasting Service and Ethics Resource Center. 1988. Ethics in American business. (Aired November 17).

Raelin, J. A. 1987. The professional as the executive's ethical-aide-de-camp. *Academy of Management Executive 1*, 171–82.

Rotten at the core. 1991, August 17. *The Economist*, pp. 69–70.

Salwen, K. G. 1991, November 20. SEC chief's criticism of ex-managers of Salomon suggests civil action likely. *Wall Street Journal*, p. A18.

Schein, E. 1985. *Organizational culture and leadership*. San Francisco, CA: Jossey-Bass.

Schwartz, S. 1989, March 31. Why Mike Milken stands to qualify for Guiness book. *Wall Street Journal*, p. A1.

Stead, W. E., Worrell, D. L., & Stead, J. G. 1990. An integrative model for understanding and managing ethical behavior in business organizations. *Journal of Business Ethics 9*, 233–42.

Sterngold, J. 1988, January 10. Too far, too fast. *The New York Times Magazine*, pp. 18–27, 59.

Taylor, J. 1989. *Circus of ambition*. New York: Warner Books.

Vitell, S., & Festervand, T. 1987. Business ethics: Conflicts, practices and beliefs of industrial executives. *Journal of Business Ethics 6*, 111–22.

Weiss, G. 1991, August 26. The Salomon shocker: How bad will it get? *Business Week*, pp. 54–57.

Welles, C., & Galen, M. 1990, December 10. Milken is taking the fall for a "decade of greed." *Business Week*, p. 30.

Worrell, D. L., Stead, W. E., Stead, J. G., & Spalding, J. B. 1985. Unethical decisions: The impact of reinforcement contingencies and managerial philosophies. *Psychological Reports*, pp. 355–65.

Yukl, G. A. 1989. *Leadership in organizations*. Englewood Cliffs, NJ: Prentice-Hall, pp. 213–15.

6

Countering Unethical Behavior

With the increased emphasis on ethics in the workplace, organizations have found themselves needing to develop and implement processes to counter unethical behavior. It is important that organizations be pro-active in countering unethical behavior. A major point of this chapter is that organizations must work to improve their employees' decision-making skills when confronted with ethical dilemmas as individuals and working in groups. Therefore, organizations must ensure that their employees learn to cope with the inevitable conflicts that arise, improve the quality of their decisions by taking active steps to counter group-think and unethical behavior, and foster disagreement and contrast in the decision-making process.

This chapter will highlight several activities that organizations have and can use to counter the unethical behavior of both individuals and groups (for example, unethical behavior that is a result of groupthink). Specifically, this chapter will offer reasons why organizations should be concerned with countering unethical behavior, discuss ways in which organizations can improve individual decision making and several pop-ular frameworks for ethical decision making, then turn to a discussion on improving group decision making and managing conflict in groups. The chapter will conclude by highlighting several techniques for fostering open discussion and flexibility in groups.

WHY ORGANIZATIONS SHOULD COUNTER UNETHICAL BEHAVIOR

Besides the obvious answer that being ethical is simply the proper thing to do, organizational members should be ethical because not to do so will likely generate significant personal, organizational, and societal costs. Consider first the personal costs. If an action is illegal as well as unethical (as many such actions are), the employee who makes the questionable ethical decision can be held personally liable. The case of the Foreign Corruption Act of 1977 (which applied to U.S. based organizations) that prohibits the bribery of foreign officials to obtain overseas contracts illustrates this point (Kaikati & Label, 1980). For each violation (that is, the payment of a bribe), the organization is subject to a $1 million fine. More significant, however, the manager responsible for this payment is subject to a $10,000 fine per violation and a maximum of five years in prison. Relatedly, the courts are increasingly disposed to incarcerate executives shown to be responsible for violations of the law that endanger consumers (Laczniak & Murphy, 1986). For instance, a manager who premeditatedly decides to market an unsafe product is subject to criminal and personal liability. Criminal liability, of course, is the harshest of penalties, but there are other negative outcomes. Organizations that take their ethical reputation seriously will not hesitate to terminate employees who violate ethical and professional norms. This is an obvious gesture that communicates an organization's seriousness of purpose concerning the maintenance of an ethical culture. Needless to say, such termination will affect the future career prospects of these individuals, not to mention the personal embarrassment that goes along with being fired.

There are also substantial organizational costs resulting from unethical behavior when ethical transgressions by a company become publicized. Typically, these take the form of reduced sales and a loss of goodwill. A classic case is the experience of Beech-Nut Company. In this situation the reputation of Beech-Nut, a company marketing to children and one dependent upon fostering an image of safety and care, has probably become irreconcilably besmirched because of the actions of a few unscrupulous managers.

Finally, there are enormous societal costs that are generated by the unethical behavior of organizations. A consumer who is tricked into buying a product that he or she does not need or who ends up paying substantially more for a product or service than is justified incurs a surplus economic cost as well as some resentment toward the organization's marketing system. Some groups, such as the poor, the old, the handi-capped, the mentally feeble, children, and recent immigrants, are partic-ularly vulnerable to unethical business practices. Besides the economic or physical pain suffered by victims of unethical business practice, there is a general damage to the credibility of the existing economic system, which requires a high level of trust to operate smoothly. Whether one believes in a free market economy or a planned economy, most business analysts agree that it is the economically efficient firm with superior product that should be rewarded, rather than the dishonest firm that gains a perceived advantage via misrepresentation. Yet, when a compet-itive situation exists wherein an unethical business practice generates a short-term benefit for loss efficient firms, the advantages of the suppos-edly efficient marketplace are shortcircuited and shift toward the uneth-ical firm. Needless to say, if questionable business practices happen to a greater extent, further erosion of confidence by the U.S. public in the business system occurs.

IMPROVING INDIVIDUAL DECISION MAKING

It stands to reason that organizational decision making can be im-proved if employees can be encouraged to think ethically and to approx-imate more closely effective and ethical decision making. This should help to preclude the various biases and errors that were alluded to in Chapter 3. Many organizations have found that helping their employees learn how to deal with ethical dilemmas decreased the likelihood of employees making decisions that result in unethical behavior.

As noted in Chapter 2, ethical behavior is that which is morally accepted as "good" and "right" as opposed to "bad" or "wrong" in a par-ticular setting. Is it ethical, for example, to pay a bribe to obtain a busi-ness contract in a foreign country? Is it ethical to allow your company to dispose of hazardous waste in an unsafe fashion? Is it ethical to withhold information that might discourage a job candidate from joining your organization? Is it ethical to ask someone to take a job you know will not be good for their career progress? Is it ethical to do personal business on company time?

The list of examples could go on and on. Regardless of one's initial inclinations in response to these questions, the major point of it all is to remind you that the public-at-large is demanding that employees and the organizations they represent all act in accordance with high ethical and moral standards.

The subject of employee ethics cannot be overemphasized. We defined employee ethics as standards and principles that guide the actions and decisions of employees and determine if they are "good" or "bad" in a moral sense. Ethical employee behavior, accordingly, is that which conforms not only to the dictates of law but also to a broader moral code common to society as a whole. An ethical dilemma is a situation in which a person must decide whether or not to do something that, although benefiting oneself or the organization or both, may be considered unethical.

Ethical dilemmas are common in the workplace. Research, in fact, suggests that managers, for example, encounter such dilemmas in their working relationships with superiors, subordinates, customers, competitors, suppliers, and regulators. Common issues underlying the dilemmas involve honesty in communications and contracts, gifts and entertainment, kickbacks, pricing practices, and employee terminations (Cullen, Victor, & Stephens, 1990).

Whereas some organizations have published codes of ethics (see Chapter 10 for a more detailed discussion of codes of ethics) to help guide behavior (or counter unethical behavior) in such circumstances, in all organizations, the ultimate test is the strength of an individual employee's personal ethical framework. Because of this, more and more organizations are offering ethics training programs to help employees clarify their ethical frameworks and practice self-discipline when making decisions in difficult circumstances. An emphasis on understanding frameworks for ethical decision making is important to improving employee decision making and key to countering unethical behavior in organizations.

FRAMEWORKS FOR ETHICAL DECISION MAKING

What standards do organizational members (for our purposes in this section, managers) use in order to grapple with questions that may have ethical implications? Historically, most business executives have gravitated toward a utilitarian method of problem solving. Applied to an ethical situation in a business context, the reasoning employed by many managers would take the form of a cost/benefit analysis. Business people, because of their training, are naturally prone to talk about concepts such as "maximizing profitability" and "concern for the bottom line." Profitability essentially translates into the excess revenue over cost. It does not require a great stretch of the manager's imagination to apply a similar sort of thinking to an ethical context. Thus, managers often operate with a rule that essentially says, "make decisions such that the firm to the greatest extent possible is maximized." Depending upon how a manager defines "benefits" and "costs," one might arrive at different conclusions. If the emphasis is upon economic criteria (such as short-term profits), it is easy to see how a fair amount of the ethical analysis conducted by business executives gives great weight to economic outcomes that evaluate how various options would benefit stockholders in the near term.

Thus, looking at situations from their personal influence upon short-run profitability, one can see how an organization rationalizes taking a product (for example, a toy dart gun) that has been declared unsafe in one market and attempting to sell it in another market where the regulation might not apply. The rationale: the organization does not have to write off the inventory — a major cost. The inherent danger of the product might be arguable. Who is to say definitely that a plastic, rubber tipped dart gun is any more or less dangerous than a baseball? The sale of the product is perfectly legal, thereby protecting a revenue stream. In short, economic considerations often prevail over other possible perspectives like whether "toy guns" are a proper plaything or whether a firm should tolerate any product that has a likelihood of severely injuring a child.

This is not to say that there are not other short-hand decision rules besides utilitarian cost/benefit analysis that are used by business people. Other expeditious frameworks for ethical decision making have been articulated as useful. Laczniak (1983) lists some of the maxims that might aid an employee facing an ethical dilemma:

The Golden Rule — Act in a way that you would expect others to act toward you.

The Professional Ethic — Take only actions that would be viewed as proper by an objective panel of your professional colleagues.

Kant's Categorical Imperative — Act in a way such that the action taken under the circumstances could be a universal law of behavior for everyone facing those same circumstances.

The TV Test — A manager should always ask, would I feel comfortable explaining this action on TV to the general public?

Such maxims can have considerable value.

The work of Kohlberg (1969, 1981) has substantially influenced the thinking behind many programs designed to increase ethical behavior in organizations. Drawing heavily on the work of developmental psychologists such as Piaget, Kohlberg developed a theory of the development of seven stages of moral reasoning. The stages of moral reasoning central to Kohlberg's theory are:

Preconventional Level

Stage 1 — punishment and obedience orientation. The physical consequences of an act determine whether it is good or bad.

Stage 2 — instrumental relativist orientation. Things that satisfy your needs, and sometimes the needs of others, are good.

Conventional Level

Stage 3 — "good boy/good girl" orientation. Behavior that pleases others and earns approval is good.

Stage 4 — "law and order" orientation. Respect for authority, order, and doing one's duty determine what is right.

Postconventional Level

Stage 5 — social contract orientation. The consensus of society, which can change, defines what is right.

Stage 6 — universal ethical principle orientation. Right is defined in terms of self-chosen universal principles of good and bad.

Stage 7 — cosmic ethical principle orientation. Right is defined in terms of the oneness of the universe, leading to principles that are cosmic rather than strictly people or word oriented.

Kohlberg's theory suggests that most individuals develop their understanding of what is right and wrong over a long period of time and that the eventual definition of right and wrong adopted by the individual reflects his or her progression through a well-defined hierarchy of types of moral reasoning. Young children operate at a preconventional level, in which the definition of right and wrong depends on rules set down by others. As they mature, children move to a conventional level, in which they adopt and internalize rules and start to recognize some acts as right or wrong regardless of the rewards and punishments that might immediately accompany the act. At a postconventional level, the definitions of right and wrong flow from the set of general ethical principles the individual has chosen to follow.

Within each of the three general levels, there are a number of stages of moral development, in which right and wrong are successively defined in slightly different terms. In general, the stages proceed from self-oriented thinking and from a punishment/reward orientation to an abstract principle orientation. Each successive stage represents a higher level of reasoning regarding the definition and nature of right and wrong. A number of studies suggest that the moral reasoning of most adults is similar to that described in Stage 4 of Kohlberg's theory (Colby, 1978). And that moral reasoning at Stage 5 or beyond is relatively rare, even in educated groups such as managers (Trevino, 1986).

Kohlberg's theory might be applied to the problem of unethical behavior in organizations in two ways. First, it is possible that the selection of employees, particularly managers, whose moral reasoning is at higher, rather than lower, stages in the hierarchy might help increase ethical behavior in organizations (Trevino, 1986). Second, it might be possible to increase the sophistication of an individual's moral reasoning through training or education (Baxter & Rarick, 1987). Whatever frameworks are used, the consensus regarding what constitutes proper ethical behavior in a decision-making situation tends to diminish as the level of an analysis proceeds from the abstract to the specific. Put another way, it is easy to get a group of managers to agree in general that a practice is improper; however, casting that practice in a very specific set of circumstances usually reduces consensus.

Ethical Dilemmas

Most typically, ethical dilemmas involve risk and uncertainty and nonroutine problem situations. Just how an employee handles the ones that will inevitably appear in his or her career may well be the ultimate test of his or her ethical framework. Consider this short case (Otten, 1986):

You are a new financial analyst for a small project engineering firm. Your job is to analyze competitive proposals for the electrical portion of a construction project supervised by your firm. Three have been received so far, and one is clearly the best. Your boss's assistant puts a copy of this proposal in an envelope and tells you to hand carry it to a "friend" of the boss's who runs an electrical contracting business. "He always gets a chance to look at the other bids before submitting one himself," the assistant says. Your boss is out of town for the next two days. What should you do?

What follows is a useful seven-step decision-making checklist that some organizations encourage their employees use for resolving ethical dilemmas such as the one found in the prior case (Schermerhorn, 1989):

1. Recognize and clarify the dilemma.
2. Get all possible facts.

3. List your options — all of them.
4. Test each option by asking, "Is it legal? Is it right? Is it beneficial?"
5. Make your decision.
6. Double check your decision by asking, "How would I feel if my family found out about this? How would I feel if my decision was printed in the local newspaper?"
7. Take action.

Ethical Guidelines

A few simple guidelines, regularly used, should help in the ethical screening of decisions. The point is not to paralyze an employee's decision making but to get him or her to think seriously about the moral implications of his or her decisions *before* they are made (Johns, 1992).

Identify the stakeholders that will be affected by any decision.

Identify the costs and benefits of various decision alternatives to these stakeholders.

Consider the relevant moral expectations that surround a particular decision. These might stem from professional norms, laws, organizational ethics codes, and principles such as honest communication and fair treatment.

Be familiar with the common ethical dilemmas that are faced by decision makers in your organizational role or profession.

Discuss ethical matters with decision stakeholders and others. Do not think ethics without talking about ethics.

Decision Rules

Another approach to improving ethical behavior is the use of decision rules. Nash (1981) has proposed 12 questions to guide managers in handling the ethical dimensions of decision making:

1. Have you defined the problem accurately?
2. How would you define the problem if you stood on the other side of the fence?
3. How did this situation occur in the first place?
4. To whom and to what do you give your loyalty as a person and as a member of the corporation?
5. What is your intention in making this decision?
6. How does this intention compare with the probable results?

7. Whom could your decision or action injure?

8. Can you discuss the problem with the affected parties before you make the decision?

9. Are you confident that your position will be as valid over a long period of time as it seems now?

10. Could you disclose without qualm your decision or action to your boss, your chief executive officer, the board of directors, your family, society as a whole?

11. What is the symbolic potential of your action if understood? If misunderstood?

12. Under what conditions would you allow exceptions to your stand?

One final approach to more normatively deal with ethical dilemmas or issues is to require employees or managers to proceed through a sequence of questions like those above that essentially test whether the action that they contemplate is ethical or has possible ethical consequences. Laczniak (1983) suggests that a battery of such questions might include:

1. Does the contemplated action violate law?

2. Is the contemplated action contrary to widely accepted moral obligations? (Such moral obligations might include duties of fidelity, such as the responsibility to remain faithful to contracts, to keep promises, and to tell the truth; duties of gratitude, which basically means that special obligations exist among relatives, friends, partners, cohorts, and employees; duties of justice, which basically have to do with obligations to distribute rewards based upon merit; duties of nonmaleficence, which consist of duties not to harm others; duties of beneficence, which rest upon the notion that actions should be taken that improve the situation of others — if this can be readily accomplished.)

3. Does the proposed action violate any other special obligations that stem from the type of business organization at focus? (Such special considerations might include the special duty of pharmaceutical firms to provide safe products, the special obligation of toy manufacturers to care for the safety of children, the inherent duty of alcohol manufacturers to promote responsible drinking.)

4. Is the intent of the contemplated action harmful?

5. Are there any major damages to people or organizations that are likely to result from the contemplated action?

6. Is there a satisfactory alternative action that produces equal or greater benefits to the parties affected than the proposed action?

7. Does the contemplated action infringe upon the inalienable rights of the consumer? (Such rights might include the right to information, the right to be heard, the right to choice, and the right to redress.)

8. Does the proposed action leave another person or group less well off? Is this person or group already a member of a relatively underprivileged class?

The questions outlined need not be pursued in any lockstep fashion. If none of the questions uncover any potential conflicts, the action being contemplated is quite likely to be ethical. However, if the sequence of queries does produce a possible "conflict," this does not necessarily mean that the action being proposed is unethical per se. There may be unusual intervening factors that would still allow the action to ethically go forward. For example, suppose it is determined that the contemplated action is a violation of the law. Perhaps the law is unjust, and, thus, there could be a moral obligation for an organization to transgress the law. Similarly, suppose there is an alternative action that could be taken that would produce equal or greater good for a larger number of individuals. However, the implementation of this alternative would bankrupt the existing organization. In such a situation, the taking of the alternative action (rather than the contemplated action) is very likely not required.

Organizations that are interested in countering unethical behavior and improving employee decision making, rather than simply understanding the ethical decisions that take place, need an organizationally managed sequence of ethical reasoning that an employee or manager can utilize and organizational commitment by top management to an ethical culture.

IMPROVING THE EFFECTIVENESS
OF GROUP DECISIONS

As discussed in Chapter 3, certain advantages can be gained from sometimes using individuals and sometimes using groups to make decisions. A decision-making technique that combines the features of groups and individuals while minimizing the disadvantages would be ideal. Several techniques designed to realize the "best of both worlds" have been widely used in organizations. These include techniques that involve the structuring of group discussions in special ways, as well as improving the skills individuals may bring to the decision-making situation. However, before discussing group decison-making techniques in more detail, the next section will first provide a discussion of the importance of conflict management and the need for managing or stimulating conflict in groups as a key to countering groupthink and, subsequently, unethical behavior.

GROUP DECISION-MAKING TECHNIQUES

The most common form of group decision making takes place in face-to-face interacting groups. However, as the discussion on groupthink demonstrated, such groups often censor themselves and pressure individual members toward conformity of opinion. Devil's advocate, dialectic, brainstorming, nominal group and Delphi techniques, and electronic meetings have been proposed as ways to reduce many of the problems inherent in the traditional interacting groups. Each will be discussed in this section.

Stimulating Conflict and Managing Controversy

Smart organizations often ensure that groups are usually trained in conducting meetings and become well-versed in group problem solving and the techniques of conflict management when an organization decides to restructure into self-managing groups. However, in their haste to resolve conflict, too many groups disregard the benefits of conflict. Conflict can be exciting, stimulating, and challenging and may produce constructive outcomes and ideas of superior quality.

Groups must not disregard the benefits of disagreement and contrasting views when trying to make decisions. Recommendations for overcoming groupthink share a common characteristic: in order to assure high quality decisions, group members must value disagreement and seek contrasting viewpoints. Group members must be willing to consider a variety of alternatives and to subject these alternatives to rigorous logical testing. Once an idea is "picked apart," the plan can be revised or abandoned. However, if the plan is not subjected to a stern test of quality, its weaknesses may not be uncovered until too late.

Full-blown conflict among organizational members is hardly conducive to good decision making. Information is certain to be withheld, and personal or group goals will take precedence over developing a decision that solves organizational problems. On the other hand, a complete lack of controversy can be equally damaging, because alternative points of view that may be very relevant to the issue at hand will never surface. Such a lack of controversy is partially responsible for the groupthink effect, and it also contributes to many cases of escalation of commitment to flawed courses of action.

Stimulating conflict through the devil's advocate and dialectic methods can raise different opinions regardless of the personal feelings of the managers or members of groups. The usefulness of the devil's advocate technique was illustrated by Janis when discussing famous fiascoes such as Watergate and Vietnam (Cosier & Schwenk, 1990). Janis recommends that everyone in the group assume the role of a devil's advocate and question the assumptions underlying the popular choice. Alternatively, an individual or subgroup could be formally designated as the devil's advocate and present a critique of the proposed course of action. This avoids the tendency of agreement interfering with problem solving while still serving as a precaution for the occurrence of unethical behavior. Potential unethical behaviors are identified and considered before the decision is final.

The conflict generated by the devil's advocate may cause groups to avoid false assumptions and closely adhere to guidelines for ethical analysis in decisions. The devil's advocate raises questions that force an in-depth review of the group's decision-making process. The devil's advocate is assigned to identify potential pitfalls or unethical behavior, with a proposed course of action. A formal presentation to the key decision makers by the devil's advocate raises potential concerns. Evidence needed to address the critique is gathered, and the final decision is made and ensuing behavior monitored. The devil's advocate decision program (Cosier & Schwenk, 1990) is summarized as follows:

A proposed course of action is generated.

A devil's advocate (individual or group) is assigned to criticize the proposal.

The critique is presented to key decision makers.

Any additional information relevant to the issues is gathered.

The decision to adopt, modify, or discontinue the proposed course of action is made.

The decision is monitored.

It is a good idea to rotate people assigned to devil's advocate roles. This avoids any one person or group being identified as the critic on all group decisions. The devil's advocate role can assist organizations like Beech-Nut, E. F. Hutton, Salomon Brothers, and others in avoiding costly mistakes by hearing viewpoints that identify pitfalls instead of foster agreement.

Although the devil's advocate technique does not foster agreement between advocates of two conflicting positions, the dialectic method can program conflict into a group's decisions while offsetting potentially unethical behavior. The dialectic method calls for structuring a debate between conflicting views regardless of members' personal feelings. The benefits of the dialectic method are in the presentation and debate of the assumptions underlying proposed courses of action. False or misleading assumptions become apparent and can head off unethical decisions that are based on these poor assumptions. The dialectic method presented below can help promote ethical decisions and counteract groupthink:

A proposed course of action is generated.

Assumptions underlying the proposal are identified.

A conflicting counterproposal is generated, based on different assumptions.

Advocates of each position present and debate the merits of their proposals before key decision makers.

The decision to adopt either position or some other position, for example, a compromise, is made.

The decision is monitored.

Programming conflict into the group decision-making process allows dissent and can decrease the likelihood of groupthink and unethical behavior. Such conflict requires organizations to ensure that decisions are challenged and criticized and that alternative ideas are generated. Programmed conflict also insures that a comprehensive decision framework becomes a part of the group decision-making process.

Brainstorming

Brainstorming is the "brain child" of a Madison Avenue advertising executive (Osborn, 1957). Brainstorming is meant to overcome pressures for conformity in the interacting group that retard the development of creative alternatives (Osborn, 1941). It does this by utilizing an idea-generation process that specifically encourages any and all alternatives while withholding any criticism of those alternatives. Thus, brainstorming focuses on the generation of ideas rather than the evaluation of ideas. If a large number of ideas can be generated, the chance of obtaining a truly creative solution is increased.

In a typical brainstorming session, a half-dozen to dozen people sit around a table. The group leader states the problem in a clear manner so that it is understood by all participants. Members then "free-wheel" as many alternatives as they can in a given period of time. No criticism is allowed, and all alternatives are recorded for later discussion and analysis. That one idea stimulates others, and the fact that judgments of even the most bizarre suggestions are withheld until later encourages group members to "think the unusual."

Although the devil's advocate and dialectic methods stimulate conflict, brainstorming is merely a process for generating ideas. The next three techniques go further by offering methods of actually arriving at a preferred solution.

Nominal Group Technique

The fact that nominal (in name only) brainstorming groups generate more ideas than interacting brainstorming groups gave rise to the nominal group technique (NGT) of decision making. Unlike brainstorming, NGT is concerned with both the generation of ideas and the evaluation of these ideas.

The NGT restricts discussion or interpersonal communication during the decision-making process — hence, the term "nominal." Group members are all physically present, as in a traditional committee meeting, but members operate independently. Specifically, a problem is presented and then the following steps take place:

Members meet as a group, but before any discussion takes place, each member independently writes down his or her ideas on the problem.

This silent period is followed by each member presenting one idea to the group. Each member takes his or her turn, going around the table, presenting a single idea until all ideas have been presented and recorded (typically on a flip chart or chalkboard). No discussion takes place until all ideas have been recorded.

The group now discusses the ideas for clarity and evaluates them.

Each group member silently and independently rank-orders the ideas. The final decision is determined by the idea with the highest aggregate ranking.

As you can observe, NGT carefully separates the generation of ideas from their evaluation. Ideas are generated nominally (without interaction) to prevent inhibition and conformity. Evaluation permits interaction and discussion, but it occurs in a fairly structured manner to be sure that each idea gets adequate attention.

NGT has been used in a variety of organizational settings. The NGT has several advantages and disadvantages. This approach can be used to arrive at group decisions in only a few hours. The benefit of the technique is that it discourages any pressure to conform to the wishes of a high-status group member because all ideas are evaluated and the preferences are expressed in private balloting. The chief advantage of the NGT is that it permits the group to meet formally but does not restrict independent thinking, as does the interacting group. Its chief disadvantage would seem to be the time and resources required to assemble the group for face-to-face interaction. The Delphi technique was developed in part to overcome this problem.

The Delphi Technique

The Delphi technique of decision making was developed at the Rand Corporation to forecast changes in technology. Its name derives from the future-telling of the famous Greek Delphic Oracle (Delbecq, Van de Ven, & Gustafson, 1975). Unlike NGT, the Delphi process relies solely upon a nominal group — participants do not engage in face-to-face interaction. Thus, it is possible to poll a large number of experts without assembling them in the same place at the same time. It should be emphasized that these experts do not actually make a final decision; rather, they provide information for organizational decision makers.

The following steps characterize the Delphi technique:

1. The problem is identified, and members are asked to provide potential solutions through a series of carefully designed questionnaires.
2. Each member anonymously and independently completes the first questionnaire.
3. Results of the first questionnaire are compiled at a central location, transcribed, and reproduced.
4. Each member receives a copy of the results.
5. After viewing the results, members are again asked for their solutions. The results typically trigger new solutions or cause changes in the original position.
6. Steps 4 and 5 are repeated as often as necessary until consensus is reached.

Like the NGT, the Delphi technique insulates group members from the undue influence of others. Because it does not require the physical presence of the participants, the Delphi technique can be used for decision making among geographically scattered groups. A chief disadvantage of the Delphi technique is the rather lengthy time frame involved in the questionnaire phases. Because the method is extremely time-consuming, it is frequently not applicable where a speedy decision is necessary. Additionally, the method may not develop the rich array of alternatives that the interacting technique or NGT does. Ideas that might surface from the heat of face-to-face interaction may never arise. Despite these problems, the Delphi technique is an efficient method of pooling a large number of expert judgments while avoiding the problems of conformity and domination that can occur in interacting groups.

Electronic Meetings

The most recent approach to group decision making blends the NGT with sophisticated computer technology: the electronic meeting.

Once the technology is in place, the concept is simple. Up to 50 people sit around a horseshoe-shaped table, empty except for a series of computer terminals. Issues are presented to participants, and they type their responses onto their computer screen. Individual comments, as well as aggregate votes, are displayed on a projection screen in the room.

The major advantages of electronic meetings are anonymity, honesty, and speed. Participants can anonymously type any message they want, and it flashes on the screen for all to see at the push of a participant's board key. It also allows people to be brutally honest without penalty. It is fast, because chitchat is eliminated, discussions do not digress, and many participants can "talk" at once without stepping on one another's toes.

Experts claim that electronic meetings are as much as 55 percent faster than traditional face-to-face meetings. Yet, there are drawbacks to this technique. Those who can type fast can outshine those who are verbally eloquent but lousy typists, those with the best ideas do not get credit for them, and the process lacks the information richness of face-to-face oral communication. However, although this technology is currently in its infancy, the future of group decision making is very likely to include extensive use of electronic meetings.

TECHNIQUES FOR FOSTERING INDIVIDUAL AND GROUP DECISION MAKING IN ORGANIZATIONS

What can organizations like Beech-Nut, E. F. Hutton, and Salomon Brothers specifically do to improve their employees' decision making and counter groupthink and unethical behavior effectively? A number of useful rules can be employed. First, the organization and its managers must encourage open airing of objections and doubts. Second, one or more outsiders should be invited into the group to challenge the views of its members. Finally, after reaching a preliminary the group should hold a "second chance" meeting at which every member expresses, as vividly as possible, all his or her doubts and the group thinks through the entire issue again before making a final decision.

The following are prescriptions for helping managers reduce the probability of groupthink (Janis, 1972; Gaegler, 1989; Sims, 1992):

Prescriptions

Leader Prescriptions
1. Assign everyone the role of critical evaluator. Use "what if" statements and "which would be better, to . . . or . . . ?" questions.
2. Be impartial, do not state preferences. The group leader can refrain from stating his or her position prematurely and promote open inquiry to help explore ranges of alternatives.
3. Assign the devil's advocate role to at least one group member during meetings to challenge the majority position.
4. Use outside experts to challenge the group. The group can employ the use of experts in one of two ways: before the group reaches a decision, they can bring in experts in order to seek advice or, after a decision has been made, they can bring in experts to challenge members' views and "shoot holes" in the direction the group has decided upon.

Organizational Prescriptions
1. Do not automatically opt for a "strong" culture. Explore methods to provide for diversity and dissent, such as grievance or complaint mechanisms or other internal review procedures.
2. Set up several independent groups to study the same issue. The group could split into two subsections for independent discussion, then come back together and compare points of discussion.
3. Train all employees in ethics (these programs should explain the underlying ethical issues, legal issues (Drake & Drake, 1988), groupthink-prevention techniques, and devil's advocate and dialectic methods.
4. Establish programs to clarify and communicate values.

Individual Prescriptions

1. Be a critical thinker.
2. Discuss the group's deliberations with a trusted outsider and report back to the group.

Process Prescriptions

1. The group can make a conscious effort to obtain more suggestions for viable solutions by focusing on the process of obtaining these suggestions. For example, employ the NGT by dividing the group into subgroups and assigning the same problem or task. Discuss the results among everyone. Another example would be to use the Delphi technique.
2. Take time to study external factors.
3. Hold second-chance meetings to rethink issues before making a commitment. After a final decision is made by the group, hold a "follow-up" meeting to revisit what decision was made, how and why it was made, and basically reevaluate both the process and the content of that decision-making process.
4. Periodically rotate new members into groups and old members out.

Note that all the suggestions encourage group members to evaluate alternatives critically and discourage the single-minded pursuit of unanimity, which is a key component of groupthink. By making use of the above prescriptions, organizations can give employees the confidence to be on the lookout for groupthink and act with the understanding that what they are doing is considered correct and will be supported by top management and the entire organization.

Training Discussion Leaders

When group decision making is utilized, an appointed leader often convenes the group and guides the discussion. The actions of this leader can make or break the decision. If the leader behaves autocratically, trying to "sell" a preconceived decision, the advantages of using a group are obliterated and decision acceptance can suffer. If the leader fails to exert *any* influence, however, the group might develop a low-quality solution that does not meet the needs of the organization. One expert has argued that discussion leaders should be trained to develop the following skills:

State the problem in a nondefensive, objective manner. Do not suggest solutions or preferences.

Supply essential facts and clarify any constraints on solutions (for example, "We can't spend more than $5,000").

Draw out all group members. Prevent domination by one person and protect members from being attacked or severely criticized.

Wait out pauses. Do not make suggestions or ask leading questions.

Ask stimulating questions that move the discussion forward.

Summarize and clarify at several points to mark progress.

Notice that these skills are not vague attitudes, but specific behaviors. Thus, they are subject to training and practice. There is good evidence that this quality training can be accomplished through role-playing and that it can help counteract groupthink and unethical behavior and improve decision making in organizations.

Groupthink Checklist

Another technique for the leader to employ is to use a checklist to determine that steps and precautions were taken to avoid group-think throughout the decision-making process and to verify that groupthink was not present during a particular point throughout the entire process and content of the task at hand. Some questions that can be included in a groupthink checklist are as follows:

Were group members made aware of groupthink symptoms in order to understand and respect the delicate balance between individuality and conformity? Yes or No

Did the group bring in experts when appropriate to the problem, issue, decision at hand? Yes or No

Was someone appointed as gatekeeper to make sure all members were heard and had a voice in the decision-making process? Yes or No

Was a conscious effort made to explore nonobvious advantages and disadvantages to alternatives? Yes or No

Was a devil's advocate appointed during the project to help explore all angles? Yes or No   If yes, who was in this role and how was it played?

Was a conscious effort put forth to make the members feel comfortable in the group environment so that critical thinking would be nonthreatening to high morale and to the cohesiveness of the group? Yes or No

Was the final decision revisited and reanalyzed after it was made in order to verify that it was the right approach, considering the process for reaching that decision as well as the content of the decision? Yes or No

What efforts are employed to promote employee individual thinking?

Organizations must also ensure that they do not support financial success as the only value to be considered. Such an attitude will not promote a bottom-line mentality and an unrealistic belief that everything boils down to a monetary game. By not emphasizing short-term revenues above long-term consequences, organizations will create a climate in which individuals and groups understand that unethical behavior is unacceptable. In addition, organizations must be willing to take a stand when there is a financial cost to any group's decision. This stand will discourage ethical shortcuts by its members.

In order for values to provide the ethical "rules of the road" for employees, organizations must ensure that they are stated, shared, and understood by everyone in an organization. Formal programs to clarify and communicate important ethical values can help accomplish this objective in organizations and counteract groupthink. In addition, organizations should pay proper attention to employee recruitment, selection, and orientation.

The values of prospective employees should be examined and discussed and the results used in making selection decisions. A person's first encounters with an organization and its members also say a lot about key beliefs and values. Every attempt should be made to teach them "the ethical way we do things here." Organizations also should develop appropriate training and development opportunities to establish and maintain skills in programmed conflict methods. In addition, values can and should be emphasized, along with other important individual attributes.

Finally, organizations can make use of progressive rewards to encourage ethical behavior by individuals and groups. Rewards in the form of monetary compensation, employee benefits, and special recognition can reinforce individual values, counteract groupthink, and maintain enthusiasm in support of ethical organizational values. Organizations can find creative ways to reward employees for displaying ethical values that are considered essential to organizational success.

Enhance Group Decision Making

Organizations should see that decisions in groups are made after thoughtful consideration of counterpoints and criticism. Group members with different viewpoints must be encouraged to provide thoughts on important decisions, while widespread agreement on a key issue should be seen as a red flag, not a condition of good. For the reason just stated, groups should use the following techniques to foster open discussion, surface and manage conflict, and develop flexibility in adopting solutions in deliberations before a decision is made.

Encourage Diverse Viewpoints

Groups should recognize the need to allow different points and critical thinking into their decisions. The type of conflict that is encouraged involves different interpretations of common issues or problems. This "cognitive conflict" was noted as functional many years ago by Janis (Cosier & Schwenk, 1990). As noted in the discussion on groupthink, Janis pointed out that striving for agreement and preventing critical thought frequently leads to poor decisions.

An effective group will see themselves as a team of advisors who represent diverse viewpoints. Tunnel vision can be avoided only when a variety of perspectives are considered. If diverse viewpoints are managed properly, the group should certainly generate the kind of discussion and debate that will stimulate creative ideas and produce alternatives worth considering.

Create Incentives and Rewards for Disagreements

Disagreements should be encouraged and rewarded, not stifled and punished. However, it is important not to reward pure negativism if the creation of hard-core naysayers is to be avoided. Group members who claim that the idea under consideration "won't work" should state their reasons clearly. These reasons can then be considered and evaluated, and the idea can be supported, revised, or abandoned. This is where the interpersonal skills of the group members are particularly important. Creating incentives and rewards for disagreements requires the willingness of all group members to take responsibility for managing the group's decision-making and problem-solving process.

Take Time to Explore the Nature of the Problem

Groups must be aware of the four common mistakes that often occur during problem identification, the first step of problem solving: the tendency to define the problem in terms of a proposed solution; the tendency to focus on narrow, lower order goals; the tendency to diagnose the problem in terms of its symptoms; and the tendency to seek solutions too quickly (Williams & Huber, 1986). Before a problem can be solved and a high quality decision made and implemented, all relevant facets of the problem must be clearly articulated and understood.

The group members must encourage all angles of the problem before jumping ahead to the generation of alternative solutions.

Consider as Many Alternative Solutions as Possible

The self-managing group that considers only one solution — often the first one mentioned in the discussion or the first one that makes a favorable impression — may be preparing the organization for "a trip to Abilene." To ensure high quality decisions, it is extremely important to consider multiple alternatives, because the process of exploration and consideration is the most likely route to an innovative, creative solution. Brainstorming, the NGT (Williams & Huber, 1986), the Delphi technique (Delbecq, Van de Ven, & Gustafson, 1975), and other techniques for structured problem solving (VanGundy, 1981) are available to assist self-managing groups in the process of generating alternative solutions.

Actively Challenge Each Proposed Solution

This is the heart of the concept of fostering conflict, what Cosier and Schwenk (1990) refer to as allowing true disagreement: make certain that no proposed alternative is accepted as the final solution until it has been subjected to rigorous challenge and evaluation. Each member of the self-managing group should take responsibility for inviting group members to try to pick apart the idea; any viable challenges to the proposed solution identified in this manner can then be considered carefully and the solution modified accordingly. An alternative method would be to "program" conflict by appointing one or more devil's advocates to prepare as strong a case as possible against the proposed solution. By "trying the case," self-managing groups can come to a rational decision regarding the implementation of the idea.

Recognize that Power Struggles May Develop

Members of self-managing groups should realize that power struggles and counterproductive conflict may result from competition. What may simply be a different work style can be viewed with suspicion by a fellow group member. One person may begin to think he or she has the "right" method and the other is absolutely wrong. As the conflict escalates, minor differences can become exaggerated. The real issue — how to get the job done in the most efficient way — can become lost in a power struggle.

The group can cope with power struggles if group members assume the role of mediator. As mediators, group members attempt to reconcile the parties in counterproductive conflict by helping them define and clarify and then determine what common goals are desired. The mediator's task requires skill and sensitivity and an objective view of the situation by group members.

Encourage Sharing of Hidden Doubts

In those groups in which groupthink, unethical behavior or decisions, and the avoidance of conflict have been characteristic operating procedures, group members will find it very difficult to stimulate a lively discussion of contrasting viewpoints and an unwillingness to take on the role of mediator. The group may want to employ some of the following ideas for preventing future "trips to Abilene."

Appoint a group ombudsman who functions as a clearing house for all private matters of concern.

Periodically invite an external consultant in to interview group members about unspoken concerns.

Hold regular team-building meetings following a problem-solving format. Establish a climate where it is okay to "get it off your chest." Feelings must be aired before group members are able to move toward a solution.

Make available a form that can be filled out anonymously to describe concerns a group member feels personally but is afraid to share publicly. When possible, it is extremely helpful to have group members write down their thoughts during a group meeting. This allows group members to air their grievances and should move them toward working out a solution.

Maintain a power balance. If one person has more authority, superior verbal skills, or a more forceful personality, group members should interrupt from time to time and draw out the others. Do not let one person take over the group's conversation.

Dyer (1977) considers these to be "crutches" and argues that they should be used only in the short run.

Be Aware of Rationalizations for Justifying Unethical Behavior

An important point that must be considered in improving employees' skills in ethical decision making is that each of us can too easily use rationalizations to help justify actual or potential misconduct. The best way to prevent these rationalizations from leading us astray is to recognize them for what they are. Common rationalizations used to justify unethical behavior include pretending the behavior is not really unethical or illegal, excusing the behavior by saying it is really in the organization's or your best interest, assuming that the behavior is okay because no one else would ever be expected to find out about it, and expecting your superiors to support and protect you if anything should go wrong (Gellerman, 1986).

To counter such things as unethical behavior and groupthink, organizations must commit resources to improve individual and group decision making. The organization must strive for an environment in which openness, questioning, and honest disagreement, clearly stated, are accepted as indicators of a high level of commitment to the long-term success of the organization. At the same time, the organization must create an environment in which employees realize that by fostering conflict, one of their most difficult tasks will focus on learning to cope with inevitable counterproductive conflicts that will arise among them when working in groups and that such counterproductive conflict will occur when two or more group members believe that what each wants is incompatible with what the other wants. The group members cannot resolve the conflict until they have a clear understanding of their differences and the source of these differences.

Groups must confront counterproductive conflict and must identify this type of disagreement as quickly as possible and recognize that seemingly trivial complaints often are only symptoms of a much larger problem. If the group ignores the early warning signs, counterproductive conflict can escalate and spread to new issues. The emphasis may shift from the original issue to anything that will make the group even less effective. Trivial points just become additional fuel.

With the increased emphasis upon groups or teams in organizations, organizations must ensure that these groups make use of proven methods that can lower the level of counterproductive conflict and the likelihood of groupthink and unethical behavior. Organizations can also take steps to help these groups to reduce and effectively manage conflict. They can design specialized dispute systems (Brett, Goldberg, & Ury, 1990), or they may adopt special roles or alter structure to resolve disputes in the groups — for example, special positions might be developed to manage conflict within the groups. Organizations can also assist the groups in managing conflict by improving members' skills in both understanding and resolving counterproductive conflict. They can help reduce ambiguities that might occur in the group through such techniques as goal setting. They can make policies and rules clearer. Finally, they can develop reward systems for the group that provide an incentive for them to effectively manage conflict. In the end, using such strategies to deescalate such conflict will usually reduce its intensity, making it possible for group members to join forces to solve mutual problems and enhance their own and the organization's overall effectiveness.

REFERENCES

Baxter, G. D., & Rarick, C. A. 1987. Education for the moral development of managers: Kohlberg's stages of moral development and integrative education. *Journal of Business Ethics 6*, 243–48.

Brenner, S. N., & Mollander, E. A. 1977, January/February. Is ethics of business changing. *Harvard Business Review 55*, 50–57.

Brett, J. M., Goldberg, S. B., & Ury, W. L. 1990. Designing systems for resolving disputes in organizations. *American Psychologist 45*, 162–70.

Colby, A. 1978. Evolution of a moral development theory. In *Moral development*, ed. W. Damon. San Francisco, CA: Jossey-Bass.

Cosier, R. A., & Schwenk, C. R. 1990. Agreement and thinking alike: Ingredients for poor decisions. *Academy of Management Executive 4*(1): 69–74.

Cullen, J. B., Victor, V., & Stephens, C. 1990, Winter. An ethical weather report: Assessing the organization's ethical climate. *Organizational Dynamics*, pp. 50–62.

Delbecq, A. L., Van de Ven, A. H., & Gustafson, D. H. 1975. *Group techniques for program planning: A guide to nominal group and Delphi processes*. Glenview, IL: Scott, Foresman.

Detroit vs. the UAW: At odds over teamwork. 1987, August. *Business Week*, pp. 54–55.

Drake, B. H., & Drake, E. 1988, Winter. Ethical and legal aspects of managing corporate cultures. *California Management Review*, pp. 120–21.

Dyer, W. G. 1977. *Team building: Issues and alternatives*. Reading, MA: Addison-Wesley.

Gaegler, M. A. 1989, June. Overcoming groupthink. *Journal of Quality and Participation*, pp. 86–89.

Gellerman, S. W. 1986, July–August. Why "good" managers make bad ethical choices. *Harvard Business Review*, pp. 85–90.

Janis, I. 1972. *Victims of groupthink*. Boston, MA: Houghton Mifflin.

Johns, G. 1992. *Organizational behavior: Understanding life at work*, 3rd ed. New York: HarperCollins

Kaikati, G., & Label, W. A. 1980, Fall. America bribery legislation: An obstacle to international marketing. *Journal of Marketing*, pp. 38–43.

Kohlberg, L. 1981. *The philosophy of moral development*. New York: Harper & Row.

_____. 1969. Stage and sequence: The cognitive developmental approach to socialization. In *Handbook of socialization theory and research*, ed. D. A. Gaslin. Chicago, IL: Rand McNally, pp. 347–480.

Laczniak, G. R. 1983, January/March. Business ethics: A manager's primer. *Business*, pp. 23–29.

Laczniak, G. R., & Murphy, P. E. 1991. Fostering ethical marketing decisions. *Journal of Business Ethics 10*, 259–71.

____. 1986. Incorporating marketing ethics into the organization. In *Marketing ethics for managers*. Lexington, MA: D. C. Heath, pp. 98–100.

Nash, L. L. 1981, November–December. Ethics without the sermon. *Harvard Business Review*, pp. 79–90.

Osborn, A. F. 1957. *Applied imagination*. New York: Scribner's.

____. 1941. *Applied imagination: Principles and procedures of creative thinking*. New York: Scribner's.

Otten, A. L. 1986, July 14. Ethics on the job: Companies alert employees to potential dilemmas. *Wall Street Journal*, p. 17.

Schermerhorn, J. R. 1989. *Management for productivity*. New York: John Wiley.

Sims, R. R. 1992. Linking groupthink to unethical behavior in organizations. *Journal of Business Ethics 11*, 651–62.

Trevino, L. K. 1986. Ethical decision making in organizations: A person-situation interactionist model. *Academy of Management Review 11*, 601–17.

VanGundy, A. B. 1981. *Techniques of structured problem solving*. New York: Van Nostrand Reinhold.

Williams, J. C., & Huber, G. P. 1986. *Human behavior in organizations*. Cincinnati, OH: Southwestern, p. 323.

7

Leadership and Ethical Behavior: An Ethical Turnaround

As noted in Chapter 5, an organization's culture (like the one that developed at Salomon Brothers under John Gutfreund) socializes people. Often, it subtly (and other times not so subtly) conveys to members that certain actions are acceptable, even though they are unethical or illegal. For instance, when executives at General Electric, Westinghouse, and other manufacturers of heavy electrical equipment illegally conspired to set electrical prices in the early 1960s, the defendants invariably testified that they came new to their jobs, found price-fixing to be an established way of life, and simply entered into it as they did into other aspects of their job. One General Electric manager noted that every one of his bosses had directed him to meet with the competition: "It had become so common and gone on for so many years that I think we lost sight of the fact that it was illegal" (Greenberg & Baron, 1993). To get back on the ethical road, an organization must change.

Change is an organizational fact of life. If an organization has any chance of transforming itself from an unethical culture and experience (like Salomon Brothers), it must be able to handle change positively — to alter policies, structure, behavior, and beliefs — and do it with a minimum of resistance and disruption. It is far better to deal with the need for change — to modify it, redirect it, or disarm it — than to ignore or fight it. However, for companies like Salomon Brothers, a successful ethical turnaround does not just happen spontaneously; proper change management is the key to achieving this goal. But, in reality, can an organization like Salomon Brothers turn itself around ethically? If so, what needs to happen for an organization like Salomon Brothers to make a successful ethical turnaround? Finding an answer to that question is the focus of this chapter.

The chapter will first discuss what is needed for a successful ethical turnaround. Then, the chapter will revisit the Salomon Brothers situation by discussing Warren Buffett's efforts to change (or turn around) the ethical culture of Salomon Brothers.

IMPLEMENTING AN ETHICAL TURNAROUND

Turning around an unethical organizational culture implies decision making. Such change means that the status quo is to be abandoned and something new has been selected to take its place. In turning around an unethical organizational culture, decision making is the mechanism by which the need for abandoning the status quo is evaluated and, if change is needed, the means by which a new direction is selected. It is the premise of this book that to accomplish a successful ethical turnaround, the organization must understand the scope of the problem and be willing to make the decisions to undertake drastic measures.

In recent years, a number of organizations have been faced with the challenge of accomplishing a successful ethical turnaround. No matter what resulted in the company's culture leading to the unethical act(s), many top leaders, managers, and employees, who are accustomed to more "normal" conditions, lack an appreciation of the perspective, skills, and special actions that are necessary to accomplish a successful ethical turnaround. As a result, many efforts fail. Although achieving an ethical turnaround may seem to be an impossible task, many companies that fail do so needlessly.

For most organizational leaders, their inexperience in handling an ethical turnaround situation is the first problem. Organizational leaders and managers may incorrectly assume that business as usual can continue. In fact, drastic cultural, psychological, and behavioral changes within the company are invariably necessary. Some employees who have worked for the organization for many years will have to be fired (as evidenced in the case of Salomon Brothers), trusting relationships with customers that have been developed over the years will have to be rebuilt, and policies and procedures will need to be replaced. All too often, the people responsible for the past cannot bring themselves to make these types of sweeping changes. In cases where the ethical turnaround is entrusted to the older top management, employees, customers, suppliers, and legal interests may be dubious and suspicious of top management's actions and motives. This problem may be overcome, in time, if the organization can afford to wait that long. However, achieving an ethical turnaround in this way becomes a far more difficult and risky task.

Establishing a New Ethical Culture

A successful ethical turnaround often requires that new leadership be put in the hands of someone new, often someone without a history in the company. This person must have the freedom and ability to make changes. If he or she cannot act decisively and quickly, the company is probably doomed. The top leader may determine that some members of the existing company management (assuming they were not involved in any company wrongdoings) are ethically competent and adaptable to the changing circumstances. In some situations, some of these managers should be retained, as they provide continuity, insight, and knowledge.

Those who cannot provide help to the organization during the transition will have to be recognized and, if necessary, replaced. However, the new leadership should not adopt an attitude of change merely for change's sake; it is foolish and needlessly expensive to replace the entire management structure. Members of existing management who are retained should form a link between new management and the rest of the organization (the organization must still produce products or provide services during the turnaround period).

People are at the heart of a successful ethical turnaround. Employees of the organization must be committed to the ethical turnaround and feel personally involved in achieving it. A sense of urgency, cooperation, and participation must permeate the environment. Measures must be instituted to convert dispirited employees into believers, confident that the new leadership is committed to changing, that the company will survive, and that they will have a future as employees. The new ethical goals will be achieved through the actions of all employees, not just the few in upper management. Top management should not lose sight of this fact. In addition to motivating, training, and properly directing the activities of its current employees, management must ensure that new employees will be successfully oriented in the appropriate ethical behavior.

A successful ethical turnaround is not accomplished by reaching a consensus on what needs to be changed or which painful actions need to be taken; a major ethical change first requires the commitment and direction of top management. Although orders given by new leadership may contradict decades-long practices and ways of doing business, the process is necessary; it is futile to entrust the ethical turnaround to someone without the will or authority to impose radical change. An ethical turnaround needs a leader, not a caretaker. However, in this situation, a strong leader is not a dictator. Middle level managers must be able to assist in this process, not just carry out the leader's orders. In a situation as complex as an ethical turnaround, too many decisions must be made for one person to make them all and ensure that they are effectively carried out.

Reinforcing the New Ethical Culture

A culture is a system of shared beliefs and responses that conditions people how to behave in the organizational environment. The ethical culture of a company is defined by those things it rewards, and an employee's ethical behavior is dependent on both his or her values and the ethical climate within the organization. Both the content and the strength of an organization's culture have an influence on the ethical behavior of its managers and employees. Good people can be encouraged to do bad things when their organization's reward system positively reinforces wrong behaviors. When an organization praises, promotes, gives large pay increases, and offers other desirable rewards to employees who lie, cheat, and misrepresent, its employees learn that unethical behaviors pay off. In these situations, regardless of what management *says* is important, people in organizations pay attention to how actual rewards are handed out. Thus top management should establish new values and priorities and strive to create an organizational culture that permeates the new ethical environment.

However, top management may not realize that the old ethical culture will not instantly die. Because of the strength of the previous culture, it often lies submerged in the subconscious of employees and may quickly reappear if the new culture is not reinforced. The potential for returning to old behaviors is often high. In addition, "automatic responses" that reflect the old culture can be very detrimental. Like any change effort, the organization must use positive reinforcement and direct feedback to show employees what is expected in the new ethical culture. Employees need to be informed on why the change in attitude is necessary, and any regression to previous unethical behavior must be brought to everyone's attention and swiftly dealt with in the appropriate manner. Unlike any other organizational culture change, in which one can afford to take up to five years to replace the old culture, the new ethical culture must completely replace the unethical practices of the past in a very short period of time.

The key acceptance of change is effective communication. That involves intensive efforts to promote trust and ensure that management shares information honestly and on a timely basis with employees. Therefore, the new leadership must immediately set up an employee communications program that makes employees part of the effort to solve the organization's problems; people need information if they are to respond appropriately and be properly motivated to make the ethical turnaround successful.

The Importance of Open Communication

An ethical turnaround situation is a highly stressful environment for all concerned. All people fear the unknown, and the loss of their jobs is paramount, even when customers and the government have been affected by the unethical behavior (as was the case in the Salomon Brothers situation). Successful communications with employees can help reduce the level of personal stress. Employees should be kept informed on the status of the organization, how badly has or is the unethical behavior affecting the organization (for example, how bad are sales and losses), and what are employees expected to do. A sense of personal involvement and urgency will exist only if employees feel that they are part of the change team.

Communicating an explicit position on the importance of ethical behavior of employees and explaining the philosophy and values that are to guide the organization is a logical starting point for new leadership in turning around an unethical culture or creating an ethical culture. This can take the form of policy statements, speeches, and the like and can set the stage for more open discussion on ethical behavior and related questions.

Three suggestions adapted from Waters (1988) can be made about these communications. First, ambiguity about corporate priorities has to be eliminated. Somebody has to bite the bullet and say straightforwardly that the long-term vitality of the organization rests on the ethical integrity of its employees, that obeying the law and respecting the ethical standards of society come before and have a priority over immediate economic objectives, and that these priorities will be maintained even when the pressure is on for short-term sales and profits.

Second, these communications have to move from the "do good and avoid evil" level of abstraction to open discussion of concrete problems that would be obvious to anyone in the organization and in the industry. To avoid mentioning and taking a specific stand on the very problems with which employees in the organization are confronted not only misses an opportunity to deal with those problems but also introduces a note of ambiguity into the communication.

Third, these communications should not only point to the value of "good conversation" (an interchange of ideas where organizational members talk and listen and learn from one another) (Waters, 1988; Baker & Kolb, 1993) but also make demands that it take place routinely and regularly. In getting employees to do something, a place to start is to ask them to do it. In considering questions of ethical behavior, there is a perverse tendency to focus on the "bad guys" and ignore the "good guys." Good conversation creates the opportunity for discussions on examples of employees who exhibit ethical behavior in the organization, who, in most instances, far outnumber those who exhibit unethical behavior.

There are good reasons to believe that these communications of the new leadership's ideology are best viewed as necessary but not sufficient. First, there are problems of change and inertia. If an organization has not been operating with unambiguous corporate policies on ethical behavior and good conversation, it will take some concerted effort to break old patterns and establish new ones. Second, initial communications by the new leadership may be difficult for employees if they do not have some appreciation or understanding of the new ethical expectations, and the employees may be tentative at first.

New leadership must also recognize that they face a number of powerful constituencies who have much influence on key elements in the organizations and the success of an ethical turnaround initiative. Dealing successfully with these parties is a critical element in an ethical turnaround. Three or more groups can complicate the situation.

The first constituency is the board of directors or the parent company (in cases where a subsidiary is experiencing ethical problems). The board of directors must be convinced that the proper actions, programs, and reorganizations are being implemented and must be confident that the new management is competent and will be successful in the ethical transformation.

Lenders are the second constituency; they are most concerned with the financial resources available and such aspects as asset disposition and use of the proceeds. Unfortunately, lenders often demand leadership that is critically needed elsewhere.

Government is the third constituency. If a business is involved with the government, like Salomon Brothers was, this will be a key and very time-consuming constituency. The new leadership may have to convince government to hold back on taking legal proceedings against the organization, especially if such behavior would put the organization out of business. However, this is not a sufficient reason for government not to take legal actions against the guilty organization.

Major customers are another constituency. If customers cannot be convinced to stick with the organization during its ethical turnaround, all may be lost.

Last, major suppliers are an added constituency. They also must be reckoned with, because they must also protect their interests.

Regardless of the internal or external constituencies, the new leadership responsible for the ethical turnaround of an organization must continue to communicate a consistent message on the expected ethical standards. Although there will always be some degree of resistance to change or a period of doubt or uncertainty about the new ethical direction of the organization, the new leadership must commit to increased visibility and activity with respect to expected ethical standards. The next section offers a practical description of how Warren Buffett, as the new leader at Salomon Brothers, attempted to turn Salomon's culture around by emphasizing both institutional and individual processes.

BUFFETT'S EFFORTS TO TURN AROUND THE ETHICAL CULTURE AT SALOMON

When Warren Buffett had just become acting chief executive officer (CEO) of Salomon, he immediately began to carefully craft a new corporate culture. Like the actions of Gutfreund, the actions Buffett took are easily described according to Schein's mechanisms (which emphasize institutional as well as individual processes) introduced in Chapter 5. In each area, Buffett drastically altered the system that Gutfreund had in place. He placed a commitment to ethical standards as his top priority, and his first actions indicate this commitment.

Attention

Warren Buffett set out to quickly focus attention on the urgency and severity of Salomon's situation. With their fate in the hands of government regulators, the firm had to be prepared for an onslaught of bad publicity and, possibly, huge legal fines. Almost immediately, Buffett introduced changes in formerly accepted individual and institutional practices by eliminating many perks of Salomon employees — magazine subscriptions were canceled; cars, drivers, and secretaries were discharged; and long-distance phone services and health benefits were cut (Cohen, 1991). Signals were being sent that Salomon Brothers under Warren Buffett would be very different than it had been under Gutfreund's leadership. Thus, Buffett's initial actions demonstrated that it was important and necessary to focus employees on the fact that the culture they were working within was simply not a feasible way to continue to do business.

The new Salomon would be committed to upholding ethical principles and purging those who had a history or knowledge of unethical or illegal behavior. Buffett displayed his commitment to high ethical and legal standards by immediately issuing a memo to all Salomon senior executives declaring that they should report any but the smallest legal infractions to him directly. The full text of this memo is as follows (U.S. Securities and Exchange Commission, 1991):

Unless and until otherwise advised by me in writing, you are each expected to report, instantaneously and directly to me, any legal violation or moral failure on behalf of any employee of Salomon Inc. or any subsidiary or controlled affiliate. You are to make reporting directly to me your first priority. You should of course, report through normal chain of command when I am unavailable and, in other cases, immediately after reporting to me.

Exempted from the above are only minor legal and moral failures (such as parking tickets or nonmaterial expense account abuses by low-level employees) not involving significant breach of law by our firms or harm to third parties.

My private office telephone number in Omaha is (402) which reaches me both at the office and at home. My general office number in Omaha is (402) 346-1400. The Omaha office can almost always find me.

When in doubt, call me.

Warren E. Buffett
Chairman and Chief Executive Officer

As noted in the memo, Buffett demanded that the executives "report, instantaneously and directly to me, any legal violation or moral failure" of any Salomon employee. This was to be their "first priority," and he gave a listing of where he could be reached at any time. Buffett closed with, "When in doubt, call me." The memo should have left no doubt in the senior Salomon executives' minds that new procedures and policies were taking shape within the company.

Reactions to Crises

Buffett's tenure as interim chairman began in a crisis situation. The previous CEO had purposefully withheld information from the government regulators, and Salomon was temporarily barred from its bread-and-butter business of dealing in the U.S. Treasury auction. Buffett's reaction was swift. He began to set the tone for a new corporate culture, in preparation for a hearing before the regulators. During that hearing, Buffett's testimony and his preliminary damage control efforts were rewarded with Salomon being allowed to return to the Treasury securities market.

Briefly, it appeared that Buffett would remain friendly with Gutfreund. The night before he handed the Salomon board his resignation, John Gutfreund had dinner with Warren Buffett and Buffett's closest friend and advisor, Charles Munger, at a steakhouse in Manhattan. Gutfreund generously offered to stay on as a consultant for no charge, and Buffett replied that "I'm going to need all the help I can get" (Cohen, 1991). At the time of Gutfreund's resignation, Buffett publicly said the former chairman was someone "I like, admire and trust" (Cohen, 1991). In what appears to be his first significant step as chairman, however, Warren Buffett began to quickly separate himself and Salomon from Gutfreund and all aspects of the old regime. There is no evidence that Buffett received any additional information between the time he agreed to Gutfreund's offer for free advice and when he systematically cut off Gutfreund from the firm. It seems he believed that the future of Salomon depended on how quickly he could react and convince the regulators that the company was taking corrective measures (Cohen, 1991). On September 3, 1991, Buffett and Gutfreund agreed to never speak again. A few days after that, Buffett had Salomon's board sever all financial payments to Gutfreund and the others closely involved with the scandal (Cohen, 1991). Munger claims that when it came to Salomon's former CEO, they "had no option of forgiveness" (Cohen, 1991). John Gutfreund's association with Salomon was officially terminated, and Warren Buffett, a mythical figure in the investment community, was clearly the new man in charge. Employees could see that Gutfreund and those who followed him closely would no longer be employed by Salomon.

Role Modeling

If Salomon had searched for an upstanding and seemingly ethical investor, they could not have found a better role model than Warren Buffett. This billionaire was 61 years old when he took over the chairmanship of Salomon, Inc. Buffett had worked briefly on Wall Street in the early 1950s, after graduating from Columbia University's business school. In 1956, he returned to his hometown of Omaha, Nebraska, to begin an investment partnership (Suskind, 1991). Two years later, he bought a house for $31,500, and he still lives there today, despite his estimated fortune of $4.4 billion (*Fortune*, 1991). He has been married to the same woman for 39 years and claims, "With me, what you see is what you get" (Suskind, 1991). (He and his wife, however, have not lived together for 13 years, and Buffett lives with a companion, Astrid Menks.)

In 1969, the partnership he created was dissolved, and he made Berkshire Hathaway, a declining textile concern in which he had held a controlling interest for several years, his investment vehicle to purchase shares of other companies. Warren Buffett has been called this country's most successful investor. His close friend, CBS's Laurence Tisch, says, "There's no one in the business world who is sounder of mind than Warren. He represents the best of capitalism" (Suskind, 1991). The community of Omaha is somewhat awestruck by their home-grown billionaire, and a group of residents follows his professional and personal movements so closely that they call themselves "Buffologists." This group estimates that Buffett is responsible for approximately 200 "Buffett millionaires" in and around the city. Buffett usually sticks with a company's current management and invests for long-term, not just short-term, gains (Suskind, 1991). His philosophy is in stark contrast to that of Gutfreund and his "trader mentality" of going for short-term profit, no matter what the cost.

Susan and Warren Buffett share three children, who are all grown and will not stand to gain much should their father die. Buffett once said that inheritance "is a lifetime supply of food stamps" and will, accordingly, leave each child a mere $5 million. Munger speaks for Buffett in this way:

Peter [a son] wanted a bridge loan for his house. Warren turned him down. Howie [another son] wants this. Susie [the daughter] wants that. Warren is just as tough on his children as he is on his employees. He doesn't believe that if you love somebody that the way to do him good is to give him something he's not entitled to. And that's part of the Buffett personality. (Suskind, 1991)

Perhaps the most important thing that Warren Buffett brought to the Salomon table is his image. Although there are numerous examples of contradictions to this image, it is only important that government officials, Salomon's customers, and the investment community in general perceive him to be a paragon of U.S. heartland virtues — almost a mythical figure riding in from Omaha on his white horse to rescue the pitiful New York bankers from their ethical downfalls. Experts have stated that they believe that one of the main reasons Salomon will survive their prosecution is because of Buffett himself (Spiro, 1991). During the Capitol Hill hearings on Salomon's trading violations, Ohio Representative Dennis Eckart, referring to fictional financial villains, said, "Gordon Gekko and Sherman McCoy are alive and well on Wall Street. Mr. Buffett . . . get in there and kick some butt" (Suskind, 1991). Thus, there were those who saw Buffett as the "ideal" role model to get Salomon back on track.

Many claim this image has been carefully and consciously crafted. There is little information available about Buffett, who refuses most interview offers. The Berkshire Hathaway annual report reads like a press release about his activities for the year and serves as a vehicle to communicate his down-to-earth image. He appears as "Will Rogers with an MBA," discussing everything from his four-year-old granddaughter's birthday party to quotations attributed to Mae West (Suskind, 1991). He told shareholders at the 1991 Berkshire Hathaway annual meeting, "I tap-dance into work, and then I read and talk on the phone for seven or eight hours, and then I go home and read some more" (*Fortune*, 1991). At other meetings, Buffett has been known to wear an apron, pass out Coca-Colas (Berkshire Hathaway owns 7 percent of Coca-Cola, Inc.), sign autographs, and pose for pictures. When someone asked about his growing population of followers, he said, "They still treat me the same at the McDonald's in Omaha" (Suskind, 1991).

One aspect of this Buffett image — being a "penny pincher" — may be the most important one to regulators and others watching the Salomon recovery. Berkshire Hathaway's 22,000 employees are directed by only 11 people at its Omaha headquarters, which resembles a doctor's office more than the nucleus of a billion-dollar operation. Their offices are located in one corner of only one floor at the end of a hall that has "industrial carpet and plastic weave wall paper" (Suskind, 1991).

All of the evidence indicates that Warren Buffett, or at least the public image of Warren Buffett, is an exemplary ethical role model for Salomon employees to follow. It is drastically different from the image and the reality of John Gutfreund. In addition, Buffett does not share Gutfreund's hunger for personal cash flow. He is interested, instead, in maximizing long-term Salomon shareholder wealth.

Allocation of Rewards

Similarly, Buffett made jokes as Salomon's incoming chairman about his own salary. At his first press conference, he said, "I was thinking of making [my salary] $1 a year, but I could be negotiated with — downward" (Weiss, 1991). This is a sharp contrast from the millions made by John Gutfreund. In addition, Warren Buffett took the unusual step of taking out a two-page newspaper advertisement, which declared in part, "Employees producing mediocre returns for owners should expect their pay to reflect this shortfall. In the past that has neither been the expectation at Salomon nor the practice" (Siconolfi, 1991a). Thus began Buffett's "pay for performance" philosophy at Salomon. With Buffett, "performance" means return on equity for the stockholders, not each manager's divisional profits. In 1990, more than 106 employees earned more than 41 million in salary and bonuses, but Salomon, Inc., had a return on equity of 10 percent, which was deemed "mediocre" by Buffett. He promptly took back $110 million that had been earmarked for employee bonuses. Although employees certainly were upset with the change, investors were delighted, and the stock jumped 8.6 percent a share on the day of the announcement (Siconolfi, 1991a).

Interestingly, it appeared that Buffett was also taking steps to return to a employee-owned philosophy, which existed at the firm before Gutfreund sold out to Phibro — that is, he intended to force the bankers and traders at Salomon to take more of their pay in Salomon common stock that would not be redeemable for at least five years. This will help to reinstill a long-term focus to Salomon employees and increase their interest in its future. Although individual performance will still be recognized, special arrangements like ones that Gutfreund and certain key managers had made that paid huge bonuses to some traders will be gone. Buffett vows that top performers will, however, "receive first class compensation" (Siconolfi, 1991a). The long-term focus is key to encouraging employees to consider *all* ramifications of their actions, not just what these actions will mean to their department's profits this quarter.

Criteria for Selection and Dismissal

To further distance Salomon from the old way of life, Buffett made efforts to ensure that anyone who was even remotely connected with the scandal was no longer employed by the company. Carroll (1978) has suggested that disciplining violators of ethical standards is a positive management action to improve ethical behavior of employees. Salomon's former top legal advisor, Donald M. Feuerstine, knew of trading violations in April and had persistently advised senior officials to report them to the proper authorities. He was fired anyway and replaced by Robert E. Denham, who has been one of Buffett's lawyers for 17 years. Denham set his personal goal to "make sure Salomon operates according to the highest of ethical principles" (Galen, 1991). Creating an ethical advocate's role is another suggestion made by Carroll (1978) to improve a firm's ethics, and it appears that Denham will serve such a role at Salomon.

Not surprisingly signals of a new emphasis away from stocks and the traders toward bonds, as well as a change in culture, have led to many defections in the firm. Such a drastic shift in strategic course necessitates similarly drastic changes in personnel. More conservative, less brash bond employees will be the new rulers at Salomon; the traders' role in upper management will be limited. In November 1991, Buffett created a nine-man executive committee, primarily composed of bond executives, to replace Gutfreund's office of the chairman and board of directors. The former office of the chairman had seven vice chairmen as members, and four of them were already gone by this time (Siconolfi, 1991b). Traders no longer rule at Salomon; for example, the former head of stock trading, Stanley Shopkorn, was excluded from the committee and subsequently left the firm. Shopkorn had a history of "questionable" ethical behavior. His department had caused the firm to be fined $1.3 million on charges that it cheated customers during the crash of October 1987. He kept a handful of blackjack cards encased in Lucite to remind visitors of his skill at gambling with Salomon's money (Smith, 1991). Shopkorn's exodus signals to others that the new Salomon will be a more cautious and leaner organization committed to ethical principles.

Firings and resignations have extended past senior employees closely connected to the old regime. Approximately 15 percent of Salomon's senior investment analysts as well as many stock traders and analysts, have been fired (Siconolfi, 1991c). Buffett has been criticized for firing so many people so quickly. Alan Bromberg, a securities law professor at Southern Methodist University, claimed, "This whole thing may have been an overreaction . . . sacking and condemning highly talented peo-ple for the sake of crisis containment. . . . [Buffett] may have done more damage to Salomon's morale and its ability to conduct its business than it was worth" (Cohen, 1991). Bromberg's comments would be on target in most organizations but ignore the fact that Salomon's unique culture seems to have created an atmosphere ripe for the unethical and illegal behavior that occurred. Firing Gutfreund was not enough to change the fabric of the company. Cultural change or an ethical turnaorund for a company is a long and complicated process that cannot happen overnight or by simply firing an unethical CEO. Gutfreund had been at Salomon his entire working career and had made his impact on every part of the organization. He had surrounded himself with people who shared his ethical principles, and the same people cannot abide by Buffett's new rules. Munger argued, "When the final chapter is written, the behavior evinced by Salomon will be followed in other, similar cases. People will be smart enough to realize this is the response we want — superprompt — even if it means cashiering some people who may not deserve it" (Cohen, 1991). By bringing in Denham as an ethi-cal champion and by dismissing those Salomon employees most like Gutfreund, Warren Buffett began to pave the way for a new culture. Although it is too soon to tell if this new culture will maintain its current commitment to ethics, by clearing out the vestiges of the previous one, Buffett is taking the first step.

Buffett's Efforts To Turn Around Salomon's Culture

Through Buffett's efforts, Salomon was able to survive both the neg-ative publicity and the federal penalty. In a sense, one could say that the government needed access to Salomon's massive capital base and was also willing to put its faith in Warren Buffett and the new management philosophy. John Gutfreund's culture was so deeply ingrained in the fiber of Salomon, Inc., however, that simply removing him and other top managers was not enough. Further steps were taken to kill the culture and return the firm's ethical credibility. Warren Buffett was ready to accept this challenge and took many of the necessary steps (through Schein's [1985] mechanisms by which a leader can influence a corporate culture) to ethically turn around Salomon's culture:

Attention — He began to focus attention on improving the moral fiber of the firm.

Reactions to Crises — He swiftly reacted to crises facing the company by complying with authorities and firing ethical wrongdoers.

Role Modeling — He conveyed the image of one of the country's most ethical investors.

Allocation of Rewards — He allocated rewards according to employee's performance, and it remains to be seen how he will promote employees.

Criteria for Selection and Dismissal — He brought in employees who proclaim their commitment to ethical principles and ushered out all old employees connected to ethical misconduct.

Although dramatic change is necessary, Salomon, like any organization trying to change its culture through an ethical turnaround, will go through a difficult readjustment period. Buffett had to realize that once he had removed all of the employees who were thriving in the old culture, the remaining employees needed to be assured that their positions were safe. Stabilization had to be an important next step for Buffett.

Avoiding Future Ethical Fiascoes at Salomon Brothers

We've never been able to figure out how to reliably prevent the cyclical decline of great civilizations, religions, armies, or corporations. But if we cannot bring ourselves to believe that man and his organizations are perfectible, at least we must believe that we can improve our own areas of responsibility according to some set of ethical standards. To do otherwise is to abdicate to the natural entropy of power. (Kelly, 1987)

Following the guidelines to determine if a firm is at ethical risk suggested by Cooke (1991) can be an effective first step by an organization interested in countering unethical behavior. Cooke warns of organizational ethics becoming trivialized, because it is such a "hot" topic. By recognizing his warning signs early, an unethical experience, such as that of the Salomon Brothers, may be avoided. Several of the danger signs were exhibited by the culture created by John Gutfreund, including short-term revenue emphasis, arbitrary performance-appraisal standards, an internal environment discouraging ethical behavior, and ethical problems being sent to the legal department. Unfortunately, at least one danger sign — primary concern for shareholders' wealth — appeared in Buffett's new culture. Once any or all of these signs have been recognized, it is imperative that a firm take corrective measures. Although Warren Buffett took several necessary steps through his leadership (establishment of a code of ethics, discipline of violators, and creation of an ethical advocate's role), it is also important that leaders committed to ethical turnarounds create a long-term strategic and ethical plan. The plan should emphasize a whistleblowing mechanism and, most importantly, a training program in business ethics to ensure that there is little ambiguity when employees face ethical and legal dilemmas in the future. In a sense, what is needed at companies like Salomon Brothers is to ensure that ethics becomes paramount in the organization.

The Salomon example is particularly difficult because so drastic a change was needed to retain the firm's viability — planned change was not an option. Some of Kanter's (1985) suggestions, such as minimizing surprises, demonstrating top management's commitment to change, offering positive rewards for new competence, and creating excitement about the future, can be particularly helpful to Buffett and other leaders responsible for ethical turnarounds in their organizations.

No matter who the leader, they must work to eliminate any inherent abstractness or the conflicting nature of the organization's ethical standards if they are going to be successful at an ethical turnaorund. An understanding of the organization's culture (and subcultures) is a must first step for the new leader that should quickly be followed by proactive steps to communicate an explicit position on the importance of ethical behavior that will guide the future organization.

Kanter (1985) has made many suggestions about how to address the human side of change, which are applicable to an ethical turnaround:

Allow room for participation in the planning of change.

Leave choices within the overall decision to change.

Provide a clear picture of the change, a "vision" with details about the new state.

Share information about change plans to the fullest extent.

Divide a big change into more manageable and familiar steps; let people take a small step first.

Minimize surprises; give people advance warning about new requirements.

Allow for digestion of change requests — a chance to become accustomed to the idea of change before making a commitment.

Repeatedly demonstrate your own commitment to the change.

Make standards and requirements clear — tell exactly what is expected of people in the change.

Offer positive reinforcement for competence; let people know they can do it.

Look for and reward pioneers, innovators, and early successes to serve as models.

Help people find or feel compensated for the extra time and energy change requires.

Avoid creating obvious "losers" from the change. (But if there are some, be honest with them — early on.)

Allow expressions of nostalgia and grief for the past — then create excitement about the future.

REFERENCES

Anthony, P. 1990. The paradox of the management culture, or "He who leads is lost?" *Personnel Review 19*(4): 33–45.

Baker, A., & Kolb, D. 1993. Diversity, learning, and good conversation. In *Diversity and differences in organizations: An agenda for answers and questions*, ed. R. R. Sims and R. F. Dennehy. Westport, CT: Quorum Books, pp. 17–32.

Bridges, W. 1986. Managing organizational transitions. *Organizational Dynamics 15*(1): 24–33.

Carroll, A. B. 1978. Linking business ethics to behavior in organizations. *Advanced Management Journal 43*(3): 4–11.

Cohen, L. P. 1991, November 8. Buffett shows tough side to Salomon — and Gutfreund. *Wall Street Journal*, p. A6.

Cooke, R. A. 1991. Danger signs of unethical behavior: How to determine if your firm is at ethical risk. *Journal of Business Ethics 10*, 249–53.

Galen, M. 1991, September 9. The lawyer who'll ride herd on Salomon's cowboys. *Business Week*, p. 65.

Greenberg, J., & Baron, R. A. 1993. *Behavior in organizations*. Needham Heights, MA: Allyn and Bacon.

Kanter, R. M. 1985, April. Managing the human side of change. *Management Review*, pp. 52–56.

Kelly, C. M. 1987, Summer. The interrelationship of ethics and power in today's organizations. *Organizational Dynamics*, pp. 5–18.

Schein, E. 1985. *Organizational culture and leadership*. San Francisco, CA: Jossey-Bass.

_____. 1983, Summer. The role of the founder in creating organizational culture. *Organizational Dynamics*, pp. 13–28.

Siconolfi, M. 1991a, October 30. Salomon's Buffett moves to slash sky-high paychecks. *Wall Street Journal*, p. C1.

_____. 1991b, November 7. Salomon's executive panel tilts to bond sector. *Wall Street Journal*, p. C1.

_____. 1991c, November 14. Salomon's banking division to see staff cuts. *Wall Street Journal*, p. C23.

Smith, R. 1991, November 7. Buffett's rebuffs, change of culture said to have led Shopkorn to resign. *Wall Street Journal*, p. C1.

Spiro, L. N. 1991, October 7. How bad will it get? *Business Week*, pp. 122–23.

Suskind, R. 1991, November 8. Warren Buffett's aura as folksy sage masks tough, polished man. *Wall Street Journal*, p. A1.

The billionaires: More than ever in 1991. 1991, September 9. *Fortune*, p. 62.

U.S. Securities and Exchange Commission. 1991, September 4. From the testimony of Richard S. Breeden, SEC Chairman. Washington, DC: U.S. Securities and Exchange Commission.

Van Maanen, J., & Barley, S. 1984. Occupational communities: Culture control in organizations. In *Research in Organizational Behavior 6*, pp. 287–365.

Waters, J. 1988. Integrity management: Learning and implementing ethical principles in the workplace. In *Executive integrity: The search for human value in organizational life*, ed. S. Srivastva. San Francisco, CA: Jossey-Bass, pp. 172–96.

Weiss, G. 1991, August 26. The Salomon shocker: How bad will it get? *Business Week*, pp. 54–57.

Weiss, G. 1991, September 2. Clearing the wreckage. *Business Week*, pp. 66–70.

8

Ethics Training in Organizations: Can We Teach People to Become Ethical?

Organizations like E. F. Hutton, Salomon Brothers, and others assumed that the ethical side of business would take care of itself. Other companies, like Heinz, further assumed that signed statements annually from senior executives would forestall unethical behavior. In the case of each organization, the assumptions proved to be wrong.

Similar unwarranted assumptions afflicted Drexel Burnham Lambert. It was never clear how much chief executive officer Fred Joseph knew about Michael Milken's activities. The outcome indicates that he was ethically naive. There are no media accounts that suggest that Joseph tried to set the ethical tone in his organization (Henderson, 1992).

Fred Joseph accepted an invitation from Dean Lester Thurow of the Massachusetts Institute of Technology's Sloan School of Management to sit in on an ethics panel convened at that institution in 1988. The scandal that virtually destroyed the company was still embryonic. At this little-publicized event, Fred Joseph supported training in ethics, on the one hand, but fell victim to a questionable assumption, on the other. He spoke candidly about the investment banking business: "There are opportunities every day to act unethically many times. I favor special training in ethics for investment bankers along with tough, clear standards" (Henderson, 1992, p. 193). These words did not carry the ring of deep conviction. Joseph pointed out that Dennis Levine and Martin Seigel, both convicted of insider trading while employed by Drexel Burnham Lambert, were not trained by Drexel Burnham Lambert. Joseph did not describe any ethics seminars or workshops as an integral part of the training at Drexel Burnham Lambert. He replied during the panel discussion, instead, that "people will be ethical if you expect it of them" (Henderson, 1992, p. 193). He did not say how top management communicates that expectation. Was he a victim of an unwarranted assumption? Clearly. He is not alone. Many of today's business leaders share the assumption that ethics is something you should not have to talk about. You suspect that some are too embarrassed to talk about ethics. They prefer to just expect people to behave properly. Unfortunately, Fred Joseph's star pupil, Michael Milken, completely shattered his assumption, his company, his professional life. The training in investment banking was obviously sufficient. The training in the ethics of investment banking was obviously *not* sufficient. Failure to be aware of unwarranted assumptions leaves too much room for unethical behavior to occur in an organization. Training offers one way of helping an organization ensure that appropriate ethics are learned and practiced on the job. That is the focus of this chapter.

It is the thesis of this chapter that ethics can be learned and that effective ethics training can occur if there is agreement about the goals or objectives of ethics training in an organization, ethics training is perceived as relevant by employees, a debriefing (processing) phase is included as part of ethics training, and if the design and implementation of ethics training is renewed by a well designed and implemented outcomes assessment process.

CAN ETHICS BE LEARNED?

Ethics training has been identified as an important component in countering unethical behavior in organizations. As a result, there has been a sharp increase in the number of organizations that have developed some form of ethics training in the United States and abroad (Sims & Sims, 1993). Training in ethics now occurs in both academic and business settings. For example, nearly 50 percent of all business schools offer courses on social responsibility and business ethics (Weber, 1990). Although the content of these courses varies greatly, the best programs seem to focus on ethical awareness (that is, increasing sensitivity to ethical dilemmas at work) and ethical reasoning (that is, learning strategies for solving ethical dilemmas). Harrington (1991) notes that 30 percent to 45 percent of the companies she surveyed have in-house ethics training. As in academic settings, the content varies considerably, but this training often involves statements from the CEO emphasizing ethical business practices, discussions of the corporate code of ethics, and descriptions of procedures for dealing with or reporting unethical behavior (Murphy, 1993). Approximately 80 percent of the largest corporations have formal ethics programs, and 44 percent of these firms provide ethics training. Forty-five of the 46 largest U.S. defense contractors report that they conduct employee ethics training programs (Geary & Sims, in press).

What proponents of ethics training expect to achieve with these programs differs, depending on the organization and the training effort. Ethics trainers include among their goals stimulating moral thought recognizing ethical dilemmas, creating a sense of moral obligation, developing problem-solving skills, and tolerating or reducing ambiguity. There is also a lack of agreement on the objectives of ethics training. Such training efforts have been and continue to be problematic, particularly because there are conflicting views on whether or not ethics can be taught and conflicting expectations about whether and how the teaching of ethics should lead to more ethical behavior. Thus, many ask whether we can teach people ethics. A more pointed question is whether ethics can be learned. Although the answer should be obvious, there are still those who doubt it, and people are clearly divided on answering the question of whether or not ethics can be taught.

Critics argue that ethics are based on values, and value systems are fixed at an early age. By the time people start working in most organizations, their ethical values are already established. It is not unusual to hear critics make the following argument:

In my opinion, we should not, and perhaps could not even if we wished, teach moral standards of behavior, as such — the goals, norms, beliefs, and values held by a person. These are personal and reflect the teachings and experiences of a lifetime. I think this is what some people have in mind when they say, as I'm sure you've heard, that you can't teach people ethics They tell you that a person's ethics is something learned at home, in church, and in school, pretty well established in a person's early years. Trying to inculcate these by lecture would be a waste of time — and wrong, since it would amount to little more than indoctrination. (Hall, 1993, p. 160)

The critics also claim that ethics cannot be formally taught but must be learned by example. Leaders set ethical examples by what they say and do. If this is true, the ethics training is relevant only as part of leadership training.

It is also not unusual for supporters of ethic training to take the stance that

A course on ethical analysis would probably not have changed the value rankings or the moral standards of Ivan Boesky, Dennis Levine, or Timothy Tabor (though ethicists are always filled with hope), but it would have reinforced the value rankings and moral standards of their associates and peers. Those people would have felt more confidence in their own norms, beliefs, and standards, and would have been more willing to take actions based upon those norms, beliefs, and standards. (Hosmer, 1987, p. 14)

The supporters of ethics training argue that values *can* be learned and changed after early childhood. Even if they could not, ethics training would be effective because it gets employees to think about ethical dilemmas and become more aware of the ethical issues underlying their actions.

In reality, if we can learn bad ethics without trying, we can learn good ethics with training and a little personal effort. As noted in previous discussions in this book, ethical or unethical behavior is a direct result of the culture that develops in an organization. Like culture, ethics is also invented, discovered, and developed in response to particular situations. If unethical behavior is learned, it can be unlearned.

Despite the many advocates for and discussions on providing opportunities for employees to learn about ethical applications, it is the contention of this chapter that organizations should give more attention to ethics training in their efforts to develop ethically oriented employees. An important starting point in ethics training is to come to agreement on the objectives of ethics training.

AGREEMENT ON ETHICS TRAINING OBJECTIVES

People are more often nonethical than unethical, that is, they lack ethical standards and values (Tracey, 1990). If one accepts the premise that nonethical or unethical people can learn to behave ethically, then training can be a valuable tool for enhancing such learning. It is our premise that people are not born with values and standards. They are learned (or not learned) at home, in church, synagogue, or mosque, at school, and in the workplace. Inappropriate standards can be replaced with their own values. Voids in standards can be filled. As noted earlier, more and more organizations are now conducting their own ethics workshops and seminars for employees, sending them to public seminars, or contracting with ethics training specialists for tailored courses.

Agreement about ethics training goals is not an easy task. The disagreement about ends is reflected in the remarkable diversity of ethics training efforts. However, with this in mind, it is critical that management does not overlook the need to build consensus regarding the goals of ethics training in their organization. These goals should reflect the values of the organization.

This process is similar to the development of a mission statement. The ethics training mission often focuses on awareness training, discernment, analysis, judgment, and reflection. In developing agreement among members of an organization, one could start with the following six goals for ethics training adapted from Callahan (1980, pp. 64–74): relate the training to moral issues, recognize situations and issues in the organization that have ethical implications, develop a sense of moral obligation or responsibility, develop the abilities needed to deal with ethical conflicts or dilemmas, learn to deal with the uncertainties of the workplace, and set the stage for a change in ethical behavior.

If the goal or objective of ethics training is ethical awareness, then the initial effort to increase ethical awareness should occur at the orientation session for new employees. A discussion of the mission, leadership vision, and values will facilitate an understanding of ethics guidelines in employee behavior and decision making. When the organizational leadership successfully identifies the goals and values of the organization and adheres closely to those goals through effective communication and control, it is easier for employees to recognize ethical difficulties and to bring problems into the open.

Basic information on the ethical practice of the organization is critical in helping new employees begin their work experience in the organization with the understanding and confidence that will support their making ethical decisions. The following are areas to be addressed in new employee orientation and training:

a clear and concise statement by the CEO on expectations concerning the ethical behavior of all employees;

the formal codes of ethics, policies, rules, and procedures within which they must operate and the penalties for not observing them;

the organization's management philosophy — mission and values — and rules, how the rules are enforced, what safeguards exist against groundless accusations or unfairness, how disciplinary codes are enforced, and what are the appeals procedures;

what constitutes ethical practice in the organization, what are the dilemmas most commonly faced by employees at different levels of the organization (conflict of interest, outside employment, gifts and favors, information that may or may not be disclosed, whistleblowing, and so forth), and the resources that are available to discuss and receive advice about potential ethical dilemmas or clarification about the above areas.

In addition to a common understanding of the goals of ethics training, the organization must also develop a plan to make their goals operational. One suggestion is that the organization develop a strategic plan for its ethics training efforts as part of its overall institutionalization of ethics process.

THE CHALLENGE OF RELEVANCE

The challenge of relevance is to achieve a direct connection between personal choices and real problems and issues. Ethics training should provide both a theoretical and a experiential framework that employees can apply in evaluating a situation and choosing between conflicting moral demands. In such a program or course, the analysis relies on human reason to raise important questions of morality and to provide logically defensible responses.

For employees to derive the most from ethics training, organizations must insure that their efforts reflect those issues that their employees need to realistically understand, that is, ethics training must be geared to the more immediate and personal issues that employees are likely to encounter throughout their careers. To accomplish this goal, ethics training must avoid the tendency to use training approaches that reflect a strong bent toward dilemmas that have no direct relevance to the roles that employees will occupy in organizations. For example, not all or even most employees will be top managers, yet, in our experience, too many ethics training efforts reflect a strong bent toward dilemmas encountered by top managers.

Relevant ethics training should provide a process for resolving ethical issues, one that can be demonstrated using case studies and experiential learning. Employees can receive training in using the following steps when dealing with ethical problems:

Define the problem, considering the organization's expressed values and guidelines. What are the facts involved? Are your values in conflict with the policies of the organization? With other individuals with whom you must work? With those of the groups or individuals who are most affected by the decision?

Determine whether it is an ethical problem or a straightforward management decision.

Define the desired outcome for the entire situation where ethical issues have been identified. Who will be affected by the decision? Who else needs to be involved in determining a course of action?

Identify those elements of the problem that are ethical concerns.

Identify difficult obstacles to resolving the ethical issues, and determine how to overcome them.

Develop alternative solutions to the problem, and determine their acceptability from legal, moral, and sound business practice perspectives. Does the solution support the organization's mission and values and the image it wishes to have with key stakeholders (for example, employees, customers, suppliers)?

Select the best solution that can be implemented at reasonable cost, both short- and long-term, with a minimum of disruption and with a high probability of success.

Resolve the ethical issue.

In summary, the challenge of relevancy can be expressed in terms of the following operational objectives: create and foster awareness of the ethical components of the organization; legitimize the consideration of ethical components as an integral part of organizational decision making; provide a conceptual framework for analyzing the ethical components of decision making and making choices; and help employees apply ethical analysis to the very real and practical, day-to-day organizational activities.

METHODS OF ETHICS TRAINING

The most common method of ethical training is a stand-alone course in a business school. However, there has been a growing trend toward educational curricula that integrate ethics into many or most facets of the academic training curriculum. Also, an increasing number of institutes and research centers are now devoted to the study and advancement of business ethics. Training programs usually include exposure to ethical theories (often Kohlberg's theory), together with practice in applying the principles to typical business situations.

Although questions have been raised about the role of such ethics training approaches, in our view, there have been both strengths and weaknesses of past efforts focused on ethics training. It is a strength that employees are typically expected to be aware of professional ethics and to gain factual mastery of the rules of their organization's ethical codes. However, many ethical problems do not have specific "correct" solutions like those problems encountered in some ethics training programs. Furthermore, an emphasis on factual rules important to success can create an expectation that is especially unwelcoming to the unstructured and ill-defined ethical problems that employees will face. Thus, the problem is twofold: the emphasis on learning facts to produce correct solutions to specific situations and problems is too narrow a focus, and the training approaches customarily applied to analyze ethical issues are not the right approach when the objective is to develop the ability to make independent ethical judgments or decisions.

To overcome these two problems, employees need to have an experiential awareness of the types of ethical dilemmas they will face, and they need to be able to evaluate and identify possible courses of action when confronted by ethical dilemmas. Role playing, for example, provides employees with the opportunity to participate with a high level of personal involvement. Or, rather than memorize an existing organizational code, employees could be asked to help develop and critique a code of ethics for their organization. Similarly, ethical cases and dilemmas can provide another training vehicle to actively engage employees in analyzing ethical problems and identifying creative resolutions. Providing employees with problems involving improper gifts, kickbacks, and conflict of interest will develop their ability to analyze unstructured ethical dilemmas and discern alternative courses of action. These training approaches all emphasize high participation and active, rather than passive, learning.

Cases involving ethical issues relevant to their particular organization and industry often provide the opportunity for employees to work in groups. The added benefit of group work means that a single assignment will contribute to analytical development, ethical awareness, and team interaction. In selecting an appropriate problem for discussion, it is critical that the problem present a true dilemma, that is, there must be adverse consequences associated with all the choices. For example, the ethical case may be a single parent with two dependent children who is asked by the department head to commit an inappropriate act (covering an unapproved purchase) where refusing to comply with the request has negative ramifications for the employee (such as being fired). Each group could be asked to analyze and resolve the ethical dilemma and develop a response that is then presented to the rest of the class. During discussion of each group's recommendations, employees can also elect to use role playing (one employee is the department head, another is the employee).

Another training approach that can be highly effective is to schedule discussions that are focused on current organizational problems or dilemmas with ethical ramifications. Discussion can focus on how these problems could have been avoided. It is equally valuable to ask employees to examine how their organization's ethical code would suggest they address the problem or dilemma.

Ethics training that extends beyond the rote mastery of facts of a corporate code of ethics should strive to be an intensive, interactive experience in which participants are asked to identify with a problem and take a stand. These experiences offer tremendous potential for employee development and growth. However, there is also the potential for confusion, misunderstanding, and alienation. To manage the potential for adverse consequences, it is critical that experiential exercises be carefully designed, safely and thoughtfully executed, and carefully debriefed.

DEBRIEFING THE ETHICS TRAINING EXPERIENCE

Debriefing refers to the post-experience analysis designed to provide insight into the cases, journalizing, role plays, or other experiential learning approaches used in ethics training. In our view the debriefing phase should be an active experience that is involving and interesting, even exciting. Thus, debriefing is the cessation of this experience and the deliberate decision to reflect on the actual action of the experience.

In the debriefing phase of ethics training, employees are challenged to make sense of what has been taught or experienced, to operate on experience by organizing reflections, to emphasize some elements and not others, and to relate the ethical experience encountered in the training program to other events or ideas. Thus, debriefing is used to facilitate positive cognitive, behavioral, and affective change and learning. As a result, debriefing is the part of the process in which the reflection takes place and from which the change in the persons will occur, because it is the part of the activity that focuses on the complex processes that took place in each individual and in the group as a whole.

The debriefing phase can be conceptualized as a dialogue or conversation between the trainer/facilitator (debriefer) and the program participants. The debriefing phase can provide the opportunity to address questions such as: What is the difference between ethical and unethical behavior? What causes unethical behavior? How can unethical behavior be countered? How can ethics be institutionalized in organizations?

What is the responsibility of the employee in the area of ethics? Is there a difference between legal authority and moral authority?

In structuring the debriefing phase it is important to establish a structure that will provide a framework to contain the discussion. The model developed by Pagano (1987) can be very useful for this purpose. This model consists of six clear questions to ask. Pagano suggests that using the six test (or questions) can provide useful insights into the ethics of a particular action.

1. Is it legal? — this is a core starting point.

2. The benefit-cost test — the utilitarian perspective of the greatest good for the greatest number.

3. The categorical imperative — do you want this action to be a universal standard? If it's good for the goose, it's good for the gander.

4. The light of day test — what if it appeared on TV? Would you be proud?

5. Do unto others (golden rule) — do you want the same to happen to you?

6. Ventilation test — get a second opinion from a wise friend with no investment in the outcome.

During the debriefing phase, employees will often express deeply held views. Thus, the trainer or facilitator must challenge the program participants to create a climate that is conducive to trust and open to spontaneous communication. Conditions that suggest an ideal environment for the debriefing phase in ethics training are human involvement from a felt need to communicate; an atmosphere of openness, freedom, and responsibility; dealing with the *real* issues and ideas relevant to the communicator; appreciation of individual differences and uniqueness; acceptance of disagreement and conflict with the desire to resolve them; effective feedback and use of feedback; mutual respect and, hopefully, trust; sincerity and honesty in attitudes toward communication on ethical issues in organizations; a positive attitude for understanding and learning about ethics in organizations' public administration in general; and a willingness to admit error and allow persuasion. Conscious awareness of the ideal environment will contribute to the success of the debriefing phase. Such awareness may also help to explain why the intended experiential learning objectives were not achieved.

Managing the debriefing phase can be especially challenging to ethics trainers whose preferred training methodology is more closely aligned with the traditional methods of lecture and structured question and answer exchanges. When organizational trainers are asked to experiment with a new, and perhaps unknown, training method, it is important that they believe that the goal is appropriate and that they be given the necessary support to develop new skills. Facilitation skills workshops sponsored within the organization and through professional associations provide an excellent vehicle for bringing trainers (and others) who have well-developed debriefing skills together with colleagues who are just beginning to experiment with experiential learning and debriefing. Also, trainers should be encouraged to work in teams to contain both the knowledge of the organizational environment and the facilitating skills needed to debrief a controversial ethical issue.

In summary, the debriefing phase of experiential ethics training is a critical component of the educational process. This phase provides the reflection and introspection necessary to process the experiences and complete the learning. Managing the debriefing phase requires a structured process and conscious awareness of the risks and problems associated with an open discussion of controversial ethical dilemmas. If ethics education in organizations is to move beyond the mastery of factual material into the arena of ethical dilemmas, organizational leaders and trainers must recognize the importance of debriefing and either acquire the necessary experience or form teams with others who have the ability to provide leadership during the debriefing phase.

EVALUATING ETHICS TRAINING: OUTCOMES ASSESSMENT

In spite of many organizations' emphasis and concern for accountability, one area of ethics training that has not been adequately discussed is the issue of evaluating outcomes, especially behaviorally specific outcomes. After an employee has received ethics training, how will trainers and the organization know that the employee has learned and will behave according to the organization's ethical standards? The question of whether or not ethics training works depends in part on the criteria and the methods used to evaluate such training. In our opinion, outcomes assessment in ethics training should not be equated with measuring performance on examinations. Yet, if the trainer has presented a highly structured unit on the organization's code of ethics, a pencil and paper test may well be an appropriate choice to assess how well the learning objectives have been met. If, however, the learning objective is to develop the ability to make well-informed ethical judgments, assessment is more complex than simply measuring the ability to master a body of factual knowledge.

In our view, ethics training programs should be evaluated against four distinct criteria developed by Kilpatrick (1977): reactions, learning, behavior, and results. First, it is useful to examine individuals' reactions to the content and delivery of the ethics training. If individuals see the training as irrelevant or contrary to the norms of the organization, it is unlikely that the training will change their behavior. Second, individuals' learning might be tested. If individuals never learn or retain critical information in the ethics training program, they will not be able to apply it. Third, you might look for changes in behavior; it seems logical to attempt to measure this behavior and compare behavior designs employed in these comparisons. Finally, you might examine the results of training. It is possible that the training can be successful in teaching ethical principles and in changing the behavior of the individuals who receive training but that the results of those changes might not be relevant, worthwhile, or quite what the organization expected. For example, an organization plagued by extensive expense padding by managers might put all its managers through ethical training. If the training is successful in changing the behavior of 90 percent of all mangers but leaves the 10 percent who were doing most of the padding untouched, the results might be disappointing. If the other 90 percent are now more willing to question the status quo, blow the whistle, or put ethical issues before any considerations of profit, the net results of this "successful" training program might not look so good to the organization after all.

In our view, the goal of evaluating ethics training or, simply, "outcomes assessment" is to produce reliable data that can be used to aid in the evaluation of efficiency and effectiveness. Outcomes assessment data provide feedback on what has gone before and suggest what should come next.

To adequately assess experiential ethics training in an organization, the assessment model must emphasize process rather than outcomes. Assessment is conceptually well-specified by the four dimensions of reactions, learning, behavior, and results. However, the actual implementation of the assessment effort must be guided by an action-based model that is designed to assess processes rather than specific outcomes. One model especially well-suited to this task is the life cycle approach based on the work of Sims (1989). The five life cycle stages are: entrepreneurial, collectivity, formalization, elaboration, and renewal or decline. Each phase of the life cycle suggests how the ethics training program can be improved and where there are weaknesses in the process.

The five stages of the life cycle prompt questions. What are the purposes or incentives for outcomes assessment of ethics training? Is there consensus about the goals to be achieved and the means to be employed? What type of outcomes assessment data will be collected as part of the evaluation effort? How will outcomes assessment findings be disseminated? Where will we go from here?

The entrepreneurial stage of the life cycle model is primarily concerned with identifying the goals and the means. Key components of this stage are identifying needs and intended uses for outcomes assessment results, identifying key audiences and obtaining their support, shifting modes of thinking from input measures to output measures, reexamining the mission and goals/objectives of ethics training, and developing a general mission for the outcomes assessment effort. This stage also includes the identification of one individual or group who is responsible for managing the assessment.

The collectivity stage focuses more closely on the execution of the assessment effort. Who initiated the effort? Who is interested in the results? What will be assessed? How will the assessment be carried out? Cooperation and support so essential to a successful assessment effort are jeopardized if interested and affected parties are not included in the assessment process.

The formalization stage is essential to the development of formal assessment procedures, such as setting the time schedule for the outcomes assessment effort, selection of appropriate assessment instruments, and collection and analysis of data. If the results are to be persuasive, it is important to have agreement and discussion when these design decisions are made.

The elaboration stage stresses the dissemination and incorporation of assessment results into the decision-making process in the ethics training program. This stage is critical to establishing the link between outcomes assessment of ethics training data as a reflection of program (and particular module) quality. It is important at this stage to make sure that all recipients of the data have the knowledge required to successfully interpret the results.

The renewal or decline stage is highly dependent on the use and evaluation of the outcomes assessment results in the elaboration stage. Renewal or decline depends on if and how the feedback is used. Renewal typically is accompanied by a redesigning and streamlining of the ethics training efforts. Decline suggests that experiential ethics training will probably disappear and that external demands for ethics training may be perfunctorily satisfied with rule based drills on topics such as mastering the organization's code of ethics.

As noted earlier, it is important to determine what is the expected impact of teaching ethics, incorporating a longitudinal dimension in assessment designs (pre- and post-course analyses), and going beyond rather simplistic measurement of ethical awareness and reasoning by utilizing Likert scale and a comparison of frequencies and means to using various ethical frameworks (for example, Kohlberg's standard Issue Scoring method [see Colby & Kohlberg, 1987]).

Those responsible for planning outcomes assessment of ethics training should address the following questions to ensure evaluation of program outcomes:

Does the evaluation design fit the objectives of the outcomes assessment effort?

Does the design address important issues such as employee, trainer, and organization needs and expectations and organizational culture (for example, expectations about authority, how hard to work)?

Does the evaluation method meet standards discussed by the developers of the outcomes assessment program?

Does the structure for the program provide a framework where emergent issues can be addressed? Can the design be modified to address key stakeholders' felt needs without sacrificing objectives?

Can the design be carried out in the time allotted?

Does the design provide a mix of evaluation activities that appeal to different data gathering methodologies?

Is the evaluation logically sequenced?

Is there redundancy in information gathered in the evaluation effort? Should there be?

Does the evaluation design allow for on-going development of an organizational climate conducive to continued outcomes assessment efforts?

Assessment of ethics training efforts is not complete without a follow-up plan for the improvement of the controllable variables (for example, employee and trainer performance, choice of training materials, choice of training methods, and program assessment). In order to encourage an honest and accurate evaluation, involved parties should be urged to identify real problems associated with the outcomes assessment effort.

Once problems are identified, a priority listing should be established for the improvement program. Those items that if uncorrected will be most limiting to attaining the goals should have the highest priority. Associated with this priority list should be an accurate estimate of resources needed and potential constraints to implementing the necessary changes.

Finally, it is important to emphasize the need to continue with those initiatives that are working well. In reality, there is little net gain result from a program that stresses deficiencies and at the same time permits strengths to deteriorate. Additionally, overemphasis on improving weak areas, along with failure to recognize strengths, may dampen motivation and commitment to excellence that are essential to improving the outcomes assessment of ethics training.

ETHICS TRAINING THAT CAN SUCCEED

Like the institutionalization of ethics training in general, successful ethics training requires the support of top management. Ethics training programs work best from the top down. High level managers first are trained to identify and resolve ethical issues, and they then are able to reinforce the training their employees receive.

The most effective ethics training initiatives are comprehensive and pervasive. Periodic reinforcement is important, using such methods as follow-up training and statements from top management stressing the importance of paying attention to ethical issues.

An "ethics audit" is another means of letting employees know the positive effects of their efforts and emphasizing the desirability of such efforts. Managers are encouraged to review with their employees all decisions on ethical issues, asking, What did we do right? What did we do that we should have done? What should we do in future similar situations?

Another important aspect of ethics training is reinforcing the importance of communication and listening to employees. Top management must have the courage to listen in order to monitor where the organization is to provide the leadership to move it in the right direction ethically.

Human resource management (HRM) personnel, in their capacity as primary training agent for the organization, play a significant role here. They are often responsible for gaining enthusiastic top management support for the ethics training. Next, they must locate a credible and qualified trainer or team of trainers. The next step is to identify and analyze the specific ethical issues, problems, and opportunities that exist. (This step is essential if the content of the training is to be relevant to those who attend.) Using those problems and issues, the task becomes one of selecting and developing case studies, role playing skits, and other experientially oriented exercises that are work-related situations and using them as the basis for discussion and resolution by participants in the training program.

The experience of many companies has taught us that certain conditions are essential to the success of ethics training. Here are some of the most critical:

If possible, conduct the training away from the plant or office — in neutral territory.

Allow enough uninterrupted time for the sessions.

Bring in a knowledgeable resource person unconnected with the company, a consultant.

Do not preach; allow people to identify their own ethical values and level of ethical behavior; challenge their reasoning; make them aware of different viewpoints.

Teach people the process of analysis leading to higher levels of ethical behavior.

Use realistic ethical dilemmas, problems, and cases — issues that are likely to arise in the organization — for presentations, discussions, simulations, experiential learning exercises, and role playing.

Successful ethics training must also be reinforced through continuous training, because organizations have a continuously changing group that needs training (new people from outside, promotions, retirements, all those factors that result in personnel changes at different employee levels); people forget, and they get busy; people lose the enthusiasm that immediately follows a good educational experience; they do not get exposed to new ideas; significant ethical dilemmas do not arise every day for everyone; and people lose some of their sensitivity (they may fail to recognize moral issues when they do come up) and need reinforcement, the new ideas and the renewed interest that come from reinforcement and continuous training. This does not mean repeating the ethics training program periodically (say, annually) but tailoring training to the situation. Such follow-up training, the reinforcement, should consider the makeup of the participants and should build on what has gone before.

Citicorp provides a model for ethics training. The corporate HRM group has developed a board game based on realistic business scenarios requiring decisions having an ethical component. Employees play the game in teams and try to reach consensus on the best solution for each scenario. There are four levels of play, corresponding to the decisions faced by entry-level employees, supervisors, middle managers, and executives. Thus far, the game has been used by more than 30,000 Citicorp employees around the world (Ireland, 1991).

Ethics training should create a dialogue on training. It is also very important for top management to model and reinforce ethical behavior and for organizational policies to state clearly that unethical behavior will not be tolerated. Citicorp embodies these ideas by distributing a 60-page booklet on corporate ethics to all officers and by having top managers sit in each time the ethics game is played by employees.

Top management can demonstrate their commitment to high ethical performance by ensuring that employees at all levels of the organization are sensitized to ethical and value issues — and to the means of dealing with them — through training. Ethics training can sensitize employees to the importance of enduring ethical principles and can help develop skills for analyzing the application of such principles to ethical and value issues. Moreover, there are many rules of varying degrees of clarity and specificity as to what constitutes ethical behavior. Ethics training can foster understanding of what these rules mean in practice and can stimulate formal changes in rules that are unrealistic.

Also, as Andrews (1989) has noted:

Since policy cannot be effective unless it is understood, some companies use corporate training sessions to discuss the problems of applying their ethical standards. In difficult situations, judgments in making the leap from general policy statements to situationally specific action can be informed by discussion. Such discussion, if carefully conducted, can reveal the inadequacy or ambiguity of present policy, new areas in which the company must take a unified stand, and new ways to support individuals in making the right decisions. (p. 102)

As will be noted in Chapter 10, codes of ethics can serve a useful complementary purpose in ethics training by articulating the rules of appropriate behavior and providing a framework for discussion of ethical issues. Ethics courses provide opportunities for applying a code to the resolution of specific issues and for consulting those affected by a code on its appropriate content and form. In addition, these ethical training courses can provide an intellectual basis and stimulus for a continuing dialogue on ethical issues. They can, therefore, advance Jackson's (1987) objective of having employees reason about moral judgments persistently. Given the complexity of ethical issues, combined with the need for exemplary role models in the senior ranks of business organizations, such training courses provide formal opportunities for these leaders to articulate their values and assess the extent to which these values are shared by their colleagues.

Training is an important vehicle for helping organizations institutionalize ethics and encourage employees to act ethically. Rather than being strictly compliance oriented, the goals of effective training should be to:

Increase awareness of ethical consequences of business decisions, that is, among other things, to train employees to recognize and focus on ethical problems, to develop and refine appropriate methods of moral reasoning, and to be sensitive to the nuances and ambiguity of ethical situations.

Develop an understanding of decision models that encourage employees (and particularly managers) to see their responsibility to make a commitment to the highest standards of honor and personal integrity, to appreciate the ethical dimension in decision making (just as they appreciate the financial and management dimensions, for example), and to accept the multiple and sometimes conflicting responsibilities of working in organizations.

Integrate relevant cases and vignettes that reinforce the organization's code.

Encourage critical evaluation of value priorities.

Increase awareness of societal realities.

Improve understanding of the importance of public image and public/society relations.

Bring about a greater degree of fairness and honesty in the workplace.

Respond more completely to the organization's social responsibility.

Can ethics be learned? An affirmative answer comes easily if the task of ethics training is to achieve mastery of factual knowledge related to codes of ethics. The answer is more controversial if the task is defined as the ability to make careful and well-considered ethical judgments. The training challenge is straightforward: How can ethics be taught to employees so that effective learning takes place?

Quality and depth of training are obviously important factors. Certainly, an informal training program conducted by persons without adequate exposure to ethical concepts, dilemmas, and analysis techniques would not achieve the same results as more structured teaching. However, organizations must strive to develop well-organized ethics training programs.

Trainers must accept the responsibility to broaden ethics training in organizations to include ethical dilemmas and decision making that are relevant to the life experiences of employees at all levels. An experiential based training approach is a critical component of effective ethics training, and the debriefing phase is an essential part of this experiential methodology. Experience alone is not adequate; employees must reflect on their experiences to complete the learning process. The debriefer should strive to provide a supportive atmosphere for inquiry and conversation during the debriefing phase. Employees have the ability to learn from their experiences but often need help in finding the appropriate ways to achieve this learning. The debriefer should facilitate the dialogue and create a shared sense of community characterized by concern, responsibility, and respect. It is the debriefer's responsibility to provide the path to learning.

A critical phase that should not be omitted in ethics training is outcomes assessment. Assessment provides feedback needed to improve and renew the training process. An understanding of the factors that contribute both to success and to failure provide the means for an organization's trainers to engage in continuous quality improvement in the design and delivery of ethics training.

If an organization's key stakeholders reach consensus on the goals of ethics training, make wise training choices emphasizing active rather than passive learning strategies, incorporate a well-structured and well-implemented debriefing phase, and provide for feedback through an effective assessment process, ethics training will be an integral and vital component of an organization's efforts to institutionalize ethics, as suggested in Chapter 10.

REFERENCES

Andrews, K. R. 1989, September/October. Ethics in practice. *Harvard Business Review*, p. 102.

Callahan, D. 1980. Goals in the teaching of ethics. In *Ethics teaching in higher education*, ed. D. Callahan and S. Bok. New York: Plenum Press, pp. 61–80.

Colby, A. L., & Kohlberg, L. 1987. *The measurement of moral judgment: Theoretical foundations and research validations, and standard issues scoring manual*. Cambridge: Cambridge University Press, vols. 1 and 2.

Geary, W., & Sims, R. R. In press. Can ethics be learned. *Accounting Education*.

Hall, W. D. 1993. *Making the right decision: Ethics for managers*. New York: John Wiley & Sons.

Harrington, S. J. 1991. What corporate America is teaching about ethics. *Academy of Management Executive 5*, 21–30.

Henderson, V. 1992. *What's ethical in business?* New York: McGraw-Hill.

Hosmer, L. T. 1988, July/August. Adding ethics to the business curriculum. *Business Horizons*, pp. 9–15.

Ireland, K. 1991, March. The ethics game. *Personnel Journal*, pp. 72–75.Jackson, M. 1987, September. The eye of doubt: Neutrality, responsibility and morality. *Australian Journal of Public Administration 46*, 287.

Kilpatrick, D. L. 1977. Evaluating training programs: Evidence vs. proof. *Training and Development Journal 31*, 9–12.

Murphy, K. R. 1993. *Honesty in the workplace.* Pacific Grove, CA: Brooks/Cole.

Pace, C. R. 1984, Fall. Historical perspectives on student outcomes: Assessment with implications for the future. *NASPA Journal 22*, 10–18.

Pagano, A. M. 1987, August. Criteria for ethical decision making in managerial situations. In *Proceedings* of the National Academy of Management, New Orleans.

Sims, S. J. 1989. *The origins and development of Virginia's student assessment policy: A case study.* Unpublished doctoral dissertation, The College of William and Mary, Williamsburg, VA.

Sims, S. J., & Sims, R. R. 1993. Diversity and difference training in U.S. organizations. In *Diversity and differences in organizations: An agenda for answers and questions*, eds. R. R. Sims and R. F. Dennehy. Westport, CT: Quorum Books.

_____. 1991. Student assessment: A proactive response for the 21st century. In *Managing institutions of higher education into the 21st century: Issues and implications*, ed. R. R. Sims and S. J. Sims. Westport, CT: Greenwood.

Tracey, W. R. 1990. *Leadership skills.* New York: American Management Association.

Weber, J. 1990. Measuring the impact of teaching ethics to future managers: A review, assessment, and recommendations. *Journal of Business Ethics 9*, 183–90.

9

Maintaining Ethical Employee-Employer Contracts

Present and future organizations and their employees are being challenged by corporate relocations, mergers and acquisitions, new chief executives, major corporate reorganizations or restructurings, downsizings or retrenchments, layoffs, foreign competition, unanticipated crises, and new strategic initiatives. These large system changes precipitate and require new attitudes and behaviors on the part of all organizational members if they are to be successful. For example, managers must orchestrate and cope with the day-to-day operational changes; they also must use the system changes as opportunities to position the company for attaining future goals and objectives. In addition, as organizations change, what they expect of employees may be completely different from what that same organization expected before the change (for example, employees may be required to work in teams, work with fewer resources, and, in some instances, take a pay cut and lose benefits in the process).

The forces of demography also pose challenges for organizations and demand responses. For example, baby boomers (those born between 1946 and 1956) are hitting middle age, and they have brought new expectations to the job that made traditional definitions of success obsolete. Quality of life and personal growth are at least as important as raises and a corner office. They want to pursue new, less frantic careers. Community, family, security, and meaning are distinctly more important to them today.

These demographics, along with the shrinking labor pool and an expected increase in the number of minorities entering the workplace, are revolutionizing the work force. Employees of every race, sex, and age are insisting on corporate policies that respond to their changing expectations and still satisfy their professional ambitions, expectations that must also be balanced with every changing organizations. It is the premise of this chapter that the extent to which today's and tomorrow's changing employee-employer relationships are understood and managed determines the likelihood that unethical behavior will occur in the organization.

The implications of these changes for organizational ethics is the focus of this chapter. More specifically, this chapter will highlight the origins of changing employee-employer relationships and discuss the importance of creating and maintaining an ethical climate in the midst of changing employees and organizations.

THE ORIGINS OF THE CHANGING PSYCHOLOGICAL CONTRACT

The seeds of change are taking root, and, with these changes, new psychological contracts are developing between organizations and their members. No longer is the traditional psychological contract that existed between the organization and the employee valid. Changes like those cited thus far have profoundly changed the ways in which organizations and their employees relate.

Companies in the United States from 1950 to 1980 enjoyed prosperity and world leadership. It was not unusual for many employees and their children to spend their entire working lives at one organization. Organizations invested considerable time and money in employee training and management development, and employees in turn embraced the corporate culture. Firing of long-term employees was an unheard of practice, often resulting in a family-like atmosphere in many organizations. As a result, employees and management believed in a "cradle-to-grave" psychological contract: hard work and loyalty would be rewarded with job security and steady rewards (financial and promotional).

Traditional psychological contracts existed in organizations where there was stability, predictability, and growth. Organizations expected steady increases in revenue and the number of employees. Organizations saw their work force as permanent and tried to build loyalty among their employees by making financial investments in training and by providing guaranteed long-term employment. Employees were committed to the organization and expected steady advancement up the corporate ladder. On the climb up the corporate ladder, the symbols of success were visible: vertical job growth (career paths were linear, job preparation generally meant one-time learning, and education and professional training were usually job specific), steady salary increases, employee recognition plans, and perks like cars and country clubs for managers. Pensions, life insurance, and health-care plans that addressed long-term needs were funded by the organization.

Today, there are change, uncertainty, and continuous cuts in human resources in organizations. Reorganizations, downsizing, mergers, and acquisitions threaten job security and career paths. An organization's work force is flexible; employees are recruited, hired, and retained for their particular skills for the short run as organizations focus less and less on long-term performance. Opportunities for advancement are limited by slower growth and leaner organizational structures with fewer levels of management. Dwindling career opportunities and greater emphasis on economy have forced managers to reexamine their reliance on this definition as a motivator of performance. In addition, employees have learned that good performance is no longer a guarantee, even of job security. Not only have the tangible symbols of success become less available, but also the entire strata of career positions have been obliterated in corporate downsizing. More and more employees recognize that they can expect multiple careers, have more responsibility for assessing and designing their own careers, must seek new definitions of success, and need to put more emphasis on life-long learning to avoid obsolescence of job skills.

The changing psychological contract also has implications for the organization. For example, with more and more well-qualified workers competing for a shrinking number of managerial jobs, the problems for organizations have changed from coaching employees with skill deficiencies to finding ways to motivate bright people with the carrot of promotion. In addition, old-style management techniques no longer apply and familiar incentives have evaporated, which make the management of a brave new work force considerably more challenging. The unilateral cancellation of the implied contract (for example, from downsizings) profoundly affects the surviving employees as well. Some of their most basic tenets — beliefs in fairness, equity, and justice — have been violated. Their sense of security has been destroyed, their identity and self-esteem are threatened, and organizations must be concerned about the implications that employees feel they can no longer trust management or the organization to look out for their welfare or to be truthful to them (that is, the contract has become null and void). It is not surprising that company loyalty is quickly becoming extinct. Indeed, the employee-employer relationship is changing; thus, the need arises to understand, clarify, and manage the psychological contract.

Employee Rights in the Workplace

All of the prior changes and trends create pressures for new ways of organizational thinking and for new relationships between organizations and employees who work for them. Human rights and social justice are increasingly revered in the workplace, as they are in the world at large. All organizations (and their managers), accordingly, must be willing to deal with:

Pressure for self-determination. People seek greater freedom to determine how to do their jobs and when to do them. Pressures for increased worker participation in the forms of job enrichment, autonomous work groups, flexible working hours, and compressed work weeks will grow.

Pressures for employee rights. People expect their rights to be respected on the job as well as outside work. These include the rights of individual privacy, due process, free speech, free consent, freedom of conscience, and freedom from sexual harassment.

Pressures for job security. People expect their security to be protected. This includes their physical well-being in terms of occupational safety and health matters and their economic livelihood in terms of guaranteed protection against layoffs and provisions for cost-of-living wage increases.

Pressures for equal employment opportunity. People expect and increasingly demand the right to employment without discrimination on the basis of age, sex, ethnic background, or handicap. Among these demands will remain a concern for furthering the modest but dramatic gains made by women and other minorities in the workplace. "Progress" will be applauded, but it will not be accepted as a substitute for true equality of opportunity.

Pressure for equity of earnings. People expect to be compensated for the "comparable worth" of their work contributions. What began as a concern for earnings differentials between women and men doing the same jobs has been extended to cross-occupational comparisons. Questions such as why a nurse receives less pay than a carpenter and why a maintenance worker is paid more than a secretary are asked with increasing frequency. They will require answers other than the fact that certain occupations (such as nursing) have traditionally been dominated by women, whereas others (such as carpentry) have been dominated by men.

Smart organizations will understand and respond to these and related social pressures. Failure to do so will have an impact on the employee-employer contract and on employee loyalty and will increase the likelihood of unethical behavior.

Unfortunately, some organizations are not always clear as to what their expectations of employees are, either. As a result, they do not talk about many areas nor pay attention to them. Mismatches between employee and employer expectations can occur by accident, out of neglect.

What is needed in today's organizations is for employees and organizations to carefully consider all areas of expectations in order to overcome the problem of clarity, which, if not addressed, can lead to dire circumstances for one or both parties. Too often this step does not occur because organizational managers and employees do not regularly consider it as important. Creating and maintaining an ethically oriented culture can be enhanced if proactive attempts are made to increase the number of matches in the employee-employer contract and efforts are made to first ensure that the employee-employer contract is ethical.

CLARIFICATION OF THE
EMPLOYEE-EMPLOYER CONTRACT

Clarifying the new employee-employer contract is an important step in the management of and maintenance of ethical employee-employer contracts. This section discusses several employee-employer interactions (the employee-job relationship, the employee-organizational training relationship, and the employee-organization relationship in the promotion and institutionalization of organizational ethics) that, if appropriately managed, can help maintain an ethical employee-employer contract.

The Realistic Job Preview: A Vehicle for Maintaining
Ethical Employee-Employer Contracts

Once a new employee has been recruited and selected, he or she must adjust to the new job and organization. As evidenced by the high rate of turnover among hires in the first few months, problems obviously arise at this point. One reason for the turnover may be that the job did not match the newcomer's expectations or desires, resulting in a perceived violation of the employee-employer contract. The recruitment process may be partly responsible for this mismatch, as organizations and their recruiters tend to present jobs in very favorable terms in order to increase the number of employees hired. When these processes do not function well, unfortunate problems can arise (thus violating the employee-employer contract), as illustrated in the following scenario:

When she began to major in marketing as a junior in college, Sandy Sherman knew that someday she would work in that field. Once she completed her MBA, she was more positive than ever that marketing would be her life's work. Because of her excellent academic record, she received several outstanding job offers. She decided to accept the offer from one of the nation's largest consulting firms, believing that this job would allow her to gain experience in several areas of marketing and to engage in a variety of exciting work. Her last day on campus, she told her favorite professor, "This has got to be one of the happiest days of my life, getting such a great career opportunity."

Recently, while visiting the college placement office, the professor was surprised to hear that Sandy had told the placement director that she was looking for another job. Because she had been with the consulting company less than a year, the professor was somewhat surprised. He decided to call Sandy and find out why she wanted to change jobs. This is what she told him: "I guess you can say my first experience with the real world was a 'reality shock.' Since joining this company, I have done nothing but gather data on phone surveys. All day long, I sit and talk on the phone, asking questions and checking off the answers. In graduate school, I was trained to be a manager, but here I am doing what any high school graduate can do. I talked to my boss, and he said that all employees have to pay their dues. Well, why didn't they tell me this while they were recruiting me? To say there was a conflict between the recruiting information and the real world would be a gross understatement. I'm an adult. Why didn't they provide me with realistic information and then let me decide if I wanted it? A little bit of accurate communication would have gone a long way."

Sandy Sherman's experience illustrates inconsistent decision making and shows how an organization can violate an employee-employer contract. In such situations, these types of decisions affect people's lives and well-being, and ethics play a major role. Was Sandy provided with realistic and truthful information about the job? If not, was there a breach of ethics on the part of the recruiter? Organizations must avoid violations of the employer-employee contract if they are committed to creating and maintaining an ethically oriented organizational culture.

To increase the likelihood of a satisfactory employee-employer contract at the employee entry stage, organizations can see to it that their human resource management department regularly uses the realistic job preview (RJP), a down-to-earth presentation of both the favorable and unfavorable aspects of the job. Ideally, organizational personnel must ensure that each stage of recruiting is honest and realistic. An RJP may take the form of a booklet or film about the job, realistic information delivered by an interviewer, or a work sample test that exposes the candidate to actual job conditions and activities.

Overall, RJPs can reduce turnover, lower recruits' expectations about the job, slightly reduce the job-offer acceptance rate, and slightly increase job satisfaction and commitment to the organization among new hires. Several reasons RJPs have these effects are the following:

Self-selection. If the RJP helps the applicant realize that the job will not be personally satisfying, the applicant may choose not to take the job or select himself or herself out of the organization's selection process. Without this realistic information, the applicant might have accepted the offer and could have become an early turnover statistic (the result of a mismatch or the perception of a violation of the employee-employer contract).

Commitment to the decision. When the RJP is presented before the candidate accepts or rejects the job offer, the candidate feels that she or he has made an informed decision about the job. Having accepted a job known to include difficult moments or distasteful duties, a newcomer feels less justified in reversing the decision and quitting when an unpleasant event actually occurs.

Lowered expectations. The aim of an RJP is to lower, or make more realistic, the expectations that the newcomer holds about the job. One theory of job satisfaction states that dissatisfaction is a function of the discrepancy between what one expects and desires on a job and what one actually gets. Lowering expectations reduces the gap between expectations and reality; consequently, dissatisfaction decreases. Because dissatisfaction is one cause of turnover, this mechanism can explain both attitudinal and behavioral differences between RJP and no-RJP groups.

Coping. Unpleasant events are less stressful and more effectively dealt with if they are expected rather than if they are surprises. It is possible that the RJP operates by improving the ability of new hires to cope with negative aspects of the job. The RJP may stimulate newcomers to mentally rehearse their reactions to anticipated job problems and so increase their ability to deal with problems when they occur.

RJPs are most useful when organizational personnel present them early in the recruiting process (so that the self-selection and commitment processes can occur). RJPs are particularly effective for jobs in which there tends to be early high turnover and for entry-level jobs in which applicants are unlikely to have an accurate picture of the job or occupational field prior to applying, make the most sense when there are numerous applicants for the available openings (if some decide to decline offers, the jobs can still be filled), and are most effective in reducing turnover when unemployment is low. In this situation, applicants will be most likely to turn down a job offer that does not suit them because they know that other jobs are readily available.

The RJP can be used by organizational personnel to help clarify the psychological contract both at the early stages of the employee-employer relationship and during job reassignments (laterally, promotions, or demotions). However, like other means of clarifying the employee-employer contract, organizational personnel must make sure that RJPs are tailored to the needs of the organization and that they include balanced presentations of positive and negative job information.

Clarifying the Employee-Employer Contract in Training

Effective use of the RJP provides an organization with the potential for better matches between employees and jobs, but additional training and development are usually required to convey job-specific knowledge, skills, and abilities (KSAs) to employees in order to build increasing skills over the course of a career. The training function, now popularly called human resource development, coordinates the provision of training and development experiences in organizations.

Technological innovations such as robots, desktop publishing, and computer-aided design require training for affected employees. Competitive pressures are also changing the way organizations operate and the KSAs that their employees need. For instance, more and more organizations are providing quality management training and customer service training in an attempt to keep up with rising consumer expectations. Restructuring and downsizing mean that many employees need to be trained to take on expanded responsibilities.

The declining level of new-hire literacy and numeracy, coupled with greater diversity in the labor force, has stimulated a number of employers to furnish education in reading, mathematics, writing, and English as a second language. This same diversity has prompted many organizations to offer training on dealing effectively with diversity and multiculturalism in the work force. The aging of the work force means that more retraining is necessary and that some training methods must be adapted to better fit the needs of older learners. In addition, the long arm of the federal government is also reaching into the organizational training room with a growing list of mandated training topics.

Acknowledging the above, organizational personnel will encounter more times when their expectations and those of trainees are not congruous. To better communicate expectations, organizations must spend more time discussing with trainees and their supervisors the objectives of a training program, the training needs, and the strategies to be used to develop employees' KSAs and attitudes. As in other situations, the psychological contract in training is an implicit, yet important, agreement among trainees, organizations, and the organizational personnel responsible for training. The psychological contract should specify what each expects to give and receive from the others in the training relationship. The process goes to the heart of motivation, productivity, training program satisfaction, involvement, and the management of the training environment. Companies like IBM, Dana Corporation, Walt Disney Productions, and McDonald's are actively investing in improving the employee-employer contract with their employees by helping employees select and achieve meaningful goals and objectives through their training and education efforts.

A number of general points that will be instrumental in developing the climate for learning in a training program result from organizational personnel taking the time to clarify the employee-employer contract. First, the importance of the development of an employee-employer contract early in the training process requires careful management. It has been shown that the attitudes and expectations of trainees as they begin a training program can affect both their reaction to the program and the amount they learn (Noe, 1986). Second, what you don't know *can* hurt you. A clear understanding of one's own expectations and those of the other party will assist in the development of better contracts. Third, the key to contract formulation is achieving a match or the best fit. Fourth, if a training program participant and the organization's training personnel have a number of basic mismatches in their expectations, these mismatches may be counterproductive for all involved in the training program. Finally, the development of matches in the employee-employer contract begins the process of self-directed learning and setting personal directions for learning by the training program participants.

Organizational training programs developed with clearly defined objectives should come close to meeting the expectations of trainees. The organization's training personnel should also have the KSAs to help create sound employee-employer contracts that will help to develop the learning climate and to improve the organization's training efforts. In the final analysis, the trainee, the human resources management staff, and the organization all stand to gain.

To further clarify the employee-employer contract, organizations might ask the following types of questions of trainees and their supervisors:

What two or three concepts, activities, discussions are most important to you in this training program?

Do you feel that your training needs are being fully addressed in this training program? Previous organizational training programs? Why or why not?

If you had complete freedom to reconstruct this training program, what changes would you make?

How well does/has the organization's training program(s) meet/met your personal and professional needs?

What do you think this training program expects of you at this point (for example, preparation, active participation)?

What have you learned are the objectives of this training program?

Although not all-encompassing, these questions can help define changing expectations and current fit between an organization's training program and the trainees' expectations and current fit. Consider the question: How well does the organization's training program meet your personal and professional needs? If the answer is primarily negative, modification or improved management of the training program or some change in training methods may be necessary. However, a positive answer may indicate that the training personnel and trainee should move on with the training effort. Training personnel can influence the attitude of potential trainees by involving them in the needs assessment phase and/or by giving them a realistic training preview — a synopsis of what benefits they can expect from the training program and how it fits into their career plans.

Clarifying the Employee-Employer Contract on Organizational Ethics

Ethical issues are a daily component of business. They are more important today than ever and are involved in all facets of a business: decision making, arbitration, marketing and sales, financial reporting, personnel, appraisal, and leadership. Maintaining an ethical employee-employer contract can go to the heart of an organization's efforts to promote, institutionalize, and manage ethics within the organization. If appropriately reinforced and managed, the ethical requirements of the organization can serve as the foundation of the employee-employer contract, with the organization providing a culture that encourages and rewards the ethical behavior of employees. If an employee's expectations are that an organization encourages ethical behavior but she or he finds out through experience that the opposite is true, the employee-employer contract has been violated.

It is important for organizations to understand that clarity, discussion, and some give-and-take are often not enough to resolve some ethical mismatches. The major obstacles to the process are organizational norms that define some items as not legitimate areas for discussion. In addition, contract participants may be unwilling or unable to find a commonality of ethical expectations, and small but significant differences between the expectations of employees and of the organizations may result in mismatches concerning ethical behavior.

There are also times when neither party in the contract fully knows all that must be included over the length of the contract. However, each party may act as though a stable frame of reference exists in which to define the relationship. The institutionalization and management of organizational ethics must be perceived and treated as an evolving set of mutual understandings as new ethical issues and concerns arise in organizations and in our society in general.

Top executives and managers are interdependent agents and must understand that ethical behavior does not develop automatically but is communicated and reinforced from the top down. Organizations must make sure that those individuals acting on the organization's behalf (with top management support) can give life to the formal employment agreement (especially during new hire orientation training), meaning of the organizational structure, and very often the ethical behavior of an organization's employees. Early in their organizational careers, managers and employees develop enduring attitudes and expectations that are important to their future performance and success. Those attitudes and aspirations are directly related to the manager's and employee's expectations of them (for example, those people who are not stretched early in their organizational careers or, conversely, are assigned work beyond their skills and abilities may not reach their full potential). Just as a mismatch of challenges and capabilities or of personal aspirations and company expectations may sharply reduce an employee's long-term productivity, a similar mismatch regarding ethical expectations can result in unethical behavior.

Finding the Employee-Organization Match in Ethical Expectations

The psychological contract specifies what the individual and the organization expect to give and receive from each other in the relationship, and the process can go to the heart of the institutionalization and management of ethics within an organization, that is, if appropriately reinforced and managed, the ethical requirements of the organization can serve as the foundation of a psychological contract, with the organization providing a culture that encourages and rewards the ethical behavior of employees. Therefore, if an employee's expectations are that an organization encourages ethical behavior (or vice versa) but he or she finds out through experience that the opposite is true, then the psychological contract has been violated.

It is the contention of this chapter that psychological contracts made up primarily of matches in expectations of ethical behavior will lead to greater institutionalization of ethics within the organization, lead to ethical employee behavior, and increase the length of time the individual and the organization are mutually committed to the institutionalization of ethics. The following four propositions further explain the relationships involved in the match between the ethical contributions and inducements in the psychological contract.

Proposition 1: Understanding Ethical Expectations

The clearer an organization and employees understand each others' ethical expectations, the higher the probability is of matching them. This can be accomplished to the degree to which the individual and the organization have clearly thought out their ow expectations toward giving and receiving; the amount of open discussion of expectations initiated by the organization, the individual, or both; and the degree to which the individual understands the organization's expectations and vice versa. Therefore, the institutionalization of organizational ethics can be enhanced through increases in the number of matches in the psychological contract.

Proposition 2: Barriers to Matching Ethical Expectations

Clarity, discussion, and even some give-and-take are often not enough to resolve some ethical mismatches. The major obstacles to the process are organizational norms that define some items as not legitimate to talk about. In addition, contract participants often may be unwilling or unable to find a commonality of ethical expectations. There may be small but significant differences between the expectations of individuals and the organizations that might result in mismatches concerning ethical behavior.

Proposition 3: Evolving Ethical Expectations

The psychological contract typically is not static; rather, it is an evolving set of mutual expectations. Neither party of the contract fully knows everything it wants over the length of the contract. However, each party may act as if a stable frame of reference exists, defining the relationship. The institutionalization and management of organizational ethics must also be perceived and treated as an evolving set of mutual expectations as new ethical issues and concerns arise in organizations and our society in general.

Proposition 4: Interpreting the Ethical Contract

Top executives and managers are agents of interdependence and must understand that ethical behavior does not develop automatically but is communicated and reinforced from the top down. Interpreting the ethical contract is the function of the people in authority (particularly, top executives) acting on the organization's behalf. It is they who give life to the formal employment agreement, meaning of the organizational structure, and, very often, the ethical behavior of an organization's employees. Early in their organizational careers, managers and employees develop enduring attitudes and expectations that are important to their future performance and success. Those attitudes and aspirations are directly related to their organization's expectations of them (for example, those people who are not stretched early in their organizational careers or who are assigned work beyond their skills and abilities may not reach their full potential). Just as a mismatch of challenges and capabilities, of personal aspirations and company expectations may sharply reduce an employee's long-term productivity, a similar mismatch on ethical expectations can result in unethical behavior.

When organizations attend to the need for matching an organization's ethical expectations with those of its employees, the organization is in a better position to improve the institutionalization of ethics. The greater the extent to which employees are expected by the organization to behave ethically and employees indeed have similar expectations of themselves result in ethics being more institutionalized within the organization. Top management will have a far greater effect on developing the employees' ethics than will their peer group. The match of ethical expectations should also lead to a long-term organization and employee commitment to the persistence of ethical behavior. Boeing, Champion, International Chemical Bank, General Mills, Arthur Andersen, GTE, Hewlett-Packard, Johnson & Johnson, and Xerox are a few companies that have experienced the benefits of managing the employee-employer contract with their employees in their efforts to create and maintain an ethically oriented organization.

Creating and Maintaining
Ethical Working Conditions

Velasquez (1992) has noted that although more attention is now being paid to worker safety, occupational accident rates have not necessarily been declining. Between 1961 and 1970, the number of injuries per million working hours in manufacturing industries rose by almost 30 percent: from 11.8 injuries per million to 15.2 per million (Association of Military Surgeons, 1987). By 1973, the rate had moved up to 15.3 per million, and by the late 1970s, the incidence of disabling injuries continued to be 20 percent higher than in 1958 (Velasquez, 1992).

Risk is, of course, an unavoidable part of many occupations, and as long as they are fully compensated for assuming these risks and freely and knowingly chose to accept the risk in exchange for the added compensation, we may assume that their employer has acted ethically (Settle & Burton, 1978) and has not violated the employee-employer contract.

To maintain the likelihood of ethical employee-employer contracts related to working conditions, the employer must take steps to ensure that employees are not being unfairly manipulated into accepting a risk unknowingly, unwillingly, or without due compensation. In particular, employers should offer wages that reflect the risk-premium prevalent in other similar but competitive labor markets; insure their workers against unknown hazards by providing them with suitable health insurance programs; and collect information (singly or together with other firms) on the health hazards that accompany a given job and make all such information available to workers (Velasquez, 1992). Reducing the potential for workplace hazards like the more obvious categories of mechanical injury, electrocution, and burns but also extreme heat and cold, noisy machinery, rock dust, textile fiber dust, chemical fumes, mercury, lead, beryllium, arsenic, corrosives, skin irritants, and radiation (Lowrance,

1976) is important to the maintenance of ethical employee-employer contracts.

Dismissing or Firing Employees: The Importance of Fair and Equitable Treatment

There are few actions that managers find harder to take than dismissing or firing an employee. Many managers confide that this task is especially hard when the reason is cost cutting. It is typically easier to justify firing someone who has not performed well — you can attribute the action to the employee: "If they had done a good job, I wouldn't have to let them go." But when an organization is downsizing or laying off large numbers of people, the task is tougher. It is often not the employee's fault. "I had eight years of excellent performance reviews," said a fired graphics arts specialist. "They showed them to me. What have I done wrong?" (Greenberg & Baron, 1993).

Managers may argue that they have no alternatives. In many instances, for example, during downsizing, if the organization is to be competitive, costs have to be trimmed. Those organizations that "have a heart" and do not make the tough decisions will eventually fail in the marketplace to organizations that are "lean and mean." But do organizations have a moral obligation to repay their employees' long-term loyalty by providing job security?

Being fired can be devastating. Losing a job is not unlike suffering a divorce or the death of a close family member. It undermines people's self-esteem. It forces many to question their identity. It can cause mental illness, family breakups, and even suicides. And finding a new job can be a long and dehumanizing experience. For instance, one 44-year-old computer executive who was laid off reported that he sent out 100 letters, answered 200 ads, made 2,500 phone calls, and exhausted $25,000 of savings during his job hunt. One study found that among laid-off workers over 55 years of age, one in three is forced to leave the work force altogether (Greenberg & Baron, 1993).

It is not as if there are no alternatives to firing people. For example, a few organizations are spreading the cutbacks among all their employees. Instead of firing 20 percent of their staff, they are having all employees cut their hours by 20 percent and take a commensurate pay cut. In the end, the extent to which organizations downsize in an ethical manner, the greater is the likelihood that employees will perceive that the organization is treating them equitably.

Employees who are satisfied with their jobs, status, compensation, benefits, job security, and prospects for advancement are likely to be loyal to their organization. Employees who believe they are overworked and underpaid, are not given the recognition they deserve, or are dissatisfied with their working conditions (for example, the approach an organization uses in dealing with issues of layoffs and firings during downsizing or retrenchment) are likely to become disgruntled and angry. They may, and often do, develop a desire to "get even" or strike back. The result is all too often dishonesty, stealing, or some other unethical act.

Organizations can make a major difference here. They can provide training for supervisors and managers that focuses on the goal of fair and equitable treatment of employees and they can be the impetus for corporatewide programs to improve the working conditions and to improve the employee-employer relationship.

Organizations can also make a difference in the employee-employer contract when they recognize and address those situations where there may be organizational flaws that generate conflicts, mismatches, or violations of the psychological contract. Three causes of such conflict are organizational incongruence, that is, built-in opposition between task responsibilities; inadequate performance measures, for example, a purchasing department evaluated on the basis of the negative measures of excess inventory may fail to purchase adequately, and this, in turn, may lead to conflict with the sales department; and ambiguity, that is, organizational complexity results in ambiguous communication, allowing employees to read what they want into communications. In such cases, utility for the organization and fairness to its employees dictates that the flaws be remedied, and dismissals based on conflicts originating in such flaws do not and should have a just cause foundation.

An employer can also exhibit fair and equitable treatment to its employees by stating in writing the reasons for discharge (that is, under situations other than those resulting from economic reasons). No employee should have to experience the following:

Do you have any idea why you were fired? — I think ultimately because they didn't like me. I think it's probably that simple. There are still people in the company who are quasi-alcoholics or who don't do any work. They're still there. And people who don't make waves. I had a lot of people working for me, and I was under a lot of pressure. I'm probably the kind of person who under those circumstances is not invisible. Probably what it came down to was simply that I was not liked. But I don't really know. (Maurer, 1979, p. 20)

There is no moral basis for the anxiety, self-doubt, and resentment often caused by such terminations. Dismissal may be justified in some cases, but the discharged employee cannot learn from the action if he or she does not understand its rationale. In addition, a written explanation of reasons for dismissal would encourage the manager to give the same reasons to his or her superiors, the discharged employee, and those responsible for the organization's due process procedure (the second element, after just cause) in an ethical discharge system.

It is important that the organization and the employee realize that there are termination costs for both of them. In the case of just dismissals, where an employee has a good performance record, discharge may reduce efficiency, and many dismissals are harmful to morale and company image. Even just dismissals entail a waste of training and often a disruption of continuity. Therefore, organizations should take a close look at the impact of terminations. It should start with a close look at its recruitment, selection, and performance appraisal systems.

As noted in the discussion on RJPs, a major factor in separations may be underhiring and overhiring of employees. A great deal of the agony of separation could be eliminated by working harder at the front end — the selection process — making sure not only that candidates can do the job, which is the easy part of the procedure, but also that they *will* do the job.

There are three questions related to performance that, if sufficiently answered, would prevent many terminations and resignations (that is, violations of the psychological contract): Was the employee's job description regularly reviewed to determine if the employee was performing the duties prescribed? Was the correlation between the employee's salary and his or her job description reviewed? Were the employee's performance reviews carefully studied? The main point here is that even if an organization has an ethical discharge system, with just cause, due process, and mitigation mechanisms, the organization should be structured so that the dismissal issue seldom arises, other than as the result of economical necessity.

The following are some characteristics of an ethical due process system:

It must be a procedure; it must follow rules. It must not be arbitrary.

It must be visible and well enough known so that potential violators of rights and victims of abuse know it.

It must be predictably effective. Employees must have confidence that previous decisions in favor of rights will be repeated.

It must be "institutionalized," that is, it must be a relatively permanent fixture in the organization, not a device that is here today, gone tomorrow.

It must be perceived as equitable. The standards used in judging a case must be respected and accepted by a majority of employees, bosses as well as subordinates.

It must be easy to use. Employees must be able to understand it without fear that procedural complexities will get the best of them.

It must apply to all employees.

There are a variety of ways that an ethical due process system can be institutionalized, and the best method will be somewhat dependent on the size and type of the organization.

Maintaining Ethical Employee-Employer Contracts during Mergers

Although employees can reap benefits from mergers, they often provide dire consequences for the average employee, who may find that some form of job displacement ensues. How the organization manages the merger process can go a long way in maintaining an ethical employee-employer contract. The possibility of a successful ethical employee-employer contract during mergers is best accomplished when the organization keeps in mind one of the oldest theories of moral conduct based upon the assertion that a person's actions toward another should be considered in light of how that person would wish to be treated in the same situation. This perspective calls for key organizational leaders to examine the effects from the vantage point of those impacted. For example, in a merger situation, those initiating the consolidations should seriously consider the effect on employees from the vantage point of the employees. Would the top managers want to be treated in this way? If the answer is negative, then a reexamination of the process may be in order. According to this model, the dignity and importance of employees must be preserved in the process of consolidation in order to maintain an employee-employer contract. If this is not possible, the process must be questioned, because the negative effects on employees impact the organization.

Organizations should take measures to alleviate or to remove the negative consequences, if possible. When organizations are committed to maintaining ethical employee-employer contracts, they should adopt this framework of ethical analysis during the merger process while also addressing questions like the following:

Are there ways to consolidate or merge that will not have negative consequences for employees?

Will each employee be treated with dignity and respect in the merger process?

If negative effects are unavoidable, are there mechanisms to alleviate or lessen the impact?

If there are negative consequences, can these be shared among various employee groups so that no individual group bears the full brunt of the consequences?

If any employees suffer loss, are there measures that can be taken to alleviate the loss?

In conclusion, four requirements must be met in order for contracts to be ethical (Drake & Drake, 1988):

1. Both of the parties to a contract must have full knowledge of the nature of the agreement they are entering.
2. Neither party to a contract may intentionally misrepresent the facts of the contractual situation to the other party.
3. Neither party to the contract must be forced to enter the contract under duress or coercion.
4. The contract must not bind the parties to an immoral act (Velasquez, 1982).

These contracts apply to the initial employment contract, to any changes made in the contract after an employee is hired, and to organizational changes (that is, during reorganizations).

When organizations pay attention to the development, clarification, and management of changing employee-organization relationships, they create progressive organizational cultures that are concerned with maintaining ethical employee-employer contracts. Top management personnel can and should play an active role in the development of such a culture and the ensuing employee-employer contracts. Because of continuing changes in the business environment, organizations, and employees, there must be corresponding changes in such areas as organizational recruiting, training and development, motivating, leading, communicating, and retaining strategies. Such changes require that managers at all levels of the organization be role models and champion ways of facilitating the needed changes in the organization to maintain ethical employee-employer contracts. Such contracts are more likely when organizations develop comprehensive employment strategies and policies that recognize that today's contract is one of shared destiny and mutual benefit rather than one of job security and company loyalty.

More than ever before, an organization's management personnel have to ensure that they devote time and energy to staying in touch with their employees. Through the use of meetings, surveys, and informational videos, management personnel can stay in close contact with employees. In addition, management personnel must see to it that talking and listening to employees are requirements included in a company's management development efforts for individuals holding top- and middle-level management positions. Today's employee-employer contract requires an emphasis on talking *with* people, not *at* people.

Employee-employer contracts should see that employees are treated as valuable assets that cannot be ignored. Management personnel have a responsibility to see to it that their organization recognizes that each employee has unique needs that may be different from those of top- and middle-level managers. By ensuring that their organizations hold regular meetings to exchange ideas, express needs, and debate goals, management personnel improve the potential success of the new psychological contract. For example, chief executive officers and other managers benefit from meetings because they learn what others feel are important. The employees learn from meetings how the chief executive officer views them, the organization, issues like ethics, and the progress of the firm.

As organizations become more competitive, as the contract between employees and employers continues to change, and as downsizing becomes a common practice, it is a necessity for employees and organizations to observe, study, interpret, and communicate with each other regarding their expectations. As the twenty-first century approaches, ethical employee-employer contracts are a valuable link in the individual and organizational performance process. Whether it is before (recruitment) or after (orientation or training) the employee enters, the organization must work to decrease the likelihood of either party experiencing living by anything other than an ethical employee-employer contract.

REFERENCES

Association of Military Surgeons. 1987. Opening general session, Annual Meeting of the Association of Military of the United States, Las Vegas, November 9, 1987.

Drake, B. H., & Drake, E. 1988, Winter. Ethical and legal aspects of managing corporate cultures. *California Management Review*, pp. 107–23.

Greenberg, J., & Baron, R. A. 1993. *Behavior in organizations*. Needham Heights, MA: Allyn & Bacon.

Lowrance, W. W. 1976. *Of acceptable risk*. Los Altos, CA: William Kaufmann, p. 147.

Maurer, H. 1979. *Not working*. New York: Holt, Rinehart, and Winston, p. 20.

Noe, R. A. 1986. Trainees' attributes and attitudes: Neglected influences on training effectiveness. *Academy of Management Review 11*(4): 736–49.

Settle, R. F., & Burton, B. A. 1978. Occupational safety and health and the public interest. In *Public interest law*, ed. B. Weisbord, J. F. Handler, & N. K. Komesar. Berkeley: University of California Press.

Velasquez, M. G. 1992. *Business ethics: Concepts and cases*, 3rd ed. Englewood Cliffs, NJ: Prentice-Hall.

10

Institutionalizing Ethics in Organizations

Institutionalizing ethics may sound ponderous, but its meaning is straightforward. It means getting ethics formally and explicitly into daily business life. It means getting ethics into company policy formation at the board and top management levels and through a formal code getting ethics into all daily decision making and work practices down the line, at all levels of employment. It means grafting a new branch on the corporate decision tree — a branch that reads "right/wrong." (Purcell & Weber, 1979, p. 6)

Institutionalizing ethics is an important task for today's organizations if they are to effectively counteract the increasingly frequent occurrences of blatantly unethical and often illegal behavior within large and often highly respected organizations. One need only look at some of the literature on ethics in organizations to recognize the importance of finding a way to institutionalize ethics (see Snoeyenbos, 1992). In reality, the institutionalization and management of ethics is a problem facing all types of organizations — educational, governmental, religious, business, and so on.

The purpose of this final chapter is to discuss the importance of developing and institutionalizing organizational ethics. The chapter discusses the importance of institutionalizing ethics in organizations by highlighting several variables (organizational commitment, organizational culture and value system, the role of top and middle management, and a code of ethics) introduced throughout this book that are keys to the institutionalization process.

THE PROCESS OF INSTITUTIONALIZING ETHICS

The importance of understanding more about institutionalizing organizational ethics should be apparent. Today it would seem plain good strategy for a company to be concerned about and adopt institutional ethics. If an organization is truly interested in bringing about a long-term ethical system, then they must first define institutionalization while at the same time increasing their understanding about why some organizations and their employees remain ethically viable while others decline. This section will focus on defining institutionalization and present some currently accepted mechanisms organizations may use to institutionalize ethics.

The approach emphasized in this chapter is to understand the existence of an ethical system via the concept of institutionalization, that is, institutionalization should be examined in terms of specific behaviors or acts. A basic premise of this chapter is that the persistence of an ethical organization can be understood and studied by analyzing the persistence of the specific behaviors associated with an organization and its employees behaving ethically. An institutionalized act is defined as a behavior that is performed by two or more individuals, persists over time, and exists as a part of the daily functioning of the organization (Goodman & Dean, 1981). It should be clear from this definition of institutionalization that an act is not all-or-nothing. An act may vary in terms of its persistence, the number of people in the organization performing the act, and the degree to which it exists as part of the organization.

Ethical principles can be institutionalized within organizations in a variety of ways by considering both long- and short-term factors (Dunham, 1984). For the long term, organizations should develop their organization's culture so that it supports the learning — and, if necessary, relearning — of personal values that promote ethical behavior. For example when decisions are made, managers should explicitly and publicly explain the ethical factors that accompany each alternative considered. An organization should create and continue to nurture an organizational culture that supports and values ethical behavior. This can be done, for example, by encouraging organization members to display signs of ethical values through whistleblowing. In the short term, organizations can make public statements that ethical behavior is important and expected. The goal of such activities is to ensure that ethical concerns are considered in the same routine manner in which legal, financial, and marketing concerns are addressed.

Today, more and more corporations are relying on committees to monitor the ethical behavior of the organization. These committees are often called "social responsibility" or "public policy" committees and serve two functions within an organization. First, they lend legitimacy to the consideration of an ethics agenda at the highest level of organizational decision making. Second, they symbolically communicate to the employees and external stakeholders of the organization its commitment to ethical principles in conducting business.

Another mechanism for the institutionalization of ethics within an organization is the use of a code of ethics, which will be discussed in more detail later in this chapter (Beneish & Chatov, 1993; Sims, Veres, & Sims, 1989). Within an organization, this code describes the general value system of the organization, defines the organization's purpose, and provides guidelines for decision making consistent with these principles.

Another method that has gained in popularity is the implementation of ethics training programs, as noted in Chapter 8. 3M, Arthur Andersen, Boeing, Champion, International Chemical Bank, General Dynamics, General Mills, GTE, Hewlett-Packard, Johnson & Johnson, and Xerox are a few of the companies who have formal programs designed to teach ethics (Dunham & Pierce, 1989). Interestingly enough, often the most visible companies in the ethics business are those struggling to repair their damaged reputations. General Dynamics developed an ethics program so that it could remain eligible for its Navy contracts after allegations about improper contracting procedures surfaced. General Dynamics has even gone to the point of implementing an "ethics hot line" to aid employees when confronted with an ethical decision. Corporations that have not been guilty of wrongdoing have initiated formal ethics programs in an effort to avoid public-relations problems, raise employee morale and productivity, and make their organizations more honest.

KEYS TO INSTITUTIONALIZING ETHICS

Organizations can enhance the institutionalization of ethics by first recognizing and then managing the importance of a number of key variables. This section revisits the concept of organizational culture discussed earlier in this book and then focuses on organizational commitment and its importance to the institutionalization of ethics.

Organizational Culture and Ethical Behavior

What guides the behavior of managers and employees as they cope with ethical dilemmas they may pose? As noted earlier in this book, Trevino (1986) has developed a model that suggests that individual's standards of right and wrong are not the sole determinant of their decisions. Instead, these beliefs interact with other individual characteristics (such as locus of control) and situational forces (such as an organization's rewards and punishments and its culture). All of these factors shape the ethics of decisions and the behavior that results from them (see Stead, Worrell, & Stead [1990] for an additional description and application of the importance of these factors to understanding and managing ethical behavior). This interactive process is illustrated in Figure 1 of Trevino's article. It shows how people can choose to engage in acts they consider unethical when the culture of an organization and its prevailing reward structure overwhelm personal belief systems. As evidenced in Trevino's work, organizational culture is a key component when looking at ethical behavior.

Institutionalization operates to produce common understandings among organizational members about what is appropriate and, fundamentally, meaningful behavior (Zucker, 1983; Richardson, 1986). When an organization takes on institutional permanence, acceptable modes of ethical behavior become largely self-evident to its members. This is essentially the same thing that organizational culture does. An understanding of what makes up an organization's culture and how it is created, sustained, and learned will enhance one's ability to explain, predict, and manage the behavior of people at work.

Four major components can assure and contribute to the institutionalization of an ethical culture within an organization and convey this culture: selection, socialization, training, and mentoring (Northcraft & Neale, 1990). Selection serves as a means for bringing into the organization the "right kind" of individuals — those who have values and beliefs consistent with the organization or who can be inculcated with the organization's values. Once the individual is an organizational member, then the actual process by which an ethically responsible culture is conveyed and commitment is produced — organizational socialization begins. Organizational socialization is the process of conveying the organization's goals, norms, and preferred ways of doing things to the new employee. Socialization molds the new employee to fit the organization and serves as a key step in the institutionalization of ethics.

Through organizational socialization, the employee comes to appreciate the values, abilities, expected behaviors, and social knowledge essential for assuming an organizational role and participating as an organizational member (Louis, 1980; Van Maanen & Schein, 1979). In essence, organizational socialization conveys the organization's culture and can strongly influence the behavior of new organization members.

Pascale (1985) suggests that organizational socialization is necessary for organizational effectiveness. He suggests a seven-step approach to successful organizational socialization: selection, humility-inducing experiences, training, meticulous attention to systems of measuring operational results and rewarding individual performance, careful adherence to the firm's transcendent values, reinforcement folklore, and consistent role models. These seven steps suggest that how people are brought into the organization can have a major impact on their future relationship with the organization and subsequent ethical behavior.

Analysis and Change of Culture if Necessary

A comprehensive analysis of the organization culture or ethical climate should be undertaken (for example, recruitment, performance appraisal, and reward system) in order to institutionalize and monitor the ethics process within the organization. The primary objectives of the audit are to uncover sources of contributing factors to unethical behavior and to identify ways that the corporate culture may inadvertently reinforce unethical behavior.

It is important to look beyond surface data in auditing systems. The audit must be an in-depth analysis, and the assistance of an external ethics expert is strongly advised. The results of the audit must be translated into an agenda for specific changes in the organization culture and systems that management must then work to implement.

It is also important that the organization make regular use of questionnaires aimed at determining the ethical climate of an organization. Here we suggest consideration of questions like those in the *Organizational Integrity Perception Audit* developed by the Center for Ethics, Responsibilities, and Values (1987). The survey has 40 questions, for example, on overall ethical motivation and habits, ethical responsiveness of the organization's mission and structure, and ethical sensitivity in problem solving. The survey should be administered anonymously, with everyone given an opportunity to respond, at least in the inaugural round. Employees should be told the findings for their own major department of the organization and for the organization overall. The findings should be used to help understand the current ethical climate and should not be used to reward or punish individual managers.

Follow-up

The final component, follow-up consists of monitoring change, evaluating the results, and ultimately institutionalizing the changes as part of the organization's regular ongoing processes. Like other management efforts, there is a need for accountability and control for an ethical orientation to persist in an organization. Accountability for overseeing the change process might initially be assigned to the ethics task force or, if available, the standing ethics committee. Ultimately, however, accountability for preserving the changes must be established by every manager. Changes in the performance appraisal and reward processes are often needed to accomplish this. Follow-up activities should include additional training, repetition of the systems audit, and use of focus groups for ongoing discussions about ethical issues.

ORGANIZATIONAL COMMITMENT

Individuals react in very different ways to the organizations in which they work. Some employees give little thought to the organization, whereas others have very strong feelings, ranging from contempt and disgust to a high degree of loyalty to and identification with the organization. Social scientists and organizational researchers have devoted considerable attention to the concept of organizational commitment and to understanding its nature, causes, and consequences.

Upon entering an organization, employees are provided opportunities to become schooled in and committed to the organization's goals, objectives, and ways of conducting business (Northcraft & Neale, 1990). A variety of definitions of organizational commitment have been suggested (see Eisenberger, Huntington, Hutchinson, & Sowa, 1986). Simply defined, organizational commitment is the relative strength of an individual's identification with an involvement in particular organization (Mowday, Porter, & Steers, 1982).

It usually includes three factors: a strong belief in the organization's goals and values, a willingness to exert considerable effort on behalf of the organization, and a strong desire to continue as an organizational member. Organizational commitment, then, is not simply loyalty to an organization. Rather, it is an ongoing process through which organizational actors express their concern for the organization and its continued success and well-being.

There are many reasons why an organization should want to increase the level of organizational commitment among its members. For example, the more committed the employee is to the organization, the greater is the effort expended by the employee in performing tasks; highly committed workers are likely to remain with the organization for longer periods of time — that is, there is a positive relationship between the level of organizational commitment and job tenure; and finally, given the contribution a highly productive, trained employee can make to organizational productivity, keeping such an employee should be a high priority for the organization.

Factors Influencing Commitment

What is it about employees' experiences that leads them to be more or less committed to the organization? To answer this question, we must first consider exactly what leads to the phenomenon of commitment. Salancik (1977) suggests four key factors for understanding the concept of organizational commitment, and the following sections draw from this work. The visibility, explicitness, and irreversibility of one's behavior and personal volition for one's behavior are the factors that commit an individual to their acts (to include ethical behavior).

Visibility

One major determinant of how committing a particular behavior may be is how observable that behavior is to others. Behaviors that are secret or unobserved do not have a committing force behind them, because they cannot be linked to a specific individual. One of the most simple and straightforward ways to commit individuals to ethical behavior in an organization is to make their association with the organization public information. If they are part of the organization, they (by association) support that organization and its goals. Many organizations are already taking advantage of this visibility notion to increase employee commitment. When a new employee joins an organization, the employee's photograph and a formal announcement are sent to the local newspaper, in-house publications, and other such outlets to inform others of the new arrival. The same vehicles can be used by organizations to educate its new (and old) employees on its expectations of ethical behavior.

Maintaining visibility of expected ethical behavior is not a difficult task. Very little additional effort is required to associate individuals with their work, their accomplishments, and their organization. Organizations can follow the lead of General Electric in the late 1970s, for example, by annually issuing a booklet listing employees who have done socially good works both within and outside the company. In addition, might not a code provide for similar recognition of employees who have acted ethically? The more visible the organizations and individuals and their ethical contributions, the more committed they are likely to be to the organization's incentives for positive ethical behavior. The simple presence of an ethical code and a corporate ethics committee can increase the visibility of expected ethical behavior and the institutionalization of ethics within an organization.

Explicitness

Visibility alone is not sufficient to commit individuals to ethical behaviors. It must be combined with explicitness; the more explicit the expected behavior, the less deniable it is. Thus, explicitness is the extent to which the individual cannot deny what behavior is expected by the organization. How explicit the behavior is depends on two factors: its observability and its unequivocality. When a behavior cannot be observed but only inferred, it is less explicit. Equivocality is the difficulty of pinning down the act or behavior. It can be seen in the way people qualify the statements they make (such as "It sometimes seems to me that . . ." versus "I think . . ."). Explicitness is indeed a key component for the institutionalization of organization ethics. Explicitness can be enhanced by having all executives, managers, and employees sign a letter affirming their understanding of an organization's ethics policy and stating that they will review the policy annually and report all cases of suspicious (unethical) behavior.

Irreversibility

Irreversibility, on the other hand, means that the behavior is permanent — it cannot easily be revoked or undone. The importance of irreversibility can be observed in the circumstances that committed Great Britain and France to building the Concorde (Salancik, 1977). The Minister of Aviation, James Avery, included a clause in the 1961 agreement with France that made both France's and Britain's decision to produce the Concorde virtually irreversible. The clause required that if either of the two partners withdrew from the collaboration, the entire development cost up to that point would be borne by the withdrawing party. Interestingly, the more rational it became to withdraw (because of escalating costs), the more committed the parties were to continuing.

This type of commitment is typically referred to as behavioral commitment or escalation (Staw, 1976).

Organizations also are aware of the committing aspect of irreversible acts. Many organizations have developed benefit packages that are not transferable from one firm to another. The irreversible loss of these benefits should an individual choose to leave the organization commits the individual to continued employment. In addition, the orientation and training of employees on expected ethical behavior may reassure employees that an ethical stand will be supported and rewarded by the organization.

Organizational attempts to assimilate the individual in organizational relationships (for example, creating a network of relationships at work that become important to an employee is a primary way of connecting workers to the organization) increase organizational commitment. Employees' perceptions of the irreversibility of their positions in an organization develop naturally over time. The longer they are employed by an organization, the more their skills are tailored to the unique demands of that firm. What they know and how they think about an organization become, in reality, what they know and how they think about the particular way their organization does business. The irreversibility of behavior is important because it influence the psychological contract. An organization can use both explicitness and irreversibility as tools for institutionalizing ethics through the creation of incentives and reinforcers (for example, by encouraging and rewarding organization member to display signs of ethical values through whistleblowing).

Volition

To this point, the importance of irreversibility in the commitment process has been emphasized, but there is still a piece of the puzzle missing. Volition, then, and its observable equivalent — personal responsibility — is the fourth mechanism available to organizations for binding individuals to ethical behaviors. Without volition, behaviors are not committing. "Because I have no choice," one might reason, "I really cannot be held responsible for the consequences of my behavior." When individuals try to separate themselves from their actions, they might protest that they did not like what they were doing, but the money was too good to refuse. Another way in which individuals try to distance themselves from certain behaviors (usually those associated with unpleasant circumstances, like the consequences of committing an unethical act) is to insist that they have little personal responsibility for the behavior or the outcome, for example, the classic example of a student trying to explain why he did not turn in a homework assignment because the dog ate it; because the student could not control the dog eating the homework assignment, he believes that his not turning in the homework assignment was not volitional.

Enhancing employees' personal responsibility for their actions is critical to establishing their commitment to the organization, the accompanying expectations of ethical behavior, and the institutionalization of ethics within the organization. At this point, there should be no question that visibility, explicitness and irreversibility, and volition are important in the creation of organization members' commitment to ethical behavior. Further, commitment to an organization's ethical expectations and its goals is important because individuals will adjust their attitudes and expectations in situations to which they are committed. Although enhancing organizational commitment to ethical behavior is an ongoing process, it is probably most critical early in an employee's association with an organization.

A number of factors may lead to greater organizational commitment early in an employee's tenure with an organization and can be used to institutionalize ethics. According to this view, commitment depends on personal factors such as the employee's initial level of commitment (deriving from initial job expectations, the psychological contract, and so on), organizational factors such as an employee's initial work experiences and subsequent sense of responsibility, and nonorganizational factors such as the availability of alternatives after the initial choice has been made (for example, jobs). Each of these three factors can serve as mechanisms for the organization to institutionalize and manage ethics. Individuals who are ethically committed to an organization's ethical policies at entry are likely to remain committed throughout their tenure with the organization. Consistency between organizational, work-group, and individual goals (expectations) on ethics will increase commitment to those goals. Finally, when the organization provides disincentives for unethical behavior and accepts no alternatives but ethical behavior, then organization members will behave in an ethically responsible manner.

Commitment to the organization and its goals is a major factor in predicting ethical behavior. Thus, it is critical that organizations have mechanisms to enhance the development of organizational commitment among new employees. In fact, one way in which organizations with high levels of employee commitment differ from organizations with low levels of employee commitment is that the former tend to be "strong culture" firms. For employees to be part of such an ethical culture, they must be educated as to the expectations and practices of the organization. The extent of their commitment to the organization may well hinge on their ability to understand, accept, and become a part of the organizational culture — "The way we do things around here" (Ott, 1989).

Top Management Role in the Institutionalization Process

Probably nothing is more important to the institutionalization of ethics than the moral tone and example set by top management — the chief executive officer (CEO) and the board of directors. The role of top management in the institutionalization process does not involve procedures; it is not something anyone in the company — or, for that matter, anyone outside — can make studies, establish procedures, or do anything to make it happen. The personal values of the CEO and other top executives (powered by their authority), the belief that these values are important and must be observed, regardless of cost, and the willingness to be an example even when it is difficult or inconvenient set the ethical tone of an organization. The following highlights the importance of top management standing up and being counted as setting the ethical tone for an organization.

The way the CEO exercises moral judgment is universally acknowledged to be more influential than written policy. The CEO who orders the immediate recall of a product at the cost of millions of dollars in sales because of a quality defect affecting a limited number of untraceable shipments sends one kind of message; the executive who suppresses information about a producer's actual or potential ill effects or, knowingly or not, condones overcharging sends another.

Policy is implicit in behavior. The ethical aspects of product quality, personnel, advertising, and marketing decisions are immediately plain. CEOs say much more than they know in the most casual contacts with those who watch their every move. Pretense is futile. "Do not *say* things," Emerson once wrote. "What you *are* stands over you the while, and thunders so that I can not hear what you say to the contrary." It follows that "if you would not be known to do anything, never do it" (Andrews, 1989, p. 102).

Champions of ethical orientations are needed — people who will take strong personal stands on the need for adhering to high ethical standards, role model the behaviors required for such behavior, and assist with the work of moving the organization forward ethically. Top management must take responsibility for seeing that answers are found to questions like the following: Are resources (rewards) being provided for ethical behavior? Is this item prominently featured in the corporate strategy and consistently made a part of senior level staff meetings? Is there a willingness to change human resource management systems such as performance appraisal and bonuses to reinforce an ethical climate? Is there a willingness to consistently hold people accountable for their actions? If the answer to all of these questions is yes, the organization has genuine commitment toward an ethical orientation and institutionalization; if not, then a potential problem with leadership is indicated.

Top management commitment is crucial but not sufficient. Champions are also needed at lower organizational levels, especially key line managers. Many organizations are addressing the leadership requirement by the formation of task or advisory committees on ethics, often headed by a senior manager. Some companies also have a standing committee that oversees ethical behavior company-wide. This chapter advises using the standing ethical behavior committee in addition to, rather than as a substitute for, a broader involvement team such as an ethics task force. This is especially important when an organization has been involved in some illegal or unethical behavior and is committed to not making the same mistakes (as was the case in Salomon Brothers after Warren Buffett took over for John Gutfreund, as discussed in Chapter 5).

The Board of Directors' Role in the Institutionalization Process

Traditionally, directors have functioned as guardians of the financial interest of stockholders, with a specific concern for earnings and dividends. Even this role has been performed in a largely passive manner. Now, in the aftermath of major business scandals, the system of corporate governance and the role of directors have become subjects of special interest.

To help counter unethical behavior and to help in the institutionalization of ethics, process boards must extend their oversight beyond traditional matters of profits to areas of ethics. A concern for ethical performance is not necessarily consistent with stockholder interest, of course, but directors should recognize that there is a connection between ethics and profits.

The board of directors should demand moral leadership, because as directors, they presumably have power to require ethical performance by management. The overall institutional impact of a board that demands ethical performance is greater than that of a president or vice president who does the same.

Recognition of the growing responsibility of directors as a result of more and more boards being held accountable by the courts and the Securities and Exchange Commission should also serve as an impetus to increasing directors' involvement in the institutionalization of ethics process. In holding board members responsible, the Securities and Exchange Commission has taken the position that anyone in a position to know what is going on and to do something about it will be held liable. Overt action or direct participating in a fraud is not necessary for a judgment of liability. Directors presumably have access to the facts, or they should probe sufficiently to get the facts. Although there is some question as to the power board of directors have in reality, they must recognize that they can play a significant role in an organization's efforts to institutionalize ethics.

Middle Management's Role in the Institutionalization Process

In order for an organization to institutionalize ethics (develop sound ethical practices), middle managers must also assume responsibility for convincing employees and for influencing their concern for moral values and ethical practice. Middle management must make certain that every department and employee fosters compliance with corporate ethical standards. They must ensure that ethical policies are followed in their department, focusing on things that are likely to crop up as moral or ethical dilemmas in connection with the activities of their departments. They must see that their people clearly and explicitly understand what is expected of them in the way of ethical behavior. They must tell employees not only what to do and what not to do but also how violations will be dealt with. They must encourage employees to spot and report potential ethical problems. They must develop a radar system that keeps them in touch with the ethical climate of their department and the organization (for example, ensuring that climate and attitude surveys are conducted). The following analogy illustrates this requirement. In talking of the international environmental situation, one can conceive of the world as a ship commanded by 15 different captains, all of whom speak different languages and all of whom, being nearsighted, can see only five feet in front of the ship. Yet, the ship must have ten feet clearance in order to maneuver. This dilemma can easily face middle managers. By the time they have identified potential ethical problems, they are upon them.

They need something comparable to radar to inform them of potential ethical obstacles. If they fail to anticipate them, they will surely bump into them. They must be willing to get as much help and input as possible — ask their people for recommendations for changes in policies and procedures, and they must ensure that the organization has a hotline for anonymously reporting unethical behavior.

The Organization's Value System

Both top and middle management have responsibility for developing the organization's value system, which is a cornerstone to institutionalizing ethics. According to the president of a consulting firm that specializes in individual and organizational performance, "Our experience with scores of clients correlates excellence most closely with consistent, clear and serious management value system" (Weiss, 1989). One company with a clearly defined value system is Merck & Co., a pharmaceutical firm. The effectiveness of its value system is reflected in Merck's consistently high quality performance. For three successive years, Merck was voted the most admired U.S. company in *Fortune* magazine's polls of CEOs.

In many corporations, managers and employees tend to be self-serving, more concerned with protecting themselves and their interests than with any kind of ethics. Not so at Merck. For example, the company's field marketing representatives try to determine what is right for the doctor and the patient instead of how a particular sale might affect total sales volume. Such a focus is unusual in a highly competitive field like pharmaceuticals (French, 1990).

Merck's example shows that a positive approach is one key to success. When management compromises on quality, worker morale suffers and production slows down. It is easy for management to pay a great deal of lip service to ethics and values, but what is more important is to put them into action and to act as examples.

Managers can keep in mind several guidelines for establishing values that can help institutionalize ethics:

Values cannot be taught, they must be believed. Employees do what they have seen done, not what they are told. If their superiors engage in unethical behavior, they will become lax in their own work habits.

Values must be simple and easy to articulate. Managers should ask themselves whether the values are realistic and whether they apply to daily decision making.

Values apply to internal as well as external operations. In other words, managers cannot expect workers to treat customers well if they in turn do not treat their workers well in terms of honesty, frankness, and performance-based rewards.

Values are first communicated in the selection process. It is easier to hire people who share the corporate values than it is to train someone who does not identify with them to begin with. One executive recruiter says, "The best run organizations place a premium on the candidate's approach to issues of ethics and judgment. Anyone can read a balance sheet, but not everyone can handle a product quality or conflict of interest problem." (Weiss, 1989, p. 40)

An organization should constantly monitor its value system and make efforts to revise it when appropriate. Such a revision would be necessary from time to time, especially when downsizing, layoffs, decline in organizational performance, attrition, or redeployment of the work force is necessary; significantly different groups are combined; traditional values are inappropriate for the new climate; there has been a transgression of ethics, morals, or the law; or there has been a significant strategic redirection.

Pastin (1986) recommends a set of four principles that high-ethics firms employ to help develop values that support a climate of moral consciousness. The four principles are:

1. High-ethics firms are at ease interacting with diverse internal and external stakeholder groups. The ground rules of these firms make the good of these stakeholder groups part of the firm's own good.

2. High-ethics firms are obsessed with fairness. Their ground rules emphasize that the other person's interests count as much as their own.

3. In high-ethics firms, responsibility is individual rather than collective, with individuals assuming personal responsibility for actions of the firm. These firms' ground rules mandate that individuals are responsible to themselves.

4. The high-ethics firm sees its activities in terms of a purpose. This purpose is a way of operating that members of the firm value, and purpose ties the firm to its environment.

Codes of Ethics: Vehicles for Communicating Ethical Expectations

In an increasingly competitive environment, the potential for unethical behavior increases as competitors strive for the slightest strategic advantages over key competitors. In light of this type of operating climate, much attention has been focused upon methods for achieving more ethical behavior within organizations. One of the more pervasive methods is the establishment of a company code of ethics.

The articulation and communication of ethical expectations (rules and standards) through written codes and standards is a must in the institutionalization of ethics process (that is, building, sustaining, or transforming an unethical organization into an ethical one). Codes of ethics or conduct should not be confused with statements of values. Indeed, in some organizations the two may be the same or may at least overlap. However, they fill different roles. Rather than stating broad values held by the organization, written codes of ethics should be a series of clear, specific, positive, and direct statements from the top leadership of the organization and should be well-circulated throughout the organization.

A code of ethics can serve the purpose of mandating behavior standards and clarifying responsibilities. It communicates in unmistakable terms the ethical standards that the organization demands be met. What is critical is that there be no doubt in anyone's mind exactly where the organization stands on how it wants its employees to conduct the business affairs of the organization.

Based upon available literature, we believe the following suggestions should be considered when constructing or revising a code of ethics:

The code should include an effective date, general statement of policy, and scope of coverage.

Codes of ethics should be reasonably consistent with reality.

A code of ethics should not be in conflict with the values of the organization, the top management group, company employees, or its various stakeholders.

A code of ethics should be reasonably consistent internally.

Codes should not be arbitrarily imposed on employees.

Codes should be subject to debate or change, not carved in stone, and periodically updated to reflect changing environmental conditions.

Codes of ethics should be in-depth, in written format, and easily understood (in other words, leave out the lawyer "gobbledygook").

Codes of ethics should clearly indicate what is expected of both management and employees.

Clear specifications for the implementation and administration of the code should be given.

Procedures for reporting violations need to be clearly specified.

Sanctions or disciplinary actions need to be clearly stated.

Codes of ethics should be enforced and sanctions taken when appropriate.

Ideally, the code is developed by a group of employees representing the various levels and functions of the organization. Jones (1982) stresses the importance of understanding that writing down the organization's guides of conduct is not as easy as it might first appear. In addition, he cautions that there are potentially two almost completely opposite traps one must be aware of.

The first impulse is to write the code of ethical conduct in broad, ringing declarations. The trouble with these sweeping generalities is that they quickly take on the air of motherhood statements. They are so broad and general that they give people little or no guidance in their day-to-day behavior. Going to the other extreme may be even more dangerous, however. Setting out detailed rules in an attempt to cover all conceivable situations creates such a huge volume of specifics that people tend to use the rule book as a complete guide to action. There is a tendency to substitute rules for judgment. The hidden danger is the temptation to use the absence of a direct rule as a reason for plunging ahead even when one's conscience says "No." In too many instances, rules that are set down initially with the expectation that they will be floors for ethical behavior soon become interpreted as ceilings for it, and as suggested by Jones (1982), people rationalize their actions by saying, "It's not covered in the Rule Book so it must be okay."

To improve the likelihood that written statements in the code of ethics are useful to the employees in the organization, they have to be somewhere between the two extremes. They have to be guides for behavior and standards for conduct but not mixed rules by which all decisions are controlled. A few of the many topics that should be included in a code of ethics are: acceptance of costly entertainment, gifts, travel, payments, loans, services, or favors; business with foreign governments; corporate political contributions; discovery and reporting of violations; environmental compliance; equal opportunity; extortion and kickbacks; Foreign Corrupt Practices Act of 1977; insider information; protection of confidential information; quality and testing; relationships with government officials; theft; and whistleblowing. The comprehensive nature of Caterpillar, Inc.'s code of worldwide business conduct and operating principles is illustrated by the following list of its section headings:

Business Purpose

Business Ethics

Involvement of People

Human Relationships

Privacy of Information about Employees

Ownership and Investment

Board Stewardship

Corporate Facilities

Disposal of Wastes

Product Quality and Uniformity

Competitive Conduct

Relationships with Suppliers

Sharing Technology

Accounting Records and Financial Reporting

Intercompany Pricing

Currency Transactions

Differing Business Practices

Public Responsibility

Observance of Local Laws

Relationships with Public Officials

Disclosure of Information

Inside Information

International Information Flow

Free Enterprise, Worldwide

Reporting Code Compliance. (Lane, 1991, p. 31)

Regardless of the reasons companies implement codes of ethics, it is important that the content of it is recognized as an integral part of the institutionalization process.

It has not been the intent of this book to suggest that ethics is an easy phenomenon to understand. Ethics in business is concerned with dilemmas — the clash of two or more moral values. It relies on reason and not on religion. It focuses on business actions and practices, and it makes judgments about those actions in the light of some human value. Ethical behavior best serves the ideals of honesty, integrity, morality, and good management.

It has been the contention of this book that the roots of ethical or unethical behavior can be traced to an organization's culture, values of the CEO and top managers, poor decision making, individual personal values, and professional codes, among other things, and that pressures to behave unethically come from several sources: self-interest, superiors, peers, subordinates, and the organization itself.

Organizations that want to build an ethical organization culture have several avenues. They can convince top management to be visible examples and actively demonstrate their concern for ethical business practices. They can guide the process of developing and communicating the organization's code of ethics. They can activate a number of countermeasures, including training, ethical audits, sanctions, and rewards for ethical conduct. Organizations can also enhance an ethically oriented culture by paying particular attention to principled organizational dissent. Principled organizational dissent is an important concept linking organizational culture to ethical behavior. Principled organizational dissent is the effort by individuals in the organization to protest the status quo because of their objection on ethical grounds to some practice or policy (Graham, 1986). Organizations committed to promoting an ethical climate should encourage principled organizational dissent instead of punishing such behavior.

The importance of decision making and groupthink in the ethics equation has also been a major point emphasized in this book. In particular, it has been our contention that poor decision making in the form of groupthink is not an easy phenomenon to overcome, especially because there is some evidence that the symptoms of groupthink as related to unethical behavior presented in this book thrive in the sort of climate outlined in the following critique of corporate directors in the United States (Baum, 1986): "Many directors simply don't rock the boat. 'No one likes to be the skunk at the garden party,' says [management consultant] Victor Palmieri. 'One does not make friends and influence people in the boardroom or elsewhere by raising hard questions that create embarrassment or discomfort for management'" (p. 60). In short, policy- and decision-making groups can become so cohesive that strong-willed executives are able to gain unanimous support for poor decisions. Still, organizations committed to ethical behavior in their organizations must work toward the reduction and prevention of groupthink. However, they must first understand what is meant by groupthink and that there is, indeed, a link between groupthink and unethical behavior in some situations. Specifically, the ultimate result of groupthink is that group members become isolated from the world around them. They read positive signs as a reaffirmation of their goals and intentions; they read negative signs as an indication that there are individuals who do not understand what they are doing and that these individuals should be ignored (and perhaps even punished). During this entire process, it is common to find the group changing to a belief that its ideals are humanitarian and based on high-minded principles. As a result, no attempt is made by the members to challenge or question the ethics of the group's behavior. A second common observation is high esprit de corps and amiability among the members. This often leads them to believe that those who question their approach or intentions are acting irrationally.

Quite often groupthink is recognized only after a group has made an unethical decision. When this occurs, the members are apt to ask, "How could we have been so blind? Why didn't anyone call attention to our errors?" Unfortunately, at the time the group was making its decision(s), it is unlikely that any criticism or questioning of its actions would have been given serious consideration.

The importance of the institutionalization of ethics within an organization cannot be underestimated, nor can one tell when employees will be confronted with ethical dilemmas. Any decision they make that involves ethics is likely to be based on values they have already learned and experiences they have already had prior to joining an organization. However, organizations must take proactive responsibility for ensuring that employees do not encounter organizational policies and practices that may be inappropriate. In addition, an organization must create and nurture an environment that encourages its employees to blow the whistle on those policies and practices.

In reality, an organization that supports the institutionalization of ethics is aware of the importance of psychological contracts, organizational commitment, and an ethically oriented organizational culture, that is, the organization seeks employees who are willing to take a personal stand and perhaps put their own career at risk if necessary to expose and eliminate unethical behavior. At the same time, the organization understands that ethics will be helpful to their overall productivity and survival and that contrary to what we read and see (for example, *Wall Street*, the movie), those who are dishonest and exhibit unethical behavior do not get ahead faster than those who are honest and exhibit ethical behavior.

Although this concluding chapter has not covered all that can be done to institutionalize ethics in organizations, the actions suggested can move the organization a long way toward institutionalizing an ethical climate. By taking specific steps as suggested, many individual and group decisions that might otherwise have been wrong have a greater chance of being in line with that of an ethical climate. For example, training programs that focus on ethical awareness (that is, increasing sensitivity to ethical dilemmas at work) and ethical reasoning (that is, learning strategies for solving ethical dilemmas) also contribute to the institutionalization process. Training also often involves statements from the CEO emphasizing ethical business practices, discussions of the corporate code of ethics, lectures, workshops or seminars, case studies, films/discussions, articles/speeches, and descriptions of procedures for dealing with or reporting unethical behavior.

Organizations committed to the institutionalization of an ethically responsible culture should also consider the impact of mentors or role models (for example, through what they say and how they behave, senior executives establish norms that filter down through the organization), reward systems, and career paths — all of which reinforce the culture and expectations and contribute to the institutionalization of ethics in the organization.

In conclusion, in order for ethics to be truly institutionalized within an organization, the entire organization must agree to the importance of ethical behavior, and, more importantly, there must be a collective standard for the entire organization to follow (Maruchek & Robbins, 1988). Mayer (1970) proposes that in order for standards of ethical conduct to be maintained within one functional area, they must also apply to all other functional areas. Similarly, Bowman (1981) argues that "each manager must know that every one of his/her colleagues in the hierarchy has been required to adhere to the same standards as he/she must" (p. 62).

REFERENCES

Andrews, K. R. 1989, September/October. Ethics in practice. *Harvard Business Review*, p. 102.

Baum, L. 1986, September 8. The job nobody wants. *Business Week*, p. 60.

Beneish, M. D., & Chatov, R. 1993. Corporate codes of conduct: Economic determinants and legal implications for independent auditors. *Journal of Accounting and Public Policy 12*, 3–35.

Berenbeim, R. F. 1992. *Corporate ethics practices*. New York: The Conference Board.

Bowman, J. S. 1981. The management of ethics: Codes of conduct in organizations. *Public Personnel Management 10*(1): 59–66.

Center for Business at Bentley College. 1986. Are corporations institutionalizing ethics? *Journal of Business Ethics 5*, 77–89.

Center for Ethics, Responsibilities, and Values. 1987. *Organizational integrity perception audit*. St. Paul, MN: The College of St. Catherine.

Deal, T., & Kennedy, A. 1982. *Corporate culture: The rites and rituals of corporate life*. Reading, MA: Addison-Wesley.

Dunham, R. B. 1984. *Organizational behavior: People and processes in management*. Homewood, IL: Irwin.

Dunham, R. B., & Pierce, J. L. 1989. *Management*. Glenview, IL: Scott, Foresman.

Eisenberger, R., Huntington, R., Hutchinson, S., & Sowa, D. 1986. Perceived organizational support. *Journal of Applied Psychology 71*, 500–507.

French, W. 1990. *Human resource management*, 2nd ed. Boston, MA: Houghton Mifflin.

Goodman, P. S., & Dean, J. W., Jr. 1981. Why productivity efforts fail. In *Organization development: Theory, practice, and research*, ed. W. L. French, C. H. Bell, & R. A. Zawacki. Homewood, IL: BPI/Irwin.

Graham, J. W. 1986. Principled organizational dissent: A theoretical essay. In *Research in organizational behavior 8*, ed. B. M. Staw & L. L. Cummings. Greenwich, CT: JAI Press.

Jones, D. G. 1982. *Doing ethics in business*. Cambridge, MA: Ogleschlager, Gunn & Hain.

Kelly, C. M. 1987, Summer. The interrelationships of ethics and power in today's organizations. *Organizational Dynamics*, pp. 4–18.

Lane, M. R. 1991, February. Improving American business ethics in three steps. *The CPA Journal*, p. 31.

Louis, M. 1980, August. Culture: Yes. Organization: No. Paper presented at the annual meeting of the Academy of Management, Dallas.

Maruchek, A. S., & Robbins, L. B. 1988. Business ethics: The materials/manufacturing perspective. *Production and Inventory Management Journal 24*(4): 16–19.

Mayer, R. R. 1970. Management responsibility for purchasing ethics. *Journal of Purchasing 4*, 13–20.

Mowday, R. T., Porter, L. W., & Steers, R. M. 1982. *Employee-organization linkages: The psychology of commitment, absenteeism, and turnover*. New York: Academic Press.

Nielsen, R. P. 1989. Changing unethical organizational behavior. *Academy of Management Executive 3*(2): 123–30.

_____. 1988. Limitations of ethical reasoning as an action (praxis) strategy. *Journal of Business Ethics 7*, 725–33.

Northcraft, G. B., & Neale, M. A. 1990. *Organizational behavior*. Chicago, IL: Dryden Press.

Ott, J. S. 1989. *The organizational culture perspective*. Chicago, IL: Dorsey Press.

Pascale, R. T. 1985, Summer. The paradox of corporate culture: Reconciling ourselves to socialization. *California Management Review 27*, 26–27.

Pastin, M. 1986. *The hard problem of management: Gaining the ethics edge*. San Francisco, CA: Jossey-Bass.

Purcell, T. V., & Weber, J. 1979. *Institutionalizing corporate ethics: A case history*, Special Study No. 71. New York: The Presidents of the American Management Association.

Richardson, A. J. 1986. The production of institutional behaviour: A constructive comment on the use of institutionalization theory in organizational analysis. *Canadian Journal of Administrative Sciences*, pp. 304–16.

Richter, P. 1986, June 19. Big business puts ethics in spotlight. *Los Angeles Times*, p. C1.

Salancik, G. R. 1977, Summer. Commitment is too easy! *Organizational Dynamics*, pp. 207–22.

Sims, R. R. 1991. The institutionalization of organizational ethics. *Journal of Business Ethics 10*, 493–506.

____. 1990. *An experiential learning approach to employee training systems.* Westport, CT: Greenwood Press.

Sims, R. R., & Sims, S. J. 1991. Increasing applied business ethics courses in business school curricula. *Journal of Business Ethics 10*, 211–19.

Sims, R. R., Veres, J. G., & Sims, S. J. 1989. A training method for increasing manager's sensitivity to ethics: Developing codes of ethics. *Training and Management Development Methods 3*(3): 6.09–6.15.

Snoeyenbos, M. 1992. Management and Morals. In *Business ethics*, rev. ed., eds. M. Snoeyenbos, R. Almeder, & J. Humber. New York: Promethus Books, pp. 93–103.

Staw, B. M. 1976. Knee-deep in the big muddy: A study of escalating commitment to choose a course of action. *Organizational Behavior and Human Performance 16*, 27–44.

Stead, W. E., Worrell, D. L., & Stead, J. G. 1990. An integrative model for understanding and managing ethical behavior in business organizations. *Journal of Business Ethics 9*, 233–42.

Touche Ross. 1988. *Ethics in American business: A Special Report.* New York: Touche Ross and Co.

Trevino, L. K. 1986. Ethical decision making in organizations: A person-situation interactionist model. *Academy of Management Review 11*, 601–17.

Van Maanen, J., & Schein, E. 1979. Toward a theory of organizational socialization. In *Research in organizational behavior*, ed. B. M. Staw. Greenwich, CT: JAI Press.

Weiss, A. 1989, July. The value system. *Personnel Administrator 34*, 40–51.

Zucker, L. G. 1983. Organizations as institutions. In *Research in the sociology of organizations*, ed. S. B. Bacharach. Greenwich, CT: JAI Press.

Index

ABOUT THE AUTHOR

Ronald R. Sims is a professor of business in the Graduate School of Business, College of William and Mary. Previous works include: *Diversity and Differences in Organizations* (Quorum, 1993), *Training and Enhancement of Government Organizations* (Quorum, 1993), *Managing Higher Education in 21st Century* (Quorum, 1991), *Experiential Learning Approach* (Quorum, 1990).